THE VICTORIANS

THE
VICTORIANS

AN ANTHOLOGY CHOSEN BY
GEOFFREY GRIGSON

LONDON

ROUTLEDGE & KEGAN PAUL LTD.

BROADWAY HOUSE: 68–74 CARTER LANE, E.C.4

First published 1950

For

GEOFFREY TAYLOR

Printed in Great Britain
by T. and A. CONSTABLE LTD., Hopetoun Street,
Printers to the University of Edinburgh

PREFACE

This book is the last of a trio. The other two are The Romantics *and* Before the Romantics. *In this, the central poet is Tennyson. In* The Romantics *it was Coleridge, in the other one Dryden. Each of the books is a miscellany of poems and poetic fragments, large and small, in which the poems, so to say, are illustrated or waited upon by the prose. The poems in each are the more numerous, and* they *are why the books have been put together. The prose is their batman. It does not give orders. It does not stand for all the prose in the outer world. This time, for example, I keep the great novelists most of the while outside.*

I would like to think that each one of these books " represented" the way Englishmen, as a whole, wrote and felt in poetry in the three different but consecutive ages. But that could only happen very roughly indeed. The most wise literary historian, by himself, could only experience Augustan literature or Victorian literature, and so on, in his way. Impartiality, balance—yes, but how could he expect this individual experience to be more than individual, how could he expect it to be "true"? How could he say honestly, " This history, or this anthology does exactly reveal to you what the Victorians were about"?

Of course, we often do, as critics, claim so much; others claim it as historians, or leave it to be assumed; and very immodest we and they are at a time when the object of science is defined as " to extend the range of our experience and reduce it to order." Our experience appears to be all that we can know. Not things. Not books, not poems, but only our experience of books and poems.

I may have my notions of what, in general, was right and wrong about the poetry of the Sixties, or about the defective style of language the poets were apt to use, or about the difference between Hardy and Swinburne, or between Hopkins and Tennyson. I may affirm that Victorian literature is criticized most vitally of all by Gerard Manley Hopkins in his letters. But isn't it the critic's affair (or the affair of the anthologist, because he too is a critic) in the end, very simply indeed, but for valid

v

reasons, to affirm "Here, if you wish to read it, is what I experience as a Good Poem, which only happens to have been written in 1860 or 1760 ?"

A Good Poem ? Well, such ordered words as those which a Good Poet, Samuel Daniel, called

> the speaking Picture of the Mind;
> The Extract of the Soul, that labour'd how
> To leave the Image of her self behind.

For the sake of men, mustn't we still distrust relative standards, and all historically founded judgements of a poem ? In these days of all the universities and all their populated—their over-populated—departments of English we must remember that a good or living poem joins a man to other men; and that a poem is often the best subject for the historian of letters when it makes the junction no longer, when through some lack of authenticity in its kind it is dying or has died.

> O blessed Letters! that combine in one
> All Ages past, and make one live with all,
> By you do we confer with who are gone,
> And the Dead living unto Council call.

That is better. But most of the poems men write are not so blessed, and they collect ivy, they ruinate, they break up and vanish, in time. Or they used to; because nowadays the literary historian, a pseudo-scientist, is trying to halt the process, just as the Office of Works tries to stabilize ruination, and prevent what is now far from becoming further. It fences the ancient monument around, leaving you to enter by a revolving wicket. This preservation of castles and poems, this antiquarianism, is not kept to its bound, is not kept distinct, and is allowed to appear to be "taste"; so by prejudice it becomes a hindrance to the arts of the living.

In this, and in the other anthologies, I confess that I have not stuck to the timeless in Daniel's sense (it is, by the way, the smaller poems without much room which the more easily stay timeless through and through, not so much the long and roomier pieces). No, I come under my own ban. I mix my two methods, and while I am enjoying myself, perhaps have the best of neither.

Still, I repeat the poems outnumber and outweigh the prose; and almost all of them are poems which seem Good or Goodish to me, and which I hope will seem Good or Goodish also to you.

This time the anthology moves by way of a forecourt (Part One) into the Victorian citadel of the Fifties, Sixties, and Seventies, and then moves out (Part Five) towards poetry as we now understand it. If we came in by the forecourt, we shall be leaving, so Tennyson or Leighton would have declared, by the drain-pipe— the drain-pipe of "Danny Deever."

"Wordpainting is, in the verbal arts, the great success of our day," wrote Hopkins. "Wordpainting is in our age a real mastery and the second-rate men of this age often beat at it the first-rate men of past ages." I agree, and so have collected many of these verbal paintings. Indeed, but for the very early and late Victorianism and for the nonsense writing, I might have named this anthology "The Wordpainters," instead of "The Victorians."

GEOFFREY GRIGSON.

BROAD TOWN,
    November 25th, 1948.

CONTENTS

Dots at the beginning and the end make it clear that only part of a poem has been used. The title of the poems is always given in the notes, when they are not printed in full.

ACKNOWLEDGEMENTS

THANKS are due to Messrs. Heinemann for an extract from Whistler's *Gentle Art of Making Enemies*, three poems from the *Collected Poems* of Arthur Symons, and three poems from Swinburne's *Poems and Ballads*; to the Oxford University Press for poems by R. W. Dixon from *Lyrical Poems*, *Last Poems*, and *Selected Poems*; to the Oxford University Press and the poet's family for poems and extracts from *The Poems of Gerard Manley Hopkins*; to Messrs. G. Bell for extracts from R. A. M. Stevenson's *Velasquez*; to Messrs. Chapman & Hall for extracts from *Thomas Woolner, R.A.* by Amy Woolner; to Messrs. Allen & Unwin for an extract from Ruskin's *Praeterita*; to Messrs. Macmillan and the poet's executors for two limericks from Lewis Carroll's *Collected Poems*; to Earl Russell for an extract from the *Amberley Papers*; to the executor of the late E. F. Benson for an extract from *As We Were*; to Messrs. Constable and the Trustees of the late George Meredith for "The Old Chartist," from *Collected Poems*; to Messrs. Macmillan and Mr. H. W. Allingham for extracts from the *Diary* of William Allingham; to Messrs. Macmillan and the Trustees of the Hardy Estate for poems from the *Collected Poems* of Thomas Hardy and extracts from Mrs. Hardy's *Life of Thomas Hardy*; to Messrs. Macmillan and the author's representative for poems from the *Collected Poems* of W. E. Henley; to Messrs. Macmillan for an extract from Lord Acton's *Lectures on Modern History*; to Messrs. Macmillan and Mrs. Yeats for poems from the *Collected Poems* of W. B. Yeats; to Messrs. Burns, Oates & Washbourne and Sir Francis Meynell for Alice Meynell's *Letter from a Girl to her own Old Age*; to the Clarendon Press for poems from Robert Bridges' *Shorter Poems*; to Messrs. Methuen and Mrs. Bambridge for "Danny Deever" and "The Gift of the Sea" from Kipling's *Barrack Room Ballads*; to Messrs. Cape, Mr. T. Perceval Smith, and Mr. William Plomer for extracts from *Kilvert's Diary*; to Messrs. Cape and the literary executors of Samuel

Butler for extracts and a sonnet from *The Note-books of Samuel Butler*; to Mr. Vyvyan Holland for an extract from *The Critic as Artist* and an extract from the preface to *Dorian Gray* by Oscar Wilde; to Mr. Macmillan and Miss Nancy McIntosh for songs from *Patience*, *Ruddigore*, *Iolanthe*, and *The Gondoliers* by Sir W. S. Gilbert; to Messrs. Routledge & Kegan Paul for extracts from *The Light of Asia* by Sir Edwin Arnold, and *Dorothy* by A. J. Munby; to Mr. John Murray and Mrs. Vanessa Bell for extracts from Sir Leslie Stephen's *Hours in a Library*; to Messrs. Longmans Green and Mrs. Vanessa Bell for extracts from Sir Leslie Stephen's *Essays on Freethinking and Plainspeaking* and *Playground of Europe*; to the representatives of the late Emily Lawless for a poem from *With the Wild Geese*; the representatives of the late A. J. Munby for a poem from *Vestigia Retrorsum*; and the Society of Authors for two poems by the late A. E. Housman.

PART ONE: THIRTIES AND FORTIES

Now the Queen has recovered, and Albert's the nurse,
He puts on the child's napkins, and don't care one curse. . .

Street Ballad.

"Bless railroads everywhere," I said, "and the world's advance;
Bless every railroad share In Italy, Ireland, France; For
never a beggar need now despair, And every rogue has a
chance."

W. M. Thackeray.

And out once more in varnish'd glory shine
Thy stars of celandine. . .

Alfred Tennyson.

I hear among the trees the voices of my coming days and they
are mournful.

R. S. Hawker.

1. MAY

. . From the woods
Came voices of the well-contented doves.
The lark could scarce get out his notes for joy,
But shook his song together as he near'd
His happy home, the ground. To left and right,
The cuckoo told his name to all the hills;
The mellow ouzel fluted in the elm;
The redcap whistled; and the nightingale
Sang loud, as tho' he were the bird of day. . .

Alfred Tennyson (1809-1892).

2. NOT A MAY-GAME IS THIS MAN'S LIFE

NOT a May-game is this man's life; but a battle and a march,
a warfare with principalities and powers. No idle promenade
through fragrant orange-groves and green flowery spaces,
waited on by the choral Muses and the rosy Hours: it is a stern
pilgrimage through burning sandy solitudes, through regions
of thick-ribbed ice. *Thomas Carlyle* (1795-1881).

3. CHILDHOOD OF A FUTURE VICTORIAN

(CHARLES KINGSLEY)

A BOY friend, now a clergyman in Essex, recalls him about this
time [i.e. about 1825, when Kingsley was six], repeating his
Latin lesson to his father in the study at Barnack, with his eyes
fixed all the time on the fire in the grate. At last he could
stand it no longer; there was a pause in the Latin, and Charles
cried out, "I do declare, papa, there is pyrites in the coal."

Fanny Kingsley.

4. NATURE IN 1842

STUDY nature—not scientifically—that would take eternity, to
do it so as to reap much moral good from it. Superficial

3

physical science is the devil's spade, with which he loosens the
roots of the trees prepared for the burning! Do not study
matter for its own sake, but as the countenance of God! Try
to extract every line of beauty, every association, every moral
reflection, every inexpressible feeling from it. Study the forms
and colours of leaves and flowers, and the growth and habits of
plants; not to classify them, but to admire them and adore
God. Study the sky! Study water! Study trees! Study the
sounds and scents of nature! Study all these, as beautiful in
themselves, in order to recombine the elements of beauty;
next, as allegories and examples from whence moral reflections
may be drawn; next, as types of certain tones of feeling, etc. :
but remain in God-dependance, superior to them. Learn what
feelings they express, but do not let them mould the tone of
your mind; else by allowing a melancholy day to make you
melancholy, you worship the creature more than the Creator.

Charles Kingsley (1819-1875).

5. MOTTO FOR A LATE PICTURE BY TURNER

THE azure moon, that through the verdant clouds,
Bathes the vermilion waves with floods of blue,
Sees nought but yon gondola of pink haze,
And red-hot dots of men.

From *The Man in the Moon.*

6. POACHED EGGS AND BLADDERS OF VERMILION

(ANOTHER LATE TURNER)

(*The picture is "Slavers throwing overboard the Dead
and Dying—Typhoon coming on" which was exhibited
at the Academy in* 1840.)

ROCKS of gamboge are marked down upon the canvas; flakes
of white laid on with a trowel; bladders of vermilion madly
spirted here and there. Yonder is the slaver rocking in the
midst of a flashing foam of white lead. The sun glares down
upon a horrible sea of emerald and purple, into which chocolate-

coloured slaves are plunged, and chains that will not sink;
and round these are floundering such a race of fishes as never
was seen since the *saeculum Pyrrhae*—gasping dolphins, redder
than the reddest herrings; horrid spreading polypi, like huge
slimy poached eggs, in which hapless niggers plunge and
disappear.   *W. M. Thackeray* (1811-1863).

7. THE EVENING STAR

                . . I, that whole day,
Saw her no more, altho' I linger'd there
Till every daisy slept, and Love's white star
Beam'd thro' the thicken'd cedar in the dusk. . .
                     Alfred Tennyson (1809-1892).

8. THE PROGRESS OF SPRING

I

THE groundflame of the crocus breaks the mould,
    Fair Spring slides hither o'er the Southern sea,
Wavers on her thin stem the snowdrop cold
    That trembles not to kisses of the bee:
Come, Spring, for now from all the dripping eaves
    The spear of ice has wept itself away,
And hour by hour unfolding woodbine leaves
    O'er his uncertain shadow droops the day.
She comes! The loosen'd rivulets run;
    The frost-bead melts upon her golden hair;
Her mantle, slowly greening in the Sun,
    Now wraps her close, now arching leaves her bare
    To breaths of balmier air;

II

Up leaps the lark, gone wild to welcome her,
    About her glance the tits, and shriek the jays,
Before her skims the jubilant woodpecker,
    The linnet's bosom blushes at her gaze,

While round her brows a woodland culver flits,
  Watching her large light eyes and gracious looks,
And in her open palm a halcyon sits
  Patient—the secret splendour of the brooks.
Come, Spring! She comes on waste and wood,
  On farm and field: but enter also here,
Diffuse thyself at will thro' all my blood,
  And, tho' thy violet sicken into sere,
  Lodge with me all the year!

III

Once more a downy drift against the brakes,
  Self-darken'd in the sky, descending slow!
But gladly see I thro' the wavering flakes
  Yon blanching apricot like snow in snow.
These will thine eyes not brook in forest-paths,
  On their perpetual pine, nor round the beech;
They fuse themselves to little spicy baths,
  Solved in the tender blushes of the peach;
They lose themselves and die
  On that new life that gems the hawthorn line;
Thy gay lent-lilies wave and put them by,
  And out once more in varnish'd glory shine
  Thy stars of celandine.

IV

She floats across the hamlet. Heaven lours,
  But in the tearful splendour of her smiles
I see the slowly-thickening chestnut towers
  Fill out the spaces by the barren tiles.
Now past her feet the swallow circling flies,
  A clamorous cuckoo stoops to meet her hand;
Her light makes rainbows in my closing eyes,
  I hear a charm of song thro' all the land.
Come, Spring! She comes, and Earth is glad
  To roll her North below thy deepening dome,
But ere thy maiden birk be wholly clad,
  And those low bushes dip their twigs in foam
  Make all true hearths thy home.

v

Across my garden! and the thicket stirs,
　The fountain pulses high in sunnier jets,
The blackcap warbles, and the turtle purrs,
　The starling claps his tiny castanets.
Still round her forehead wheels the woodland dove,
　And scatters on her throat the sparks of dew,
The kingcup fills her footprint, and above
　Broaden the glowing isles of vernal blue.
Hail, ample presence of a Queen,
　Bountiful, beautiful, apparell'd gay,
Whose mantle, every shade of glancing green,
　Flies back in fragrant breezes to display
　A tunic white as May!

　　　　　Alfred Tennyson (1809-1892).

9. THE LATEST GOSPEL

THERE is a perennial nobleness, and even sacredness, in Work.
Were he never so benighted, forgetful of his high calling, there
is always hope in a man that actually and earnestly works: in
Idleness alone is there perpetual despair. Work, never so
Mammonish, mean, *is* in communication with Nature; the
real desire to get Work done will itself lead one more and more
to truth, to Nature's appointments and regulations, which
are truth.

The latest Gospel in this world is, Know thy work and do it.
"Know thyself": long enough has that poor "self" of thine
tormented thee; thou wilt never get to "know" it, I believe!
Think it not thy business, this of knowing thyself; thou art
an unknowable individual: know what thou canst work at;
and work at it, like a Hercules! That will be thy better plan.

　　　　　Thomas Carlyle (1795-1881).

10. QUEEN VICTORIA'S BABY

OH, yes, I'll sing with all my heart,
And tell you a very singular start,

That lately occurred at Buckingham Palace,
That scene of waste, confusion, and malice,
 About the baby, the dear little baby—
   Queen Victoria's baby!

About one in the morn, as I heard say,
The Queen she felt in a curious way—
She woke her husband, who said with great sorrow,
"Oh! can't you, my love, put it off till to-morrow?
 For I am so sleepy, and I don't want a baby!"
   "Ah!" says she, "but I will have a baby!"

Then there was great bustle, confusion, and hurry,
The Queen was in labour—the Prince in a flurry;
When the Princess was born the nurse loud did shout—
"Little girl, does your mother know you are out?"
   Oh, oh! little baby, etc.

Now the Queen has recovered, and Albert's the nurse,
He puts on the child's napkins, and don't care one curse;
And ladies and gentlemen, your smiles give to me,
'Twas to gain your applause I sung, d'ye see,
 About the Queen's baby, the duck of a baby,
   Queen Victoria's baby!

       Anon. (*A Street Ballad*).

11. THE BROKEN-HEARTED GARDENER

I'M a broken-hearted Gardener, and don't know what to do,
My love she is inconstant, and a fickle jade, too,
One smile from her lips will never be forgot,
It refreshes, like a shower from a watering pot.

Chorus

  Oh, Oh! she's a fickle wild rose,
  A damask, a cabbage, a young China Rose.

She's my myrtle, my geranium,
My Sun flower, my sweet marjorum.

My honey suckle, my tulip, my violet,
My holy hock, my dahlia, my mignonette.

We grew up together like two apple trees,
And clung to each other like double sweet peas,
Now they're going to trim her, and plant her in a pot,
And I'm left to wither, neglected and forgot.

She's my snowdrop, my ranunculus,
My hyacinth, my gilliflower, my polyanthus,
My heart's ease, my pink water lily,
My buttercup, my daisy, my daffydown dilly.

I'm like a scarlet runner that has lost its stick,
Or a cherry that's left for the dickey to pick,
Like a waterpot I weep, like a paviour I sigh,
Like a mushroom I'll wither, like a cucumber, die.

I'm like a humble bee that doesn't know where to settle,
And she's a dandelion, and a stinging nettle,
My heart's like a beet root choked with chickweed,
And my head's like a pumpkin running to seed.

I'm a great mind to make myself a felo-de-se,
And finish all my woes on the branch of a tree:
But I won't, for I know at my kicking you'd roar,
And honour my death with a double encore.

Anon. (A Street Ballad).

12. FAME

SEE, as the prettiest graves will do in time,
Our poet's wants the freshness of its prime;
Spite of the sexton's browsing horse, the sods
Have struggled through its binding osier rods;
Headstone and half-sunk footstone lean awry,
Wanting the brick-work promised by-and-by;
How the minute grey lichens, plate o'er plate,
Have softened down the crisp-cut name and date!

Robert Browning (1812-1889).

A*

13. TO-NIGHT THE WINDS BEGIN TO RISE

(From *In Memoriam*)

To-NIGHT the winds begin to rise
    And roar from yonder dropping day:
    The last red leaf is whirl'd away,
The rooks are blown about the skies;

The forest crack'd, the waters curl'd,
    The cattle huddled on the lea;
    And wildly dash'd on tower and tree
The sunbeam strikes along the world:

And but for fancies, which aver
    That all thy motions gently pass
    Athwart a plane of molten glass,
I scarce could brook the strain and stir

That makes the barren branches loud;
    And but for fear it is not so,
    The wild unrest that lives in woe
Would dote and pore on yonder cloud

That rises upward always higher,
    And onward drags a labouring breast,
    And topples round the dreary west,
A looming bastion fringed with fire.
            Alfred Tennyson (1809-1892).

14. PLEAD FOR ME

OH, thy bright eyes must answer now,
When Reason, with a scornful brow,
Is mocking at my overthrow!
Oh, thy sweet tongue must plead for me
And tell why I have chosen thee!

Stern Reason is to judgment come,
Arrayed in all her forms of gloom:
Wilt thou, my advocate, be dumb?

No, radiant angel, speak and say,
Why I did cast the world away.

Why I have persevered to shun
The common paths that others run;
And on a strange road journeyed on,
Heedless, alike of wealth and power—
Of glory's wreath and pleasure's flower.

These, once, indeed, seemed Beings Divine;
And they, perchance, heard vows of mine,
And saw my offerings on their shrine;
But careless gifts are seldom prized,
And *mine* were worthily despised.

So, with a ready heart, I swore
To seek their altar-stone no more;
And gave my spirit to adore
Thee, ever-present, phantom thing—
My slave, my comrade, and my king.

A slave, because I rule thee still;
Incline thee to my changeful will,
And make thy influence good or ill
A comrade, for by day and night
Thou art my intimate delight,—

My darling pain that wounds and sears,
And wrings a blessing out from tears
By deadening me to earthly cares;
And yet, a king, though Prudence well
Have taught thy subject to rebel.

And am I wrong to worship where
Faith cannot doubt, nor hope despair,
Since my own soul can grant my prayer?
Speak, God of visions, plead for me,
And tell why I have chosen thee!

Emily Brontë (1818-1848).

15. ST. AGNES' EVE

DEEP on the convent-roof the snows
   Are sparkling to the moon:
My breath to heaven like vapour goes:
   May my soul follow soon!
The shadows of the convent-towers
   Slant down the snowy sward,
Still creeping with the creeping hours
   That lead me to my Lord:
Make Thou my spirit pure and clear
   As are the frosty skies,
Or this first snowdrop of the year
   That in my bosom lies.

As these white robes are soil'd and dark,
   To yonder shining ground;
As this pale taper's earthly spark,
   To yonder argent round;
So shows my soul before the Lamb,
   My spirit before Thee;
So in mine earthly house I am,
   To that I hope to be.
Break up the heavens, O Lord! and far,
   Thro' all yon starlight keen,
Draw me, thy bride, a glittering star,
   In raiment white and clean.

He lifts me to the golden doors;
   The flashes come and go;
All heaven bursts her starry floors,
   And strows her lights below,
And deepens on and up! the gates
   Roll back, and far within
For me the Heavenly Bridegroom waits,
   To make me pure of sin.

The sabbaths of Eternity,
   One sabbath deep and wide—
A light upon the shining sea—
   The Bridegroom with his bride!

                    Alfred Tennyson (1809-1892).

16. EARLY DAWN—LOVE AND HOPE

So ends the glory of the night,
   So dreary doth the morn appear,
So pale my spirit's waning light,
   So joyless to be lingering here.

Are stars, indeed, but dying fires?
   Is dawn, indeed, so deathly cold?
Gray images of chance desires,
   That perish whilst their leaves unfold?

Is all my soul's unquenchéd love
   But the faint shadow of a dream?
Must all my hopes unstable prove
   Uncertain bubbles of a stream?

Shall all my heart's outgoings back
   Unto their silent stream return—
No mingling waters in their track?
   Dull lesson which with years I learn!

That early light repaireth not
   The ending lustre of the sky;
So sadly fails my forward thought
   I hope, to weep—I love, to die.

Oh, inward, wasting, loving flame
   That warms none other breast than mine,
Which ever burns alone, the same
   In my own being's depths to shine!

Not here affection finds its scope,
  Its heritage is fixed above.
Where shall my heart secure its hope?
  When shall my spirit rest in love?

James Smetham (1821-1889).

17. THE VISIONARY

Silent is the house: all are laid asleep:
One alone looks out o'er the snow-wreaths deep,
Watching every cloud, dreading every breeze
That whirls the wildering drift, and bends the groaning trees.

Cheerful is the hearth, soft the matted floor:
Not one shivering gust creeps through pane or door;
The little lamp burns straight, its rays shoot strong and far:
I trim it well, to be the wanderer's guiding star.

Frown, my haughty sire! chide, my angry dame!
Set your slaves to spy; threaten me with shame:
But neither sire nor dame, nor prying serf shall know,
What angel nightly tracks that waste of frozen snow.

What I love shall come like visitant of air,
Safe in secret power from lurking human snare;
What loves me, no word of mine shall e'er betray,
Though for faith unstained my life must forfeit pay.

Burn, then, little lamp; glimmer straight and clear—
Hush! a rustling wing stirs, methinks, the air!
He for whom I wait, thus ever comes to me;
Strange Power! I trust thy might; trust thou my constancy.

Emily Brontë (1818-1848).

18. CALM IS THE MORN WITHOUT A SOUND

(From *In Memoriam*)

CALM is the morn without a sound,
    Calm as to suit a calmer grief,
    And only thro' the faded leaf
The chestnut pattering to the ground:

Calm and deep peace on this high wold,
    And on these dews that drench the furze,
    And all the silvery gossamers
That twinkle into green and gold:

Calm and still light on yon great plain
    That sweeps with all its autumn bowers,
    And crowded farms and lessening towers,
To mingle with the bounding main:

Calm and deep peace in this wide air,
    These leaves that redden to the fall;
    And in my heart, if calm at all,
If any calm, a calm despair:

Calm on the seas, and silver sleep,
    And waves that sway themselves in rest,
    And dead calm in that noble breast
Which heaves but with the heaving deep.
                    Alfred Tennyson (1809-1892).

19. THE SOUL'S DEPARTURE

OH let me die at dawn,
    The stir of living men
Would call my waning spirit back
    Unto its home again.

But at the early light
  Existence seems afar,
Back in the depths of parted time
  As fading planets are.

Let me go forth alone,
  Before the sun uprise,
And meet the springing of the morn
  In its own distant skies.

Yes! let me die at dawn,
  The stir of living men
Would call my waning spirit back
  Unto its home again.

James Smetham (1821-1889).

20. THE PRISONER

(A FRAGMENT)

IN the dungeon crypts idly did I stray,
Reckless of the lives wasting there away;
"Draw the ponderous bars! open, Warder stern!"
He dared not say me nay—the hinges harshly turn.

"Our guests are darkly lodged," I whisper'd, gazing through
The vault, whose grated eye showed heaven more gray than blue;
(This was when glad Spring laughed in awaking pride;)
"Ay, darkly lodged enough!" returned my sullen guide.

Then, God forgive my youth; forgive my careless tongue;
I scoffed, as the chill chains on the damp flagstones rung:
"Confined in triple walls, art thou so much to fear,
That we must bind thee down and clench thy fetters here?"

The captive raised her face; it was as soft and mild
As sculptured marble saint, or slumbering unwean'd child;
It was so soft and mild, it was so sweet and fair,
Pain could not trace a line, nor grief a shadow there!

The captive raised her hand and pressed it to her brow;
"I have been struck," she said, "and I am suffering now;
Yet these are little worth, your bolts and irons strong;
And, were they forged in steel, they could not hold me long."

Hoarse laughed the jailor grim: "Shall I be won to hear;
Dost think, fond, dreaming wretch, that *I* shall grant thy prayer?
Or, better still, will melt my master's heart with groans?
Ah! sooner might the sun thaw down these granite stones.

"My master's voice is low, his aspect bland and kind,
But hard as hardest flint the soul that lurks behind;
And I am rough and rude, yet not more rough to see
Than is the hidden ghost that has its home in me."

About her lips there played a smile of almost scorn,
"My friend," she gently said, "you have not heard me mourn;
When you my kindred's lives, *my* lost life, can restore,
Then may I weep and sue,—but never, friend, before!

"Still, let my tyrants know, I am not doomed to wear
Year after year in gloom, and desolate despair;
A messenger of Hope comes every night to me,
And offers for short life, eternal liberty.

"He comes with western winds, with evening's wandering airs;
With that clear dusk of heaven that brings the thickest stars.
Winds take a pensive tone, and stars a tender fire,
And visions rise, and change, that kill me with desire.

"Desire for nothing known in my maturer years,
When Joy grew mad with awe, at counting future tears.
When, if my spirit's sky was full of flashes warm,
I knew not whence they came, from sun or thunderstorm.

"But, first, a hush of peace—a soundless calm descends;
That struggle of distress, and fierce impatience ends;
Mute music soothes my breast—unuttered harmony,
That I could never dream, till Earth was lost to me.

"Then dawns the Invisible; the Unseen its truth reveals,
My outward sense is gone, my inward essence feels:
Its wings are almost free—its home, its harbour found,
Measuring the gulf, it stoops and dares the final bound.

"Oh! dreadful is the check—intense the agony—
When the ear begins to hear, and the eye begins to see;
When the pulse begins to throb, the brain to think again;
The soul to feel the flesh, and the flesh to feel the chain.

"Yet I would lose no sting, would wish no torture less;
The more that anguish racks, the earlier it will bless;
And robed in fires of hell, or bright with heavenly shine,
If it but herald death, the vision is divine!"

She ceased to speak, and we, unanswering, turned to go—
We had no further power to work the captive woe:
Her cheek, her gleaming eye, declared that man had given
A sentence, unapproved, and overruled by Heaven.

Emily Brontë (1818-1848).

21. LOVE IS AND WAS MY LORD AND KING

(From *In Memoriam*)

LOVE is and was my Lord and King,
    And in his presence I attend
    To hear the tidings of my friend,
Which every hour his couriers bring.

Love is and was my King and Lord,
    And will be, tho' as yet I keep
    Within his court on earth, and sleep
Encompass'd by his faithful guard,

And hear at times a sentinel
    Who moves about from place to place,
    And whispers to the worlds of space,
In the deep night, that all is well.

Alfred Tennyson (1809-1892).

22. STARS

AH! why, because the dazzling sun
    Restored our Earth to joy,
Have you departed every one,
    And left a desert sky?

All through the night, your glorious eyes
    Were gazing down in mine,
And, with a full heart's thankful sighs,
    I blessed that watch divine.

I was at peace, and drank your beams
    As they were life to me;
And revelled in my changeful dreams,
    Like petrel on the sea.

Thought followed thought, star followed star,
    Through boundless regions, on;
While one sweet influence, near and far,
    Thrilled through, and proved us one!

Why did the morning dawn to break
    So great, so pure, a spell;
And scorch with fire the tranquil cheek,
    Where your cool radiance fell?

Blood-red, he rose, and, arrow-straight,
    His fierce beams struck my brow;
The soul of nature sprang, elate,
    But *mine* sank sad and low!

My lids closed down, yet through their veil
    I saw him, blazing, still,
And steep in gold the misty dale,
    And flash upon the hill.

I turned me to the pillow, then,
    To call back night, and see
Your worlds of solemn light, again,
    Throb with my heart, and me!

It would not do—the pillow glowed,
    And glowed both roof and floor;
And birds sang loudly in the wood,
    And fresh winds shook the door;

The curtains waved, the wakened flies
    Were murmuring round my room,
Imprisoned there, till I should rise,
    And give them leave to roam.

Oh, stars, and dreams, and gentle night;
    Oh, night and stars, return!
And hide me from the hostile light
    That does not warm, but burn;

That drains the blood of suffering men;
    Drinks tears, instead of dew;
Let me sleep through his blinding reign,
    And only wake with you!

                Emily Brontë (1818-1848).

23. UNWATCH'D, THE GARDEN BOUGH SHALL SWAY

(From *In Memoriam*)

UNWATCH'D, the garden bough shall sway,
    The tender blossom flutter down.
    Unloved, that beech will gather brown,
This maple burn itself away;

Unloved, the sun-flower, shining fair,
    Ray round with flames her disk of seed,
    And many a rose-carnation feed
With summer spice the humming air;

Unloved, by many a sandy bar,
    The brook shall babble down the plain,
    At noon or when the lesser wain
Is twisting round the polar star;

Uncared for, gird the windy grove,
    And flood the haunts of hern and crake;
    Or into silver arrows break
The sailing moon in creek and cove;

Till from the garden and the wild
    A fresh association blow,
    And year by year the landscape grow
Familiar to the stranger's child;

As year by year the labourer tills
    His wonted glebe, or lops the glades;
    And year by year our memory fades
From all the circle of the hills.

                  Alfred Tennyson (1809-1892).

24. AGED TWENTY-TWO

October 23rd, 1851.   Went to bed rather late, and read *In Memoriam*, which produced a refining melancholy.

               John Everett Millais (1829-1896).

25. A FRESH, DEEP SNOW-DRIFT

IN the range of inorganic nature I doubt if any object can be found more perfectly beautiful, than a fresh, deep snow-drift, seen under warm light.   Its curves are of inconceivable perfection and changefulness; its surface and transparency alike exquisite; its light and shade of inexhaustible variety and inimitable finish,—the shadows sharp, pale, and of heavenly colour, the reflected lights intense and multitudinous, and mingled with the sweet occurrences of transmitted light.

                    John Ruskin (1819-1900).

26. DOUBT COMES WITH THE DEVELOPMENT THEORY
(1844)

i

A CANDID consideration of all these circumstances can scarcely
fail to introduce into our minds a somewhat different idea of
organic creation from what has hitherto been generally entertained.   That God created animated beings, as well as the
terraqueous theatre of their being, is a fact so powerfully
evidenced, and so universally received, that I at once take it
for granted.   But in the particulars of this so highly supported
idea, we surely here see cause for some re-consideration.   It
may now be enquired,—In what way was the creation of
animated beings effected?   The ordinary notion may, I think,
be not unjustly described as this,—that the Almighty author
produced the progenitors of all existing species by some sort
of personal or immediate exertion.   But how does this notion
comport with what we have seen of the gradual advance of
species, from the humblest to the highest?   How can we suppose
an immediate exertion of this creative power at one time to
produce zoophytes, another time to add a few marine mollusks,
another to bring in one or two conchifers, again to produce
crustaceous fishes, and so on to the end?   This would surely
be to take a very mean view of the Creative Power—to, in
short, anthropomorphize it, or reduce it to some such character
as that borne by the ordinary proceedings of mankind.   And
yet this would be unavoidable; for that the organic creation
was thus progressive through a long space of time, rests on
evidence that nothing can overturn or gainsay.   Some other
idea must then be come to with regard to *the mode* in which
the Divine Author proceeded in the organic creation.   Let us
seek in the history of the earth's formation for a new suggestion
on this point.   We have seen powerful evidence, that the
construction of this globe and its associates, and inferentially
that of all the other globes of space, was the result, not of any
immediate or personal exertion on the part of the Deity, but
of natural laws which are expressions of his will.   What is to

hinder our supposing that the organic creation is also a result of natural laws, which are in like manner an expression of his will? More than this, the fact of the cosmical arrangements being an effect of natural law, is a powerful argument for the organic arrangements being so likewise, for how can we suppose that the august Being who brought all these countless worlds into form by the simple establishment of a natural principle flowing from his mind, was to interfere personally and specially on every occasion when a new shell-fish or reptile was to be ushered into existence upon *one* of these worlds? Surely the idea is too ridiculous to be for a moment entertained?

ii

The tendency of all these illustrations is to make us look to *developement* as the principle which has been immediately concerned in the peopling of this globe, a process extending over a vast space of time, but which is nevertheless connected in character with the briefer process by which an individual being is evoked from a simple germ. What mystery is there here—and how shall I proceed to enunciate the conception which I have ventured to form of what may prove to be its proper solution! It is an idea by no means calculated to impress by its greatness, or to puzzle by its profoundness. It is an idea more marked by simplicity than perhaps any other of those which have explained the great secrets of nature. But in this lies, perhaps, one of its strongest claims to the faith of mankind.

Robert Chambers (1802-1871).

27. IN THE GREAT METROPOLIS

EACH for himself is still the rule:
We learn it when we go to school—
     The devil take the hindmost, O!

And when the schoolboys grow to men,
In life they learn it o'er again—
     The devil take the hindmost, O!

For in the church, and at the bar,
On 'Change, at court, where'er they are,
   The devil takes the hindmost, O!

Husband for husband, wife for wife,
Are careful that in married life
   The devil takes the hindmost, O!

From youth to age, whate'er the game,
The unvarying practice is the same—
   The devil take the hindmost, O!

And after death, we do not know,
But scarce can doubt, where'er we go,
   The devil takes the hindmost, O!

  Ti rol de rol, ti rol de ro,
  The devil take the hindmost, O!
           A. H. Clough (1819-1861).

28. THE SHADOW

(A FRAGMENT)

I DREAMED a dream: I dreamt that I espied,
Upon a stone that was not rolled aside,
A Shadow sit upon a grave—a Shade,
As thin, as unsubstantial, as of old
Came, the Greek poet told,
To lick the life-blood in the trench Ulysses made—
As pale, as thin, and said:
"I am the Resurrection of the Dead.
The night is past, the morning is at hand,
And I must in my proper semblance stand,
Appear brief space and vanish,—listen, this is true,
I am that Jesus whom they slew."

And shadows dim, I dreamed, the dead apostles came,
And bent their heads for sorrow and for shame—
Sorrow for their great loss, and shame
For what they did in that vain name.

And in long ranges far behind there seemed
Pale vapoury angel forms; or was it cloud? that kept
Strange watch; the women also stood beside and wept.
    And Peter spoke the word:
"O my own Lord,
What is it we must do?
Is it then all untrue?
Did we not see, and hear, and handle Thee,
Yea, for whole hours
Upon the Mount in Galilee,
On the lake shore, and here at Bethany,
When Thou ascended to Thy God and ours?"
    And paler still became the distant cloud,
And at the word the women wept aloud.

And the Shade answered, "What ye say I know not;
        But it is true
        I am that Jesus whom they slew,
Whom ye have preached, but in what way I know not."

*   *   *   *

And the great World, it chanced, came by that way,
And stopped, and looked, and spoke to the police,
And said the thing, for order's sake and peace,
Most certainly must be suppressed, the nuisance cease.
His wife and daughter must have where to pray,
And whom to pray to, at the least one day
In seven, and something sensible to say.
Whether the fact so many years ago
Had, or not, happened, how was he to know?
Yet he had always heard that it was so.
As for himself, perhaps it was all one;
And yet he found it not unpleasant, too,
On Sunday morning in the roomy pew,

To see the thing with such decorum done.
As for himself, perhaps it was all one;
Yet on one's death-bed all men always said
It was a comfortable thing to think upon
The atonement and the resurrection of the dead.
So the great World as having said his say,
Unto his country-house pursued his way.
And on the grave the Shadow sat all day.

*   *   *   *

And the poor Pope was sure it must be so,
Else wherefore did the people kiss his toe?
The subtle Jesuit cardinal shook his head,
And mildly looked and said,
It mattered not a jot
Whether the thing, indeed, were so or not;
Religion must be kept up, and the Church preserved,
And for the people this best served.
And then he turned, and added most demurely,
"Whatever may befall,
We Catholics need no evidence at all,
The holy father is infallible, surely!"

And English canons heard,
And quietly demurred.
Religion rests on evidence, of course,
And on inquiry we must put no force.
Difficulties still, upon whatever ground,
Are likely, almost certain, to be found.
The Theist scheme, the Pantheist, one and all,
Must with, or e'en before, the Christian fall.
And till the thing were plainer to our eyes,
To disturb faith was surely most unwise.
As for the Shade, who trusted such narration?
Except, of course, in ancient revelation.

And dignitaries of the Church came by.
It had been worth to some of them, they said,
Some hundred thousand pounds a year a head.

If it fetched so much in the market, truly,
'Twas not a thing to be given up unduly.
It had been proved by Butler in one way,
By Paley better in a later day;
It had been proved in twenty ways at once,
By many a doctor plain to many a dunce;
There was no question but it must be so.
    And the Shade answered, that He did not know;
He had no reading, and might be deceived,
But still He was the Christ, as He believed.

And women, mild and pure,
Forth from still homes and village schools did pass,
And asked, if this indeed were thus, alas,
What should they teach their children and the poor?
    The Shade replied, He could not know,
But it was truth, the fact was so.

*   *   *   *

A. H. Clough (1819-1861).

29. MARY ARNOLD, THE FEMALE MONSTER

Of all the tales was ever told,
I now will you impart,
That cannot fail to terror strike,
To every human heart.
The deeds of Mary Arnold,
Who does in a jail deplore,
Oh! such a dreadful tale as this,
Was never told before.

Chorus

This wretched woman's dreadful deed,
Does every one affright.
With black beetles in walnut shells
She deprived her child of sight.

Now think you, tender parents,
What must this monster feel,
The heart within her breast must ten
Times harder be than steel.
The dreadful crime she did commit
Does all the world surprise,
Black beetles placed in walnut shells
Bound round her infant's eyes.

The beetles in a walnut shell
This monster she did place,
This dreadful deed, as you may read,
All history does disgrace,
The walnut shell, and beetles,
With a bandage she bound tight,
Around her infant's tender eyes,
To take away its sight.

A lady saw this monster
In the street when passing by,
And she was struck with terror
For to hear the infant cry.
The infant's face she swore to see,
Which filled her with surprise,
To see the fatal bandage,
Tied round the infant's eyes.

With speed she called an officer,
Oh! shocking to relate,
Who beheld the deed, and took the wretch
Before the Magistrate.
Who committed her for trial,
Which did the wretch displease,
And she's now transported ten long years,
Across the briny seas.

Is there another in the world,
Could plan such wicked deed,
No one upon this earth before,
Of such did ever see.

To take away her infant's sight,
'Tis horrible to tell,
Binding black beetles round its eyes
Placed in walnut shells.

Anon. (A Street Ballad).

30. THE WORKHOUSE BOY

THE cloth was laid in the Vorkhouse hall,
The great-coats hung on the white-wash'd wall;
The paupers all were blithe and gay,
Keeping their Christmas holiday,
When the Master he cried with a roguish leer,
"You'll all get fat on your Christmas cheer!"
When one by his looks did seem to say,
"I'll have some more soup on this Christmas-day."
    Oh the Poor Vorkhouse Boy.

At length, all on us to bed vos sent,
The boy vos missing—in search ve vent:
Ve sought him above, ve sought him below,
Ve sought him with faces of grief and woe;
Ve sought him that hour, ve sought him that night;
Ve sought him in fear, and ve sought him in fright,
Ven a young pauper cried "I knows ve shall
Get jolly vell vopt for losing our pal."
    Oh the Poor Vorkhouse Boy.

Ve sought in each corner, each crevice ve knew;
Ve sought down the yard, ve sought up the flue;
Ve sought in each kettle, each saucepan, each pot,
In the water-butt look'd, but found him not.
And veeks roll'd on;—ve vere all of us told
That somebody said, he'd been burk'd and sold;
Ven our master goes out, the Parishioners vild
Cry "There goes the cove that burk'd the poor child."
    Oh the Poor Vorkhouse Boy.

At length the soup copper repairs did need,
The Coppersmith came, and there he seed,
A dollop of bones lay a-grizzling there,
In the leg of the breeches the poor boy did vear!

To gain his fill the boy did stoop,
And dreadful to tell, he was boil'd in the soup!
And ve all of us say, and ve say it sincere,
That he was push'd in there by an overseer.
Oh the Poor Workhouse Boy.

Anon. (A Street Ballad).

31. THE ITCH WARD IN THE WORKHOUSE

IN a room opening from a squalid yard, where a number of listless women were lounging to and fro, trying to get warm in the ineffectual sunshine of the tardy May morning—in the "Itch Ward," not to compromise the truth—a woman such as HOGARTH has often drawn, was hurriedly getting on her gown before a dusty fire. She was the nurse, or wardswoman, of that insalubrious department—herself a pauper—flabby, raw-boned, untidy—unpromising and coarse of aspect as need be. But, on being spoken to about the patients whom she had in charge, she turned round with her shabby gown half on, half off, and fell a-crying with all her might. Not for show, not querulously, not in any mawkish sentiment, but in the deep grief and affliction of her heart; turning away her dishevelled head: sobbing most bitterly, wringing her hands, and letting fall abundance of great tears, that choked her utterance. What was the matter with the nurse of the itch-ward? Oh, "the dropped child" was dead! Oh, the child that was found in the street, and she had brought up ever since, had died an hour ago, and see where the little creature lay, beneath this cloth! The dear, the pretty dear!

The dropped child seemed too small and poor a thing for Death to be in earnest with, but Death had taken it; and already its diminutive form was neatly washed, composed, and stretched as if in sleep upon a box. I thought I heard a voice from Heaven saying, It shall be well for thee, O nurse of the itch-ward, when some less gentle pauper does those offices to thy cold form, that such as the dropped child are the angels who behold my Father's face!

Charles Dickens (1812-1870).

32. THE POOR MAN AND THE RICH

THE poor man's sins are glaring;
In the face of ghostly warning
    He is caught in the fact
    Of an overt act—
Buying greens on a Sunday morning.

The rich man's sins are hidden,
In the pomp of wealth and station;
    And escape the sight
    Of the children of light,
Who are wise in their generation.

The rich man has a kitchen,
And cooks to dress his dinner;
    The poor who would roast
    To the baker's must post,
And thus become a sinner.

The rich man has a cellar,
And a ready butler by him;
    The poor must steer
    For his pint of beer
Where the saint can't choose but spy him.

The rich man's painted windows
Hide the concerts of the quality;
    The poor can but share
    A crack'd fiddle in the air,
Which offends all sound morality.

The rich man is invisible
In the crowd of his gay society;
    But the poor man's delight
    Is a sore in the sight,
And a stench in the nose of piety.

The rich man has a carriage
Where no rude eye can flout him;
    The poor man's bane
    Is a third-class train,
With the daylight all about him.

The rich man goes out yachting,
Where sanctity can't pursue him;
    The poor goes afloat
    In a fourpenny boat,
Where the bishop groans to view him.
                 T. L. Peacock (1785-1866).

33. THE RAILROAD

An' while I went 'ithin a traïn,
A-ridèn on athirt the plaïn,
A-cleärèn swifter than a hound,
On twin-laid raïls, the zwimmèn ground;
I cast my eyes 'ithin a park,
Upon a woak wi' grey-white bark,
An' while I kept his head my mark,
The rest seem'd wheelèn round en.
An' when in life our love do cling
The clwosest round zome single thing,
We then do vind that all the rest
Do wheel roun' that, vor vu'st an' best;
Zoo while our life do laeste, mid nought
But what is good an' feaïr be sought,
In word or deed, or heart or thought,
An' all the rest wheel round it.
                 William Barnes (1800-1886).

34. THE SPECULATORS

The night was stormy and dark,   The town was shut up in sleep: Only those were abroad who were out on a lark,   Or those who'd no beds to keep.

I pass'd through the lonely street,   The wind did sing and blow;   I could hear the policeman's feet   Clapping to and fro.

There stood a potato-man In the midst of all the wet;
He stood with his 'tato-can In the lonely Haymarket.

Two gents of dismal mien, And dank and greasy rags,
Came out of a shop for gin, Swaggering over the flags:

Swaggering over the stone, These shabby bucks did walk;
And I went and followed those seedy ones, And listened to
their talk.

Was I sober or awake? Could I believe my ears? Those
dismal beggars spake Of nothing but railroad shares.

I wondered more and more: Says one—"Good friend of
mine, How many shares have you wrote for? In the Diddle-
sex Junction line?"

"I wrote for twenty," says Jim, "But they wouldn't give
me one;" His comrade straight rebuked him For the folly
he had done:

"O Jim, you are unawares Of the ways of this bad town;
I always write for five hundred shares, And *then* they put
me down."

"And yet you got no shares," Says Jim, "for all your
boast;" "I *would* have wrote," says Jack, "but where Was
the penny to pay the post?"

"I lost, for I couldn't pay That first instalment up; But
here's taters smoking hot—I say Let's stop my boy and sup."

And at this simple feast The while they did regale, I drew
each ragged capitalist Down on my left thumb-nail.

Their talk did me perplex, All night I tumbled and tost,
And thought of railroad specs., And how money was won
and lost.

"Bless railroads everywhere," I said, "and the world's
advance; Bless every railroad share In Italy, Ireland, France;
For never a beggar need now despair, And every rogue has
a chance."   *W. M. Thackeray* (1811-1863).

35. GREAT RAILROADS AND GREAT RAILROAD AGE

THE oily swell darkens into crisp velvet-green, till the air strikes us, and heels us over; and leaping, plunging, thrashing our bows into the seas, we spring away close-hauled upon the ever-freshening breeze. . .

Exquisite motion! more maddening than the smooth floating stride of the race-horse, or the crash of the thorn-hedges before the stalwart hunter, or the swaying of the fir-boughs in the gale, when we used to climb as schoolboys after the lofty hawk's nest; but not so maddening as the new motion of our age—the rush of the express-train, when the live iron pants and leaps and roars through the long chalk cutting; and white mounds gleam cold a moment against the sky and vanish; and rocks, and grass, and bushes, fleet by in dim blended lines; and the long hedges revolve like the spokes of a gigantic wheel; and far below, meadows, and streams, and homesteads, with all their lazy old-world life, open for an instant, and then flee away; while awestruck, silent, choked with the mingled sense of pride and helplessness, we are swept on by that great pulse of England's life-blood, rushing down her iron veins; and dimly out of the future looms the fulfilment of our primaeval mission, to conquer and subdue the earth, and space too, and time, and all things,—even, hardest of all tasks, yourselves, my cunning brothers; ever learning some fresh lesson, except that hardest one of all, that it is the Spirit of God which giveth you understanding.

Yes, great railroads, and great railroad age, who would exchange you, with all your sins, for any other time? For swiftly as rushes matter, more swiftly rushes mind; more swiftly still rushes the heavenly dawn up the eastern sky. "The night is far spent, the day is at hand." "Blessed is that servant whom his Lord, when He cometh, shall find watching!"

Charles Kingsley (1819-1875).

36. OLD ENGLAND FOREVER AND DO IT NO MORE

As the Queen and Prince Albert, so buxom and all pert,
    Were jovially conversing together one day,

Old Bull heard them talking as they were awalking,
   And V. unto A. so boldly did say
That State seems bewildering about little children,
   And we are increasing every day, you know we have four,
We kindly do treat them and seldom do beat them,
   So Albert, dear Albert, we'll do it no more.

Said A., my dearest, there's nothing thou fearest,
   Thou art loved and respected in every degree,
If Old Bull don't like it why then he may pipe it,
   And kiss our royal twins, twee diddle dee,
So do not degrade me and try to persuade me
   All pleasure and pastime to freely give o'er,
If you do I'll be jolting and off I'll be bolting,
   Right over the seas singing do it no more.

An old anti-reformer lives near Hyde Park Corner,
   A regular old swaddy who wears scarlet clothes,
There is no one bolder than this rum old soldier,
   Let him go where he will he is known by his nose,
He cried shoulder arms boys and banish alarm boys,
   The 18th of June will now shortly be o'er,
He once strong and hearty whopped old Buonaparte,
   But pipe-clay and powder will do it no more.

Now let me approach then ye cooks and ye coachmen,
   You footmen and servants of every degree,
If out in the stable or under the table
   You have danced to a hornpipe called twee diddle dee,
By noon night and morning from me take a warning,
   Such vile naughty tricks strive to quickly give o'er,
For fear of time telling the tide may be swelling,
   And you may get nicked so do it no more.

All you that are single in harmony mingle,
   And say that you'll never be left in the lurch,
Moping single don't tarry, but strive for to marry,
   Look out for a partner and toddle to church,

And when you have hurried to church and got married
 Live and be happy, each other adore,
Then you'll not be forsaken, sing fried eggs and bacon,
 The Queen and Prince Albert, and do it no more.

Anon. (*A Street Ballad*).

37. MOUNTAIN PURPLES

CONSIDER, first, the difference produced in the whole tone of
landscape colour by the introduction of purple, violet, and deep
ultramarine blue, which we owe to mountains. In an ordinary
lowland landscape we have the blue of the sky; the green of
grass, which I will suppose (and this is an unnecessary con-
cession to the lowlands) entirely fresh and bright; the green
of trees; and certain elements of purple, far more rich and
beautiful than we generally should think, in their bark and
shadows (bare hedges and thickets, or tops of trees, in subdued
afternoon sunshine, are nearly perfect purple, and of an
exquisite tone), as well as in ploughed fields, and dark ground
in general. But among mountains, in *addition* to all this, large
unbroken spaces of pure violet and purple are introduced in
their distances; and even near, by films of cloud passing over
the darkness of ravines or forests, blues are produced of the
most subtle tenderness; these azures and purples passing into
rose-colour of otherwise wholly unattainable delicacy among
the upper summits, the blue of the sky being at the same time
purer and deeper than in the plains. Nay, in some sense a
person who has never seen the rose-colour of the rays of dawn
crossing a blue mountain twelve or fifteen miles away, can
hardly be said to know what *tenderness* in colour means at all;
bright tenderness he may, indeed, see in the sky or in a flower,
but this grave tenderness of the far-away hill-purples he cannot
conceive. *John Ruskin* (1819-1900).

38. A MOONRISE

. . Last evening, when, just after dark,
 You rose up to depart,
We saw the moon, all liquid white,
 Out of the dark trees start:—

As then I felt, I felt when you
    First came upon my heart. . .
                        Coventry Patmore (1823-1896).

39. THE CAMPAGNA

PERHAPS there is no more impressive scene on earth than the
solitary extent of the Campagna of Rome under evening light.
Let the reader imagine himself for the moment withdrawn
from the sounds and motion of the living world, and sent forth
alone into this wild and wasted plain.   The earth yields and
crumbles beneath his foot, tread he never so lightly, for its
substance is white, hollow, and carious, like the dusty wreck
of the bones of men.   The long knotted grass waves and tosses
feebly in the evening wind, and the shadows of its motion shake
feverishly along the banks of ruin that lift themselves to the
sunlight.   Hillocks of mouldering earth heave around him, as
if the dead beneath were struggling in their sleep; scattered
blocks of black stone, four-square, remnants of mighty edifices,
not one left upon another, lie upon them to keep them down.
A dull purple poisonous haze stretches level along the desert,
veiling its spectral wrecks of massy ruins, on whose rents the
red light rests, like a dying fire on defiled altars.   The blue
ridge of the Alban Mount lifts itself against a solemn space of
green, clear, quiet sky.   Watch-towers of dark clouds stand
steadfastly along the promontories of the Apennines.   From
the plain to the mountains, the shattered aqueducts, pier
beyond pier, melt into the darkness, like shadowy and countless
troops of funeral mourners, passing from a nation's grave.
                        John Ruskin (1819-1900).

40. THE ENGLISHMAN IN ITALY

(PIANO DI SORRENTO)

FORTÙ, Fortù, my beloved one,
    Sit here by my side,
On my knees put up both little feet!
    I was sure, if I tried,

I could make you laugh spite of Scirocco.
    Now, open your eyes,
Let me keep you amused till he vanish
    In black from the skies,
With telling my memories over
    As you tell your beads;
All the Plain saw me gather, I garland
    —The flowers or the weeds.

Time for rain! for your long hot dry Autumn
    Had net-worked with brown
The white skin of each grape on the bunches,
    Marked like a quail's crown,
Those creatures you make such account of,
    Whose heads,—speckled white
Over brown like a great spider's back,
    As I told you last night,—
Your mother bites off for her supper.
    Red-ripe as could be,
Pomegranates were chapping and splitting
    In halves on the tree:
And betwixt the loose walls of great flint-stone,
    Or in the thick dust
On the path, or straight out of the rockside,
    Wherever could thrust
Some burnt sprig of bold hardy rock-flower
    Its yellow face up,
For the prize were great butterflies fighting,
    Some five for one cup.
So, I guessed, ere I got up this morning,
    What change was in store,
By the quick rustle-down of the quail-nets
    Which woke me before
I could open my shutter, made fast
    With a bough and a stone,
And look thro' the twisted dead vine-twigs,
    Sole lattice that's known.
Quick and sharp rang the rings down the net-poles,
    While, busy beneath,

Your priest and his brother tugged at them,
    The rain in their teeth.
And out upon all the flat house-roofs
    Where split figs lay drying,
The girls took the frails under cover:
    Nor use seemed in trying
To get out the boats and go fishing,
    For, under the cliff,
Fierce the black water frothed o'er the blind-rock.
    No seeing our skiff
Arrive about noon from Amalfi,
    —Our fisher arrive,
And pitch down his basket before us,
    All trembling alive
With pink and grey jellies, your sea-fruit;
    You touch the strange lumps,
And mouths gape there, eyes open, all manner
    Of horns and of humps,
Which only the fisher looks grave at,
    While round him like imps
Cling screaming the children as naked
    And brown as his shrimps;
Himself too as bare to the middle
    —You see round his neck
The string and its brass coin suspended,
    That saves him from wreck.
But to-day not a boat reached Salerno,
    So back, to a man,
Came our friends, with whose help in the vineyards
    Grape-harvest began.
In the vat, half-way up in our house-side,
    Like blood the juice spins,
While your brother all bare-legged is dancing
    Till breathless he grins
Dead-beaten in effort on effort
    To keep the grapes under,
Since still when he seems all but master,
    In pours the fresh plunder
From girls who keep coming and going

With basket on shoulder,
And eyes shut against the rain's driving;
    Your girls that are older,—
For under the hedges of aloe,
    And where, on its bed
Of the orchard's black mould, the love-apple
    Lies pulpy and red,
All the young ones are kneeling and filling
    Their laps with the snails
Tempted out by this first rainy weather,—
    Your best of regales,
As to-night will be proved to my sorrow,
    When, supping in state,
We shall feast our grape-gleaners (two dozen,
    Three over one plate)
With lasagne so tempting to swallow
    In slippery ropes,
And gourds fried in great purple slices,
    That colour of popes.
Meantime, see the grape bunch they've brought you:
    The rain-water slips
O'er the heavy blue bloom on each globe
    Which the wasp to your lips
Still follows with fretful persistence:
    Nay, taste, while awake,
This half of a curd-white smooth cheese-ball
    That peels, flake by flake,
Like an onion, each smoother and whiter;
    Next, sip this weak wine
From the thin green glass flask, with its stopper,
    A leaf of the vine;
And end with the prickly-pear's red flesh
    That leaves thro' its juice
The stony black seeds on your pearl-teeth.
    Scirocco is loose!
Hark, the quick, whistling pelt of the olives
    Which, thick in one's track,
Tempt the stranger to pick up and bite them,
    Tho' not yet half black!

How the old twisted olive trunks shudder,
    The medlars let fall
Their hard fruit, and the brittle great fig-trees
    Snap off, figs and all,
For here comes the whole of the tempest!
    No refuge, but creep
Back again to my side and my shoulder,
    And listen or sleep.
O how will your country show next week,
    When all the vine-boughs
Have been stripped of their foliage to pasture
    The mules and the cows?
Last eve, I rode over the mountains;
    Your brother, my guide,
Soon left me, to feast on the myrtles
    That offered, each side,
Their fruit-balls, black, glossy and luscious,—
    Or strip from the sorbs
A treasure, or, rosy and wondrous,
    Those hairy gold orbs!
But my mule picked his sure sober path out,
    Just stopping to neigh
When he recognized down in the valley
    His mates on their way
With the faggots and barrels of water;
    And soon we emerged
From the plain, where the woods could scarce follow;
    And still as we urged
Our way, the woods wondered, and left us,
    As up still we trudged
Though the wild path grew wilder each instant,
    And the place was e'en grudged
'Mid the rock-chasms and piles of loose stones
    Like the loose broken teeth
Of some monster which climbed there to die
    From the ocean beneath—
Place was grudged to the silver-grey fume-weed
    That clung to the path,
And dark rosemary ever a-dying

That, 'spite the wind's wrath,
So loves the salt rock's face to seaward,
    And lentisks [1] as staunch
To the stone where they root and bear berries,
    And . . . what shows a branch
Coral-coloured, transparent, with circlets
    Of pale seagreen leaves;
Over all trod my mule with the caution
    Of gleaners o'er sheaves,
Still, foot after foot like a lady,
    Till, round after round,
He climbed to the top of Calvano,
    And God's own profound
Was above me, and round me the mountains,
    And under, the sea,
And within me my heart to bear witness
    What was and shall be.
Oh, heaven and the terrible crystal!
    No rampart excludes
Your eye from the life to be lived
    In the blue solitudes.
Oh, those mountains, their infinite movement!
    Still moving with you;
For, ever some new head and breast of them
    Thrusts into view
To observe the intruder; you see it
    If quickly you turn
And, before they escape you, surprise them.
    They grudge you should learn
How the soft plains they look on, lean over
    And love (they pretend)
—Cower beneath them, the flat sea-pine crouches,
    The wild fruit-trees bend,
E'en the myrtle-leaves curl, shrink and shut:
    All is silent and grave:
'Tis a sensual and timorous beauty,
    How fair! but a slave.
So, I turned to the sea; and there slumbered

[1] The mastic tree (resinous).

As greenly as ever
Those isles of the siren, your Galli;
    No ages can sever
The Three, nor enable their sister
    To join them,—half-way
On the voyage, she looked at Ulysses—
    No farther to-day,
Tho' the small one, just launched in the wave,
    Watches breast-high and steady
From under the rock, her bold sister
    Swum half-way already.
Fortù, shall we sail there together
    And see from the sides
Quite new rocks show their faces, new haunts
    Where the siren abides?
Shall we sail round and round them, close over
    The rocks, tho' unseen,
That ruffle the grey glassy water
    To glorious green?
Then scramble from splinter to splinter,
    Reach land and explore,
On the largest, the strange square black turret
    With never a door,
Just a loop to admit the quick lizards;
    Then, stand there and hear
The birds' quiet singing, that tells us
    What life is, so clear?
—The secret they sang to Ulysses
    When, ages ago,
He heard and he knew this life's secret
    I hear and I know.

Ah, see! The sun breaks o'er Calvano;
    He strikes the great gloom
And flutters it o'er the mount's summit
    In airy gold fume.
All is over. Look out, see the gipsy,
    Our tinker and smith,
Has arrived, set up bellows and forge,

And down-squatted forthwith
To his hammering, under the wall there;
    One eye keeps aloof
The urchins that itch to be putting
    His jews'-harps to proof,
While the other, thro' locks of curled wire,
    Is watching how sleek
Shines the hog, come to share in the windfall
    —Chew, abbot's own cheek!
All is over. Wake up and come out now,
    And down let us go,
And see the fine things got in order
    At church for the show
Of the Sacrament, set forth this evening.
    To-morrow's the Feast
Of the Rosary's Virgin, by no means
    Of Virgins the least,
As you'll hear in the off-hand discourse
    Which (all nature, no art)
The Dominican brother, these three weeks,
    Was getting by heart.
Not a pillar nor post but is dizened
    With red and blue papers;
All the roof waves with ribbons, each altar
    A-blaze with long tapers;
But the great masterpiece is the scaffold
    Rigged glorious to hold
All the fiddlers and fifers and drummers
    And trumpeters bold,
Not afraid of Bellini nor Auber,
    Who, when the priest's hoarse,
Will strike us up something that's brisk
    For the feast's second course.
And then will the flaxen-winged Image
    Be carried in pomp
Thro' the plain, while in gallant procession
    The priests mean to stomp.
All round the glad church lie old bottles
    With gunpowder stopped,

Which will be, when the Image re-enters,
    Religiously popped;
And at night from the crest of Calvano
    Great bonfires will hang,
On the plain will the trumpets join chorus,
    And more poppers bang.
At all events, come—to the garden
    As far as the wall;
See me tap with a hoe on the plaster
    Till out there shall fall
A scorpion with wide angry nippers!

    —"Such trifles!" you say?
Fortù, in my England at home,
    Men meet gravely to-day
And debate, if abolishing Corn-laws
    Be righteous and wise
—If 'twere proper, Scirocco should vanish
    In black from the skies!

        Robert Browning (1812-1889).

41. SONNET

SAY over again and yet once over again
That thou dost love me. Though the word repeated
Should seem "a cuckoo song," as thou dost treat it,
Remember never to the hill or plain,
Valley and wood, without her cuckoo-strain,
Comes the fresh Spring in all her green completed!
Beloved, I, amid the darkness greeted
By a doubtful spirit-voice, in that doubt's pain
Cry . . . speak once more . . . thou lovest! Who can fear
Too many stars, though each in heaven shall roll—
Too many flowers, though each shall crown the year?
Say thou dost love me, love me, love me—toll
The silver iterance!—only minding, Dear,
To love me also in silence, with thy soul.

        Elizabeth Barrett Browning (1806-1861).

42. TWO LIMERICKS

THERE was a young man of Oporta,
Who daily got shorter and shorter,
　　The reason he said
　　Was the hod on his head,
Which was filled with the *heaviest* mortar.

His sister, named Lucy O'Finner,
Grew constantly thinner and thinner;
　　The reason was plain,
　　She slept out in the rain,
And was never allowed any dinner.

　　　　　　　　　　　Lewis Carroll (1832-1898).

43. LIMERICKS

i

THERE was an old Person whose habits
Induced him to feed upon Rabbits;
When he'd eaten eighteen, he turned perfectly green,
Upon which he relinquished those habits.

ii

THERE was an Old Man with a poker,
Who painted his face with red oker.
When they said, "You're a Guy!" he made no reply,
But knocked them all down with his poker.

iii

THERE was an Old Man of the Nile,
Who sharpened his nails with a file;
Till he cut off his thumbs, and said calmly, "This comes
Of sharpening one's nails with a file!"

iv

THERE was a young Lady of Tyre,
Who swept the loud chords of a lyre;
At the sound of each sweep, she enraptured the deep,
And enchanted the city of Tyre.

v

THERE was an Old Man on some rocks,
Who shut up his wife in a box.
When she said, "Let me out," he exclaimed, "Without doubt,
You will pass all your life in that box."

Edward Lear (1812-1888).

44. ASK ME NO MORE

ASK me no more: the moon may draw the sea;
   The cloud may stoop from heaven and take the shape
    With fold to fold, of mountain or of cape;
But O too fond, when have I answer'd thee ?
      Ask me no more.

Ask me no more: what answer should I give?
   I love not hollow cheek or faded eye:
    Yet, O my friend, I will not have thee die!
Ask me no more, lest I should bid thee live:
      Ask me no more.

Ask me no more: thy fate and mine are seal'd:
   I strove against the stream and all in vain:
    Let the great river take me to the main:
No more, dear love, for at a touch I yield;
      Ask me no more.

Alfred Tennyson (1809-1892).

45. PRE-RAPHAELITE DETAIL

     . . Then she press'd
Her small hand's weight of whiteness
To her richly-sloping breast. . .

Coventry Patmore (1823-1896).

46. THE SPLENDOUR FALLS ON CASTLE WALLS

THE splendour falls on castle walls
    And snowy summits old in story:
The long light shakes across the lakes,
    And the wild cataract leaps in glory.
Blow, bugle, blow, set the wild echoes flying,
Blow, bugle; answer, echoes, dying, dying, dying.

O hark, O hear! how thin and clear,
    And thinner, clearer, farther going!
O sweet and far from cliff and scar
    The horns of Elfland faintly blowing!
Blow, let us hear the purple glens replying:
Blow, bugle; answer, echoes, dying, dying, dying.

O love, they die in yon rich sky,
    They faint on hill or field or river:
Our eyes roll from soul to soul,
    And grow for ever and for ever.
Blow, bugle, blow, set the wild echoes flying,
And answer, echoes, answer, dying, dying, dying.
            Alfred Tennyson (1809-1892).

47. OF TRUTH OF COLOUR

IT had been wild weather when I left Rome, and all across the Campagna the clouds were sweeping in sulphurous blue, with a clap of thunder or two, and breaking gleams of sun along the Claudian aqueduct lighting up the infinity of its arches like the bridge of chaos. But as I climbed the long slope of the Alban Mount, the storm swept finally to the north, and the noble outline of the dome of Albano, and graceful darkness of its ilex grove, rose against pure streaks of alternate blue and amber; the upper sky gradually flushing through the last fragments of rain-cloud in deep palpitating azure, half aether and half dew. The noonday sun came slanting down the rocky slopes of La Riccia, and their masses of entangled and tall

foliage, whose autumnal tints were mixed with the wet verdure
of a thousand evergreens, were penetrated with it as with rain.
I cannot call it colour, it was conflagration. Purple, crimson,
and scarlet, like the curtains of God's tabernacle, the rejoicing
trees sank into the valley in showers of light, every separate
leaf quivering with buoyant and burning life; each, as it
turned to reflect or to transmit the sunbeam, first a torch and
then an emerald. Far up into the recesses of the valley, the
green vistas arched like the hollows of mighty waves of some
crystalline sea, with the arbutus flowers dashed along their
flanks for foam, and silver flakes of orange spray tossed into
the air around them, breaking over the grey walls of rock into
a thousand separate stars, fading and kindling alternately as
the weak wind lifted and let them fall. Every glade of grass
burned like the golden floor of heaven, opening in sudden
gleams as the foliage broke and closed above it, as sheet-
lightning opens in a cloud at sunset; the motionless masses of
dark rock—dark though flushed with scarlet lichen, casting their
quiet shadows across its restless radiance, the fountain underneath them filling its marble hollow with blue mist and fitful
sound; and over all the multitudinous bars of amber and rose,
the sacred clouds that have no darkness, and only exist to
illumine, were seen in fathomless intervals between the solemn
and orbed repose of the stone pines, passing to lose themselves
in the last, white, blinding lustre of the measureless line where
the Campagna melted into the blaze of the sea.

   Tell me who is likest this, Poussin or Turner?
                                        John Ruskin (1819-1900).

48. NOW SLEEPS THE CRIMSON PETAL

   Now sleeps the crimson petal, now the white;
Nor waves the cypress in the palace walk;
Nor winks the gold fin in the porphyry font:
The fire-fly wakens: waken thou with me.

   Now droops the milkwhite peacock like a ghost,
And like a ghost she glimmers on to me.

Now lies the Earth all Danaë to the stars,
And all thy heart lies open unto me.

Now slides the silent meteor on, and leaves
A shining furrow, as thy thoughts in me.

Now folds the lily all her sweetness up,
And slips into the bossom of the lake:
So fold thyself, my dearest, thou, and slip
Into my bosom and be lost in me.

Alfred Tennyson (1809-1892).

49. TOO LITTLE SUPERSTITIOUS

I WILL not shrink from uttering my firm conviction, that it would be a gain to this country, were it vastly more superstitious, more bigoted, more gloomy, more fierce in its religion, than at present it shows itself to be. Not, of course, that I think the tempers of mind herein implied desirable, which would be an evident absurdity; but I think them infinitely more desirable and more promising than a heathen obduracy, and a cold, self-sufficient, self-wise tranquillity. Doubtless, peace of mind, a quiet conscience, and a cheerful countenance are the gift of the Gospel, and the sign of a Christian; but the same effects (or rather, what appear to be the same) may arise from very different causes. Jonah slept in the storm,—so did our Blessed Lord. The one slept in an evil security: the Other in the "peace of God which passeth all understanding."

J. H. Newman (1801-1890).

PART TWO: CIRRUS AND MADREPORE

The crocus, in the shrewd March morn,
Thrusts up his saffron spear. . .

Coventry Patmore.

The Undertakers had all met.
They were dress'd in black a dingey set,
The picture frames black, and so were the walls,
And the window curtains were made of palls. . .

Street Ballad.

Yes! you can hammer up a coffin, you can plaster a tomb ; you
are nature's undertakers ; you cannot build it a home.

J. H. Newman.

O pale green sea,
With long pale purple clouds above. . .

William Allingham.

50. FOR US THERE MUST BE SOMETHING ELSE INTENDED

February 25, 1851.

Wordsworth's Prelude seems to me the dying utterance of the half century we have just passed through, the expression —the English expression at least—of all that self-building process in which, according to their different schemes and principles, Byron, Goethe, Wordsworth, the Evangelicals (Protestant and Romanist), were all engaged, with their novels, poems, experiences, prayers, in which God, under whatever name, or in whatever aspect, He presented Himself to them, was still the agent only in fitting them to be world-wise, men of genius, artists, saints. For us there must be something else intended—either the mere science millennium of Comte, from which good Lord deliver us, or the knowledge and life of God as the ground of all human and earthly knowledge and life.

F. D. Maurice (1805-1872).

51. A VICTORIAN SAINT: F. D. MAURICE

He was always an early riser. Hardly ever later than 6 a.m., often much earlier than that, the sound of the splash of the cold tub, which summer and winter, down to the end of his life, he invariably took both the first thing in the morning and the last at night, was to be heard, and a curiously pathetic, almost agonized "shou-shou" followed, which seemed to tell that, for a frame that was kept so low as his by constant brain-work and a somewhat self-stinted diet, the shock was almost a penance endured rather than enjoyed. Immediately after dressing he settled down to work at whatever his special task for the time might be, though very frequently if one came into his room at all suddenly, the result was to make him rise hurriedly from his knees, his face reddened, and his eyes depressed, by the intense pressure of his hands, the base of each of which had been driven and almost gouged into either eye-socket, the fingers and thumbs pressed down over forehead and head. The Greek Testament, open at some special point which had occupied him at the moment he kneeled down, lay on the chair before him; but as he rose the spirit seemed to have come back again into his face from the far-off region to which it had been travelling, and there was just the hint in the face of an involuntary sadness and almost of reproach that the spirit should be recalled from the intercourse it had been enjoying.

From the *Life of Frederick Denison Maurice*.

52. AN END

Love, strong as death, is dead.
Come, let us make his bed
    Among the dying flowers:
A green turf at his head;
And a stone at his feet,
Whereon we may sit
    In the quiet evening hours.

He was born in the spring,
And died before the harvesting.
    On the last warm summer day
    He left us;—he would not stay
    For autumn twilight cold and grey.
Sit we by his grave and sing
    He is gone away.

To few chords, and sad, and low,
    Sing we so.
Be our eyes fixed on the grass,
Shadow-veiled, as the years pass,
While we think of all that was
    In the long ago.

March 5, 1849.

Christina Rossetti (1830-1894).

53. AFTER DEATH

THE curtains were half drawn, the floor was swept
 And strewn with rushes, rosemary and may
 Lay thick upon the bed on which I lay,
Where through the lattice ivy-shadows crept.
He leaned above me, thinking that I slept
 And could not hear him; but I heard him say,
 "Poor child, poor child": and as he turned away
Came a deep silence, and I knew he wept.
He did not touch the shroud, or raise the fold
 That hid my face, or take my hand in his,
  Or ruffle the smooth pillows for my head:
 He did not love me living; but once dead
 He pitied me; and very sweet it is
To know he still is warm though I am cold.
April 28, 1849.
      Christina Rossetti (1830-1894).

54. *From* "A MODERN IDYLL"

. . Then, tired of gambols, turn into the dark
Fir-skirted margins of your father's park;
And watch the moving shadows, as you pass,
Trace their dim network on the tufted grass,
And how on birch-trunks smooth and branches old,
The velvet moss bursts out in green and gold,
Like the rich lustre full and manifold
On breasts of birds that star the curtained gloom
From their glass cases in the drawing-room. . .
      Walter Deverell (1827-1854).

55. PRE-RAPHAELITE

IN the fifteenth century, a certain feeble lamp of art arose in
the Italian town of Urbino. This poor light, Raphael Sanzio
by name, better known to a few miserably mistaken wretches
in these later days as Raphael (another burned at the same time
called Titian), was fed with a preposterous idea of Beauty—

with a ridiculous power of etherealizing, and exalting to the very Heaven of Heavens, what was most sublime and lovely in the expression of the human face divine on Earth—with the truly contemptible conceit of finding in poor humanity the fallen likeness of the angels of God, and raising it up again to their pure spiritual condition. This very fantastic whim effected a low revolution in Art, in this wise, that Beauty came to be regarded as one of its indispensable elements. In this very poor delusion, Artists have continued until this present nineteenth century, when it was reserved for some bold aspirants to "put it down."

The Pre-Raphael Brotherhood, Ladies and Gentlemen, is the dread Tribunal which is to set this matter right. Walk up, walk up; and here conspicuous on the wall of the Royal Academy of Art in England, in the eighty-second year of their annual exhibition, you shall see what this new Holy Brotherhood, this terrible Police that is to disperse all Post-Raphael offenders, had "been and done!"

You come—In this Royal Academy Exhibition, which is familiar with the works of WILKIE, COLLINS, ETTY, EASTLAKE, MULREADY, LESLIE, MACLISE, TURNER, STANFIELD, LANDSEER, ROBERTS, DANBY, CRESWICK, LEE, WEBSTER, HERBERT, DYCE, COPE, and others who would have been renowned as great masters in any age or country—you come, in this place, to the contemplation of a Holy Family. You will have the goodness to discharge from your minds all Post-Raphael ideas, all religious aspirations, all elevating thoughts; all tender, awful, sorrowful, ennobling, sacred, graceful, or beautiful associations: and to prepare yourselves, as befits such a subject—Pre-Raphaelly considered—for the lowest depths of what is mean, odious, repulsive, and revolting.

You behold the interior of a carpenter's shop. In the foreground of that carpenter's shop is a hideous, wry-necked, blubbering, red-headed boy, in a bed-gown; who appears to have received a poke in the hand, from the stick of another boy with whom he has been playing in an adjacent gutter, and to be holding it up for the contemplation of a kneeling woman, so horrible in her ugliness, that (supposing it were possible for any human creature to exist for a moment with that dislocated throat) she would stand out from the rest of the company as a Monster, in the vilest cabaret in France, or the lowest gin-shop in England. Two almost naked carpenters, master and journeyman, worthy companions of this agreeable female, are working at their trade; a boy, with some small flavour of humanity in him, is entering with a vessel of water; and nobody is paying any attention to a snuffy old woman who seems to have mistaken that shop for the tobacconist's next door, and to be hopelessly waiting at the counter to be served with half an ounce of her favourite mixture. Wherever it is possible to express ugliness of feature, limb, or attitude, you have it expressed. Such men as the carpenters might be undressed in any hospital where dirty drunkards, in a high state of varicose veins, are received. Their very toes have walked out of St. Giles's.

This, in the nineteenth century, and in the eighty-second year of the annual exhibition of the National Academy of Art, is the Pre-Raphael representation to us, Ladies and Gentlemen, of the most solemn passage which our minds can ever approach. This, in the nineteenth century, and in the eighty-second year of the annual exhibition of the National Academy of Art, is what Pre-Raphael Art can do to render reverence and homage to the faith in which we live and die! Consider this picture well.   *Charles Dickens* (1812-1870).

56. FROM THE CLIFFS: NOON

THE sea is in its listless chime:
    Time's lapse it is, made audible,—
    The murmur of the earth's large shell.
In a blue sadness beyond rhyme
    It ends: sense, without thought, can pass
    No stadium further. Since time was,
This sound hath told the lapse of time.

No stagnance that death wins,—it hath
    The mournfulness of ancient life,
    Always enduring at dull strife.
As the world's heart of rest and wrath,

Its painful pulse is in the sands.
Last utterly, the whole sky stands,
Grey and not known, along its path.

         D. G. Rossetti (1828-1882).

57. THE SEASONS

THE crocus, in the shrewd March morn,
  Thrusts up his saffron spear;
And April dots the sombre thorn
  With gems, and loveliest cheer.

Then sleep the seasons, full of might;
  While slowly swells the pod,
And rounds the peach, and in the night
  The mushroom bursts the sod.

The winter comes: the frozen rut
  Is bound with silver bars;
The white drift heaps against the hut;
  And night is pierced with stars.

         Coventry Patmore (1823-1896).

58. THERE IS NO GOD

"THERE is no God," the wicked saith,
  "And truly it's a blessing,
For what He might have done with us
  It's better only guessing."

"There is no God," a youngster thinks,
  "Or really, if there may be,
He surely didn't mean a man
  Always to be a baby."

"There is no God, or if there is,"
  The tradesman thinks, "'twere funny
If He should take it ill in me
  To make a little money."

"Whether there be," the rich man says,
  "It matters very little,
For I and mine, thank somebody,
  Are not in want of victual."

Some others, also, to themselves,
  Who scarce so much as doubt it,
Think there is none, when they are well,
  And do not think about it.

But country folks who live beneath
  The shadow of the steeple;
The parson and the parson's wife,
  And mostly married people;

Youths green and happy in first love,
  So thankful for illusion;
And men caught out in what the world
  Calls guilt, in first confusion;

And almost every one when age,
  Disease, or sorrows strike him,
Inclines to think there is a God,
  Or something very like Him.
              A. H. Clough (1819-1861).

59. IN CHANCERY

LONDON. Michaelmas Term lately over, and the Lord Chancellor sitting in Lincoln's Inn Hall. Implacable November weather. As much mud in the streets, as if the waters had but newly retired from the face of the earth, and it would not be wonderful to meet a Megalosaurus, forty feet long or so, waddling like an elephantine lizard up Holborn Hill. Smoke lowering down from chimney-pots, making a soft black drizzle, with flakes of soot in it as big as full-grown snow-flakes—gone into mourning, one might imagine, for the death of the sun. Dogs, undistinguishable in mire. Horses, scarcely better;

splashed to their very blinkers. Foot passengers, jostling one another's umbrellas, in a general infection of ill-temper, and losing their foot-hold at street-corners, where tens of thousands of other foot passengers have been slipping and sliding since the day broke (if this day ever broke), adding new deposits to the crust upon crust of mud, sticking at those points tenaciously to the pavement, and accumulating at compound interest.

Fog everywhere. Fog up the river, where it flows among green aits and meadows; fog down the river, where it rolls defiled among the tiers of shipping, and the waterside pollutions of a great (and dirty) city. Fog on the Essex marshes, fog on the Kentish heights. Fog creeping into the cabooses of collier-brigs; fog lying out on the yards, and hovering in the rigging of great ships; fog drooping on the gunwales of barges and small boats. Fog in the eyes and throats of ancient Greenwich pensioners, wheezing by the firesides of their wards; fog in the stem and bowl of the afternoon pipe of the wrathful skipper, down in his close cabin; fog cruelly pinching the toes and fingers of his shivering little 'prentice boy on deck. Chance people on the bridges peeping over the parapets into a nether sky of fog, with fog all round them, as if they were up in a balloon, and hanging in the misty clouds.

Gas looming through the fog in divers places in the streets, much as the sun may, from the spongey fields, be seen to loom by husbandman and ploughboy. Most of the shops lighted two hours before their time—as the gas seems to know, for it has a haggard and unwilling look.

The raw afternoon is rawest, and the dense fog is densest, and the muddy streets are muddiest, near that leaden-headed old obstruction, appropriate ornament for the threshold of a leaden-headed old corporation: Temple Bar. And hard by Temple Bar, in Lincoln's Inn Hall, at the very heart of the fog, sits the Lord High Chancellor in his High Court of Chancery.

Never can there come fog too thick, never can there come mud and mire too deep, to assort with the groping and floundering condition which this High Court of Chancery, most pestilent of hoary sinners, holds, this day, in the sight of heaven and earth.

On such an afternoon, if ever, the Lord High Chancellor

ought to be sitting here—as here he is—with a foggy glory
round his head, softly fenced in with crimson cloth and curtains,
addressed by a large advocate with great whiskers, a little voice,
and an interminable brief, and outwardly directing his contemplation to the lantern in the roof, where he can see nothing
but fog. On such an afternoon, some score of members of the
High Court of Chancery bar ought to be—as here they are—
mistily engaged in one of the ten thousand stages of an endless
cause, tripping one another up on slippery precedents, groping
knee-deep in technicalities, running their goat-hair and horse-
hair warded heads against walls of words, and making a pretence
of equity with serious faces, as players might. On such an
afternoon, the various solicitors in the cause, some two or three
of whom have inherited it from their fathers, who made a
fortune by it, ought to be—as are they not?—ranged in a line,
in a long matted well (but you might look in vain for Truth at
the bottom of it), between the registrar's red table and the silk
gowns, with bills, cross-bills, answers, rejoinders, injunctions,
affidavits, issues, references to masters, masters' reports, mountains of costly nonsense, piled before them. Well may the court
be dim, with wasting candles here and there; well may the
fog hang heavy in it, as if it would never get out; well may the
stained glass windows lose their colour, and admit no light of
day into the place; well may the uninitiated from the streets,
who peep in through the glass panes in the door, be deterred
from entrance by its owlish aspect, and by the drawl languidly
echoing to the roof from the padded dais where the Lord High
Chancellor looks into the lantern that has no light in it, and
where the attendant wigs are all stuck in a fog-bank! This is
the Court of Chancery; which has its decaying houses and its
blighted lands in every shire; which has its worn-out lunatic
in every madhouse, and its dead in every churchyard; which
has its ruined suitor, with his slipshod heels and threadbare
dress, borrowing and begging through the round of every
man's acquaintance; which gives to monied might, the means
abundantly of wearying out the right; which so exhausts
finances, patience, courage, hope; so overthrows the brain and
breaks the heart; that there is not an honourable man among
its practitioners who would not give—who does not often give—

the warning, "Suffer any wrong that can be done you, rather than come here!"

Charles Dickens (1812-1870).

60. THINK THAT THE GRASS UPON THY GRAVE IS GREEN

THINK that the grass upon thy grave is green;
 Think that thou seest thine own empty chair;
 The empty garments thou wast wont to wear;
 The empty room where long thy haunt hath been:
Think that the lane, the meadow, and the wood
 And mountain summit feel thy foot no more,
 Nor the loud thoroughfare, nor sounding shore:
 All mere blank space where thou thyself hast stood.
Amid this thought-created silence say
 To thy stripped soul, what am I now and where?
 Then turn and face the petty narrowing care
Which has been gnawing thee for many a day,
 And it will die as dies a wailing breeze
 Lost in the solemn roar of boundless seas.

James Smetham (1821-1889).

61. EARLY SPRING

. . So warm the day,—its influence lent
 To flagging thoughts a stronger wing,
So utterly was winter spent,
 So sudden was the birth of spring.

Wild crocus flowers by copse and hedge
 In sunlight, clustering thick below,
Sigh'd for the firwood's shaded ledge,
 Where sparkled still a line of snow.

And crowded snowdrops faintly hung
 Their heads yet lower for the heat,
While in still air all branches flung
 Their shadowy doubles at our feet. . .

Jean Ingelow (1820-1897).

62. "COME NOT, WHEN I AM DEAD"

COME not, when I am dead,
   To drop thy foolish tears upon my grave,
To trample round my fallen head,
   And vex the unhappy dust thou wouldst not save.
There let the wind sweep and the plover cry;
      But thou, go by.

Child, if it were thine error or thy crime
   I care no longer, being all unblest:
Wed whom thou wilt, but I am sick of Time,
   And I desire to rest.
Pass on, weak heart, and leave me where I lie:
      Go by, go by.
              Alfred Tennyson (1809-1892).

63. WHERE LIES THE LAND TO WHICH THE SHIP WOULD GO?

WHERE lies the land to which the ship would go?
Far, far ahead, is all her seamen know,
And where the land she travels from?   Away,
Far, far behind, is all that they can say.

On sunny noons upon the deck's smooth face,
Linked arm in arm, how pleasant here to pace;
Or, o'er the stern reclining, watch below
The foaming wake far widening as we go.

On stormy nights when wild north-westers rave,
How proud a thing to fight with wind and wave!
The dripping sailor on the reeling mast
Exults to bear, and scorns to wish it past.

Where lies the land to which the ship would go?
Far, far ahead, is all her seamen know.
And where the land she travels from?   Away,
Far, far behind, is all that they can say.
              A. H. Clough (1819-1861).

64. THE RATCATCHER'S DAUGHTER

IN Westminster not long ago,
There lived a Ratcatcher's Daughter.
She was not born at Westminster,
But on the t'other side of the water.
Her father killed rats and she sold sprats
All round and over the water,
And the gentlefolks, they all bought sprats
Of the pretty Ratcatcher's daughter.

She wore no hat upon her head,
Nor cap nor dandy bonnet,
Her hair of her head it hung down her neck
Like a bunch of carrots upon it.
When she cried sprats in Westminster,
She had such a sweet loud voice, Sir,
You could hear her all down Parliament Street,
And as far as Charing Cross, Sir.

The rich and poor both far and near
In matrimony sought her,
But at friends and foes she cocked her nose,
Did this pretty little Ratcatcher's daughter.
For there was a man cried "Lily white Sand,"
Who in Cupid's net had caught her,
And over head and ears in love,
Was the pretty little Ratcatcher's daughter.

Now "Lily white Sand" so ran in her head,
When coming down the Strand, oh,
She forgot that she'd got sprats on her head,
And cried, "buy my Lily white Sand, oh!"
The folks, amazed, all thought her crazed
All along the Strand, oh,
To hear a girl with sprats on her head,
Cry, "buy my Lily white Sand, oh!"

The Ratcatcher's Daughter so ran in his head,
He didn't know what he was arter,
Instead of crying "Lily white Sand,"
He cried "Do you want any Ratcatcher's daughter."
His donkey cocked his ears and brayed,
Folks couldn't tell what he was arter,
To hear a lily white sand man cry,
"Do you want any Ratcatcher's daughter?"

Now they both agreed to married be
Upon next Easter Sunday,
But the Ratcatcher's daughter had a dream
That she shouldn't be alive next Monday,
To buy some sprats once more she went,
And tumbled into the water,
Went down to the bottom all covered with mud,
Did the pretty little Ratcatcher's daughter.

When Lily white Sand he heard the news,
His eyes ran down with water,
Says he in love I'll constant prove,
And, blow me if I live long arter,
So he cut his throat with a piece of glass,
And stabbed his donkey arter,
So there was an end of Lily white Sand,
His ass, and the Ratcatcher's daughter!

Anon. (A Street Ballad).

65. THE CRYSTAL PALACE, 1851

WITH ganial foire
Thransfuse me loyre,
Ye sacred nymphs of Pindus,
The whoile I sing
That wondthrous thing,
The Palace made o' windows!

C

Say, Paxton, truth,
Thou wondthrous youth,
What sthroke of art celistial,
What power was lint
You to invint
This combineetion cristial.

O would before
That Thomas Moore,
Likewoise the late Lord Boyron,
Thim aigles sthrong
Of godlike song,
Cast oi on that cast oiron!

And saw thim walls,
And glittering halls,
Thim rising slendther columns,
Which I, poor pote,
Could not denote,
No, not in twinty vollums.

My Muse's words
Is like the birds
That roosts beneath the panes there;
Her wings she spoils
'Gainst them bright tiles,
And cracks her silly brains there.

This Palace tall,
This Cristial Hall,
Which Imperors might covet,
Stands in High Park,
Like Noah's Ark,
A rainbow bint above it.

The towers and fanes,
In other scaynes,
The fame of this will undo,
Saint Paul's big doom,
Saint Payther's Room,
And Dublin's proud Rotundo.

'Tis here that roams,
  As well becomes
Her dignitee and stations,
  Victoria Great,
  And houlds in state
The Congress of the Nations.

  Her subjects pours
  From distant shores,
Her Injians and Canajians;
  And also we,
  Her kingdoms three,
Attind with our allagiance.

  Here come likewise
  Her bould allies,
Both Asian and Europian;
  From East and West
  They send their best
To fill her Coornucopean.

  I seen (thank Grace!)
  This wondthrous place
(His Noble Honour Misther
  H. Cole it was
  That gave the pass,
And let me see what is there).

  With conscious proide
  I stud insoide
And look'd the World's Great Fair in,
  Until me sight
  Was dazzled quite,
And couldn't see for staring.

  There's holy saints
  And window paints
By Maydiayval Pugin;
  Alhamborough Jones
  Did paint the tones
Of yellow and gambouge in.

There's fountains there
And crosses fair;
There's water-gods with urrns;
There's organs three,
To play, d'ye see,
"God save the Queen," by turrns.

There's Statues bright
Of marble white,
Of silver, and of copper;
And some in zinc,
And some, I think,
That isn't over proper.

There's staym Ingynes,
That stands in lines,
Enormous and amazing,
That squeal and snort
Like whales in sport,
Or elephants a-grazing.

There's carts and gigs,
And pins for pigs;
There's dibblers and there's harrows,
And ploughs like toys
For little boys,
And ilegant wheel-barrows.

For thim genteels
Who ride on wheels,
There's plenty to indulge 'em;
There's Droskys snug
From Paytersbug,
And vayhycles from Bulgium.

There's Cabs on Stands
And Shandthry danns;
There's Waggons from New York here;
There's Lapland Sleighs
Have cross'd the seas,
And Jaunting Cyars from Cork here.

Amazed I pass
From glass to glass,
Deloighted I survey 'em;
Fresh wondthers grows
Before me nose
In this sublime Musayum!

Look, here's a fan
From far Japan,
A sabre from Damasco:
There's shawls ye get
From far Thibet,
And cotton prints from Glasgow.

There's German flutes,
Marocky boots,
And Naples Macaronies;
Bohaymia
Has sent Bohay;
Polonia her polonies.

There's granite flints
That's quite imminse,
There's sacks of coals and fuels,
There's swords and guns,
And soap in tuns,
And Ginger-bread and Jewels.

There's taypots there,
And cannons rare;
There's coffins fill'd with roses;
There's canvass tints,
Teeth insthrumints,
And shuits of clothes by MOSES.

There's lashins more
Of things in store,
But thim I don't remimber;
Nor could disclose
Did I compose
From May time to Novimber!

Ah, JUDY thru!
  With eyes so blue,
That you were here to view it!
  And could I screw
  But tu pound tu,
'Tis I would thrait you to it!

So let us raise
  Victoria's praise,
And Albert's proud condition,
  That takes his ayse
  As he surveys
This Cristial Exhibition.

W. M. Thackeray (1811-1863).

66. THE CRYSTAL PALACE RE-ERECTED

IT is two miles in circumference and has three stories of prodigious height; it would easily hold five or six buildings like
our Palace of Industry, and it is of glass; it consists first of an
immense rectangular structure rising towards the centre in a
semicircle like a hot-house, and flanked by two Chinese towers;
then, on either side, long buildings descend at right angles,
enclosing the garden with its fountains, statues, summer-
houses, strips of turf, groups of large trees, exotic plants, and
beds of flowers. The acres of glass sparkle in the sunlight;
at the horizon an undulating line of green eminences is bathed
in the luminous vapour which softens all colours and spreads
an expression of tender beauty over an entire landscape.
Always the same English method of decoration—on the one
side a park and natural embellishments, which it must be
granted are beautiful and adapted to the climate; on the other
the building, which is a monstrous jumble, wanting in style,
and bearing witness not to taste but to English power. The
interior consists of a museum of antiquities, composed of plaster
facsimiles of all the Grecian and Roman statues scattered over

Europe; of a museum of the Middle Ages; of a Revival museum; of an Egyptian museum; of a Nineveh museum; of an Indian museum; of a reproduction of a Pompeian house; of a reproduction of the Alhambra. The ornaments of the Alhambra have been moulded, and these moulds are preserved in an adjoining room as proofs of authenticity. In order to omit nothing, copies have been made of the most notable Italian paintings, and these are daubs worthy of a country fair. There is a huge tropical hot-house, wherein are fountains, swimming turtles, large aquatic plants in flower, the Sphinx and Egyptian statues sixty feet high, specimens of colossal or rare trees, among others the bark of a Sequoia California 450 feet in height and measuring 116 feet in circumference. The bark is arranged and fastened to an inner framework in such a manner as to give an idea of the tree itself. There is a circular concert room, with tiers of benches as in a Coliseum. Lastly, in the gardens are to be seen life-size reproductions of antediluvian monsters, megatheriums, deinotheriums, and others. In these gardens Blondin does his tricks at the height of a hundred feet. I pass over half the things; but does not this conglomeration of odds and ends carry back one's thoughts to the Rome of Caesar and the Antonines? At that period, also, pleasure-palaces were erected for the sovereign people; circuses, theatres, baths wherein were collected statues, paintings, animals, musicians, acrobats, all the treasures and all the oddities of the world; pantheons of opulence and curiosity; genuine bazaars where the liking for what was novel, heterogeneous, and fantastic ousted the feeling of appreciation for simple beauty. In truth, Rome enriched herself with these things by conquest, England by industry. Thus it is that at Rome the paintings, the statues, were stolen originals, and the monsters, whether rhinoceroses or lions, were perfectly alive and tore human beings to pieces; whereas here the statues are made of plaster and the monsters of goldbeater's skin. The spectacle is one of the second class, but of the same kind. A Greek would not have regarded it with satisfaction; he would have considered it appropriate to powerful barbarians who, trying to become refined, had utterly failed.

Hippolyte Taine (1828-1893).

67. THE UNDERTAKERS' CLUB

ONE night, being pressed by his old friend Chubb,
To go to an Undertakers' Club,
I'll furnish you all, if that I dare,
With a mournful account of this grave affair.

Chorus

For such a black looking lot is this Club of
Undertakers, such a black looking set
     You never did see.

This selfsame Club, and House of Call,
Was held at Blackheath, or else Blackwall,
The landlord's name it was Blackmore,
And an African chief hung over the door.

The Undertakers had all met.
They were dress'd in black a dingey set,
The picture frames black, and so were the walls,
And the window curtains were made of palls.

The stove black leaded not long had been,
On the table was laid Blackwood's magazine,
The carpet was black and so was each chair,
The chairman'd black whiskers and raven hair.

The supper was laid, there were lots of black game,
With polonies in mourning to match with the same,
There were blackbird pies, and nothing but good 'uns,
And a quantity of good black puddings.

The knives were black, and so were the forks,
Black strap in black bottles, with black sealed corks,
The rules of the club were done in black figures,
And the waiters and cooks were all of them niggers.

The dessert was black grapes, and black heart cherries,
Blackcurrants and mulberries and blackberries.
Prunes and elder wine were there,
Which just made up this black bill of fare.

Mr. Sable sang first, and what should he choose on
But the favourite ballad of Black eyéd Susan,
The Coal Black Steed Mr. Hatband chose,
And Mr. Merryhell sang Coal Black Rose.

The best that was sung, and that all did confess,
Was the favourite song of My bonny Black Bess,
The Chairman then whistled, when his throat was clear,
The fav'rite grand march that is played in Black Beard.

                          Anon. (*A Street Ballad*).

68. THE ARTIST AND ART

i

THE whole function of the artist in the world is to be a seeing and feeling creature; to be an instrument of such tenderness and sensitiveness, that no shadow, no hue, no line, no instantaneous and evanescent expression of the visible things around him, nor any of the emotions which they are capable of conveying to the spirit which has been given him, shall either be left unrecorded, or fade from the book of record. It is not his business either to think, to judge, to argue, or to know. His place is neither in the closet, nor on the bench, nor at the bar, nor in the library. They are for other men and other work. He may think, in a by-way; reason, now and then, when he has nothing better to do; know, such fragments of knowledge as he can gather without stooping, or reach without pains; but none of these things are to be his care. The work of his life is to be two-fold only: to see, to feel.

ii

Society always had a destructive influence upon an artist: first, by its sympathy with his meanest powers; secondly, by its chilling want of understanding of his greatest; and, thirdly, by its vain occupation of his time and thoughts.

iii

Whatever can be measured and handled, dissected and demonstrated,—in a word, whatever is of the body only,—that the schools of knowledge do resolutely and courageously possess themselves of, and portray. But whatever is immeasurable, intangible, indivisible, and of the spirit, that the schools of knowledge do as certainly lose, and blot out of their sight: that is to say, all that is worth art's possessing or recording at all; for whatever can be arrested, measured, and systematized, we can contemplate as much as we will in Nature herself. But what we want art to do for us is to stay what is fleeting, and to enlighten what is incomprehensible, to incorporate the things which have no measure, and immortalize the things that have no duration. The dimly seen, momentary glance, the flitting shadow of faint emotion, the imperfect lines of fading thought, and all that by and through such things as these is recorded on the features of man, and all that in man's person and actions, and in the great natural world, is infinite and wonderful; having in it that spirit and power which man may witness, but not weigh; conceive, but not comprehend; love, but not limit; and imagine, but not define;—this, the beginning and end of the aim of all noble art, we have, in ancient art, by perception; and we have *not*, in the newer art, by knowledge. Giotto gives it us; Orcagna gives it us; Angelico, Memmi, Pisano,—it matters not who,—all simple and unlearned men, in their measure and manner,—give it us; and the learned men that followed them give it us not, and we, in our supreme learning, own ourselves at this day farther from it than ever.

John Ruskin (1819-1900).

69. WHITSUN EVE

THE white dove cooeth in her downy nest,
Keeping her young ones warm beneath her breast:
The white moon sailest through the cool clear sky,
Screened by a tender mist in passing by:

The white rose buds, with thorns upon its stem,
All the more precious and more dear for them:
The stream shines silver in the tufted grass,
The white clouds scarcely dim it as they pass;
Deep in the valleys lily cups are white,
They send up incense all the holy night.
Our souls are white, made clean in Blood once shed:
White blessed Angels watch around our bed:—
O Spotless Lamb of God, still keep us so,
Thou who were born for us in time of snow.

May 18, 1853.

Christina Rossetti (1830-1894).

70. A NEW-YEAR'S BURDEN

ALONG the grass sweet airs are blown
    Our way this day in Spring.
Of all the songs that we have known
    Now which one shall we sing?
            Not that, my love, ah no!—
            Not this, my love, why, so!—
Yet both were ours, but hours will come and go.

The grove is all a pale frail mist,
    The new year sucks the sun.
Of all the kisses that we kissed
    Now which shall be the one?
            Not that, my love, ah no!—
            Not this, my love?—heigh-ho
For all the sweets that all the winds can blow!

The branches cross above our eyes,
    The skies are in a net:
And what's the thing beneath the skies
    We two would most forget?
            Not birth, my love, no, no,—
            Not death, my love, no, no,—
The love once ours, but ours long hours ago.

D. G. Rossetti (1828-1882).

71. THE BOY IN LOVE

THE morn rose blue and glorious o'er the world;
The steamer left the black and oozy wharves,
And floated down between dark ranks of masts.
We heard the swarming streets, the noisy mills;
Saw sooty foundries full of glare and gloom,
Great bellied chimneys tipped by tongues of flame
Quiver in smoky heat. We slowly passed
Loud building-yards, where every slip contained
A mighty vessel with a hundred men
Battering its iron sides. A cheer! a ship
In a gay flutter of innumerous flags
Slid gaily to her home. At length the stream
Broadened 'tween banks of daisies, and afar
The shadows flew upon the sunny hills;
And down the river, 'gainst the pale blue sky,
A town sat in its smoke. Look backward now!
Distance has stilled three hundred thousand hearts,
Drowned the loud roar of commerce, changed the proud
Metropolis which turns all things to gold,
To a thick vapour o'er which stands a staff
With smoky pennon streaming on the air.
Blotting the azure too, we floated on,
Leaving a long and weltering wake behind.
And now the grand and solitary hills
That never knew the toil and stress of man,
Dappled with sun and cloud, rose far away.
My heart stood up to greet the distant land
Within the hollows of whose mountains lochs
Moan in their restless sleep; around whose peaks,
And scraggy islands ever dim with rain,
The lonely eagle flies. The ample stream
Widened into a sea. The boundless day
Was full of sunshine and divinest light,
And far above the region of the wind
The barred and rippled cirrus slept serene,
With combed and winnowed streaks of faintest cloud

Melting into the blue.   A sudden veil
Of rain dimmed all; and when the shade drew off,
Before us, out toward the mighty sun,
The firth was throbbing with glad flakes of light.
The mountains from their solitary pines
Ran down in bleating pastures to the sea;
And round and round the yellow coasts I saw
Each curve and bend of the delightful shore
Hemmed with a line of villas white as foam.
Far off, the village smiled amid the light;
And on the level sands, the merriest troops
Of children sported with the laughing waves,
The sunshine glancing on their naked limbs.
White cottages, half smothered in rose blooms,
Peeped at us as we passed.   We reached the pier,
Whence girls in fluttering dresses, shady hats,
Smiled rosy welcome.   An impatient roar
Of hasty steam; from the broad paddles rushed
A flood of pale green foam, that hissed and freathed
Ere it subsided in the quiet sea.
With a glad foot I leapt upon the shore,
And, as I went, the frank and lavish winds
Told me about the lilac's mass of bloom,
The slim laburnum showering golden tears,
The roses of the gardens where they played.

    At eve I lay in utter indolence
Upon a crag's high heather-purpled head.
The sun hung o'er a sea of wrinkled gold,
And o'er him fleecy vapour, rack of cloud,
And thin suspended mists hung tremulous
In fiery ecstasy; while high in heaven,
Discerned afar between the crimson streaks,
And melting away toward the lucid east,
Like clouds of cherubs tiny cloudlets slept
In soft and tender rose.   When I returned,
The air was heavy with the breath of flowers,
And from the houses of the rich there came
Low-breathing music through the balmy gloom;

Linked lovers passed me, lost in murmurous talk:
That fragrant night of happiness and love
She seemed to lie within my heart and smile.
The village lights were sprinkled on the hill;
And on the dim and solitary loch,
Our oar-blades stirred the sea to phantom light,
A hoary track ran glimmering from the keel.
Like scattered embers of a dying fire,
The village lights had burned out one by one;
I lay awake and heard at intervals
A drowsy wave break helpless on the shore,
Trailing the rattling pebbles as it washed
Back to the heaving gloom. "Come, blessed Sleep,
And with thy fingers of forgetfulness
Tie up my senses till the day we meet,
And kill this gap of time." By sweet degrees
My slumberous being closed its weary leaves
In drowsy bliss, and slowly sank in dream,
As sinks the water-lily 'neath the wave. . .

Alexander Smith (1829-1867).

72. VOYAGE TO ENGLAND

(*At St. Vincent's, Cape Verde Islands*) *Wednesday*, *September* 27,
1854.—The women here are mostly anything but beauties,
not so finely formed as the Jago ones, nor did they appear such
a merry easy-going set of creatures altogether: I believe this
difference must be occasioned by the soil itself and influences
of the weather. Here is aridity, choking dust and no greenness
except a few scrubby pine-looking stumps, stony hills that
cannot grow a grass blade and clouds floating about that will
not rain: *there* is luxurious vegetation growing without much
attention, their hardest work seems eating rich fruit the earth
throws forth: and looking round they see green mountains
plunging into the clouds as a beast thrusts its head into a
thicket for shade: the one life is a wandering over a dust heap
for scraps, the other wallows joyously in the midst of plenty,
shining on the fat of the land. At this place I went along the

plain some distance to a well where the town gets supplied
with water: it was just such a one as we read of in extremely
old books, such as Homer and the Bible: there I saw Rebecca
standing on the stone coping of the well drawing up water,
each round dusky arm alternately down and aloft: her garments
most generously disposed: I apprehend she was scarcely well
accustomed to a European stare, for as I stood looking upon her
scarf-bound head, slightly turned aside, and watched the smile
tremulous on her lips—it might be fancy—but I thought I saw
through that dark cheek of hers the rich pomegranate flushing
into bloom. . . .

Thursday, September 28.—Dirt, noise and confusion through
the ship, for the foul process of coaling goes on with proper
vigour: when we shall get away I know not but sometime this
afternoon I suppose. The water is remarkably green; anyone
sitting near catches the reflection and looks verdant in the
extreme: fancy a green head of hair! but such is the fact, I
could not well have believed it without seeing: it is more like
green paint than an ethereal thing like reflection, several times
I have been quite deceived. The water is so clear the bottom
can be seen distinctly; there are innumerable fishes of all
kinds. I saw a shark this morning floating lazily thro' the
wave and sometimes thrusting up his dorsal fin.

Sunday, October 1.—Another vessel just hove in sight: at
first it showed like a minute sparkle on the fire waters, then
grew into a pale butterfly, now it swells a proud ship manifest
to all. The day has grown very warm. I saw one of the finest
fields of cirri at noon that ever was; every form of mottling
that could be conceived; cluster of curved shells raying in
graduated succession, breadths of vapour scarce seen curdling
into substance, and millions of whirling little manes rampant
thro' the sky.

Monday, October 2. *Night.*—When I rose this morning I
little thought the fortune of beauty was in store for me I
enjoyed to-night. A wondrous sunset! An immortal dower to
all who saw it. One might as well attempt to describe the
countless variety of form in the splashing waves of the ocean;
the universe of intricacy in a great forest or the complex
passions that agitate all the nations of the earth, as yield even a

faint notion of the heavenly splendour that shone upon our gazing as we stood looking with loving eyes upon the sun's departure to-night. North, South, East and West, the perfect circumference of the sky was crowded to astonishment with delicate to ponderous passages of fineness or power: it was a ring of magnificence, and the sun was the precious jewel in that rich setting. Round the sun was a wreath of deep burning light—the lower sky was red hot—not to be looked at, far less written down; flames dashed from the glowing sky as sparks flash from beaten iron; the water was fluid metal: above the densest body of fire lay a plain of clear crystalline sapphire, so pure, serene and beautiful, had the bright forms of silver sparkle shining there been angels of God singing everlasting joy one could not wonder more;—had a long, plaintive wail for past dismay come floating over the sea, and continued warbling love and pity to all mankind, till evil hearts melted in delicious sympathy, and giant Wrong dropt his sword and chain like things accursed to the lowest darkness of ocean, and long-suffering man, regenerated, had leapt like the morning from his long, black dream, I say these things had not given me any surprise! . . .

Friday, *October* 6.—A delightful morning, fine breeze not in our favor so much as might be wished. I felt something in the air this morning that vividly reminded me of England; I could fully believe and hold the fact that I was drawing near: it might be the iron gray sea laced over with threads of froth and bursting foam, or the hard gray sky of dark clouds fleeced with rainy vapor and shattered thro' with lovely openings of azure, or the fresh chill wind.

Sunday, *October* 8.—There was a poor weary storm-tossed lark settled on the ship this morning; it trembled with fear and weakness looking around upon us with its full clear eyes: one fellow made a dab and frightened it off: I saw it a few seconds struggling with the wind and lost it in a great glare of sunshine that lay on the water. . . .

Tuesday, *October* 10. *Night*.—Not many more of them here. Going along well, 8 knots full. After dinner soon after sun-down I saw a meteor float along the air close to the ship, it passed by the beam and half round the stern, then vanished.

I have read of souls departing in a flame of light and could almost imagine this a vital spark of some one quitting this contentious world. I hope not. It was the purest light I ever saw and the most serenely lovely.

Thursday, October 12. *Night.* — Abreast the celebrated Eddystone Lighthouse: we did not expect to hug the land so closely and the Start was to have been our next indication of land. I have seen plenty of seaweed floating in patches to-day; even this link between sea and land tho' trifling is thrice welcome. I saw dotted in various points on the horizon 13 craft at once; we spoke one and learned the war continues and Sebastopol is taken! . . .

Friday, October 13.—When I finished the above last night I went on deck and saw the Start Light; we came abreast about 10½ p.m. I saw the land when I woke this morning and could not lie in bed comfortably under the circumstances, and so dressed and came on deck to look at the dear pale cliffs, a comfort to my eyes, ease to my soul, as food to a hungry man this sight to my desires.   *Thomas Woolner* (1825-1892).

73. SEA-SAND AND SORROW

WHAT are heavy? sea-sand and sorrow:
What are brief? to-day and to-morrow:
What are frail? Spring blossoms and youth:
What are deep? the ocean and truth.

                    Christina Rossetti (1830-1894).

74. THE SEA OF LOVE

. . Love's living sea by coasts uncurb'd,
     Its depth, its mystery, and its might,
Its indignation is disturb'd,
     The glittering peace of its delight. . .

                    Coventry Patmore (1823-1896).

75. NATURE'S UNDERTAKERS

Now, were it to my present purpose to attack the principles and proceedings of the world, of course it would be obvious for me to retort upon the cold, cruel, selfish system, which this supreme worship of comfort, decency, and social order necessarily introduces; to show you how the many are sacrificed to the few, the poor to the wealthy, how an oligarchical monopoly of enjoyment is established far and wide, and the claims of want, and pain, and sorrow, and affliction, and guilt, and misery, are practically forgotten, But I will not have recourse to the common-places of controversy when I am on the defensive. All I would say to the world is,—Keep your theories to yourselves, do not inflict them upon the sons of Adam everywhere; do not measure heaven and earth by views which are in a great degree insular, and can never be philosophical and catholic. You do your work, perhaps, in a more business-like way, compared with ourselves, but we are immeasurably more tender, and gentle, and angelic than you. We come to poor human nature as the Angels of God, and you as policemen. Look at your poor-houses, hospitals and prisons; how perfect are their externals! what skill and ingenuity appear in their structure, economy, and administration! they are as decent, and bright, and calm, as what our Lord seems to name them,—dead men's sepulchres. Yes! they have all the world can give, all but life; all but a heart. Yes! you can hammer up a coffin, you can plaster a tomb; you are nature's undertakers; you cannot build it a home. You cannot feed it or heal it; it lies, like Lazarus, at your gate, full of sores. You see it gasping and panting with privations and penalties; and you sing to it, you dance to it, you show it your picture-books, you let off your fireworks, you open your menageries. Shallow philosophers! is this mode of going on so winning and persuasive that we should imitate it?

J. H. Newman (1801-1890).

76. THROUGH ME MANY LONG DUMB VOICES

(From *Song of Myself*, 1855)

. . Through me many long dumb voices,
   Voices of the interminable generation of prisoners and slaves,
   Voices of the diseas'd and despairing and of thieves and
      dwarfs,
   Voices of cycles of preparation and accretion,
   And of the threads that connect the stars and of wombs and
      of the father-stuff,
   And of the rights of them the others are down upon,
   Of the deform'd, trivial, flat, foolish, despised,
   Fog in the air, beetles rolling balls of dung.

   Through me forbidden voices,
   Voices of sexes and lusts, voices veil'd and I remove the veil,
   Voices indecent by me clarified and transfigur'd.

   I do not press my fingers across my mouth,
   I keep as delicate around the bowels as around the head and
      heart,
   Copulation is no more rank to me than death is.

   I believe in the flesh and the appetites,
   Seeing, hearing, feeling, are miracles, and each part and tag
      of me is a miracle.
   Divine am I inside and out, and I make holy whatever I
      touch or am touch'd from,
   The scent of these arm-pits aroma finer than prayer,
   This head more than churches, bibles, and all the creeds. . .

                                        Walt Whitman (1819-1892).

77. THE GEOLOGIST

   . . A pagan, kissing for a step of Pan
      The wild-goat's hoof-print on the loamy down,

Exceeds our modern thinker who turns back
The strata . . . granite, limestone, coal, and clay,
Concluding coldly with, "Here's law! where's God?" . .
Elizabeth Barrett Browning (1806-1861).

78. THE SPIRIT'S EPOCHS

Not in the crises of events,
    Of compass'd hopes, or fears fulfill'd,
Or acts of gravest consequence,
    Are life's delight and depth reveal'd.
The day of days was not the day;
    That went before, or was postponed;
The night Death took our lamp away
    Was not the night on which we groan'd.
I drew my bride, beneath the moon,
    Across my threshold; happy hour!
But, ah, the walk that afternoon
    We saw the water-flags in flower!
Coventry Patmore (1823-1896).

79. TENNYSON'S "MAUD"

August 10, 1855. — I have read "Maud" and the rest of
Tennyson's last volume. I suppose you have read it too. It
must live, like all exquisite art—and as art it is exquisite—an
episode of life with the commonest romance-plot and the
paltriest moral, but wrought out with the lyrical changefulness
of the life of this our time. A very complete story, told with
flying hints and musical echoes; as though Ariel had piped it
in the little wild island of the *Tempest*.

The poetic power which can swallow newspapers full of
business, bankruptcy courts, sanitary commissions, wars,
murders, and medical reports on the adulteration of food, and
then reproduce them, as the conjuror brings out his coloured
horn from his mouth after a meal of shavings, *is* poetic power.

What I object to in it is an objection fundamental, and it is
not so much against it as a work of art, but as a moral work.
The old tale. Thinking and feeling men, in a time when

civilisation has grown rank, and the fat weeds of peace rot on the Lethean wharf of Time, are perplexed beyond measure by the social and moral problems of their era. They have been accustomed to regard their offices of Philosopher or Poet as of vastly more importance than they are. *They* are the Regenerators. Read Tennyson's poem called "The Poet," and see how one "poor poet's scroll" is to shake the world. But they have more pride than power. Now and then such a ferment of the nations, in the disgusting rancid simmer of unregenerate peace, or in the blasts and thunder-rockings of war, arises that they feel it a solemn duty to leave their pastoral hills and pipe a prophecy to still them or to heal them. The Red Indian physician is not more powerless. The spirits "will not come when they do call on them." Their watchwords, their secrets, are as silly and as successful as Master Slender's in the procuring of a wife: "I went to her in white, and cried *mum*, and she cried *budget*, as Anne and I had appointed; and yet it was not Anne, but a postmaster's boy." The fact is that Poetry is to delight and adorn and supplement the happiness of man; it is one of the good things which God will not withhold from them that love Him. Painting has no mission but to make men happy, teaching what truth it can steal from the eternal fountains. And Philosophy is to pass round by the Cross and be baptized, and then it is to make the Intellect happy by throwing glorious magical light on truth. But the Regenerators are not these.

"Mr. Poet, what is the remedy for an evil peace?"
Mr. Poet storms and raves, and answers, "WAR"—
            That is *Mum*.
"And what is the remedy for a horrible War?"
The poet smiles, and whispers, "Pe-a-c-e"—
            That is *Budget*.
"And yet it is not Anne, but a postmaster's boy."
                                    James Smetham (1821-1889).

80. RETURN TO ITALY

                                    . . I knew the birds
And insects,—which looked fathered by the flowers

And emulous of their hues: I recognised
The moths, with that great overpoise of wings
Which make a mystery of them how at all
They can stop flying: butterflies, that bear
Upon their blue wings such red embers round,
They seem to scorch the blue air into holes
Each flight they take: and fire-flies, that suspire
In short soft lapses of transported flame
Across the tingling Dark, while overhead
The constant and inviolable stars
Outburn those light-of-love: melodious owls,
(If music had but one note and was sad,
'Twould sound just so); and all the silent swirl
Of bats that seem to follow in the air
Some grand circumference of a shadowy dome
To which we are blind: and then the nightingales,
Which pluck our heart across a garden-wall
(When walking in the town) and carry it
So high into the bowery almond-trees
We tremble and are afraid, and feel as if
The golden flood of moonlight unaware
Dissolved the pillars of the steady earth
And made it less substantial. And I knew
The harmless opal snakes, the large-mouthed frogs
(Those noisy vaunters of their shallow streams);
And lizards, the green lightnings of the wall,
Which, if you sit down quiet, nor sigh loud,
Will flatter you and take you for a stone,
And flash familiarly about your feet
With such prodigious eyes in such small heads!—
I knew them (though they had somewhat dwindled from
My childish imagery), and kept in mind
How last I sate among them equally,
In fellowship and mateship, as a child
Feels equal still toward insect, beast, and bird,
Before the Adam in him has foregone
All privilege of Eden,—making friends
And talk with such a bird, or such a goat,
And buying many a two-inch-wide rush-cage

To let out the caged cricket on a tree,
Saying, "Oh, my dear grillino, were you cramped?
And are you happy with the ilex-leaves?
And do you love me who have let you go?
Say *yes* in singing, and I'll understand."

But now the creatures all seemed farther off,
No longer mine, nor like me, only *there*,
A gulph between us. I could yearn indeed,
Like other rich men, for a drop of dew
To cool this heat,—a drop of the early dew,
The irrecoverable child-innocence
(Before the heart took fire and withered life)
When childhood might pair equally with birds,
But now . . . the birds were grown too proud for us,
Alas, the very sun forbids the dew. . .

Elizabeth Barrett Browning (1806-1861).

81. THE JAY

(AMY *sings*:)

Up went the jaunty jay,
Bough by bough, bough by bough,
Up went the jaunty jay,
Up the tall tree.

Up the tall tree where a happy bird was singing,
By his mossy home was singing,
To his callow brood was singing
In the green tree;
In the tall tree-top, in the merry tree-top,
—Alas, so merry!
In the brave tree-top,
Waving to and fro.

As a gay gallant up the stairs of pleasure,
By leaps the jaunty jay went up the tree.
Thou knowest, O mother-bird! for thou wert by,
O mother-bird, thy young, thy callow young!

When he stood o'er them as one stands at meat,
Did they not lift their heads up as to thee?
And like a fruit he plucked them one by one,
—The jay, the shining jay, the jocund jay;—
In the tall tree-top, in the merry tree-top,
—Alas, so merry!—
In the brave tree-top,
Waving to and fro.

Like a gay gallant from a ruined maiden,
The painted jay came smirking down the tree.
Oh bird, oh crying bird, oh mother bird,
Oh childless bird, could I not die for thee?
Yes, I could die for thee!

Sydney Dobell (1824-1874).

82. AN EVENING

Eastbourne, Aug. 23, 1855.

I HAVE been, in the dusk of the evening, taking a walk along Pevensey Level—a quiet, broad, seaside road; the wind soft and cool; the sky orange, most soft in the west, but with leaden, purple, ragged clouds floating here and there in masses and wild flakes about the sky, and dragging streaks of rain across the darkening downs. In the east, a large, rose-coloured, steadfast cloud arising from fresh blue-gray banks of sinking nimbi, with the summer lightning incessantly fluttering in its bosom, like thoughts.

James Smetham (1821-1889).

83. COLOUR, GIVE US COLOUR

OUR buildings should, both outside and inside, have had some of that warmth which colour only can give; they should have enabled the educated eye to revel in bright tints of Nature's own formation, while to the uneducated eye they would have afforded the best of all possible lessons, and by familiarizing it with, would have enabled it to appreciate, the proper combination of colour and form.

Besides this, if ever the day shall come when our buildings thus do their duty and teach their proper lesson to the eye, we may hope that we shall see a feeling, more general and more natural, for colour of all kinds and for art of every variety in the bulk of our people. At present it is really saddening to converse with the majority of educated men on any question of colour; for them it has no charms and no delight. The puritanical uniformity of our coats, indeed of all our garments, is but a reflection from the prevailing lack of love of art or colour of any kind. A rich colour is thought vulgar, and that only is refined which is neutral, plain, and ugly.

Perhaps in all this there may be something more than art can ever grapple with; it may be ingrained and part of the necessity of the present age; but, if so, Oh! for the days when, as of yore, colour may be appreciated and beloved, when uniformity shall not be considered beauty, nor an ugly plainness be considered a fit substitute for severity! Oh! too, for the days when men shall have cast off their shamefaced dependence on other men's works and the art of other ages, and, like true men and faithful, shall honestly and with energy, each in his own sphere, set to work to do all that in him lies to increase the power of art and to advance its best interests. All these aims and objects are more or less bound up with the best interests of a people, however old and however powerful, because they depend for ultimate and real success upon the thorough belief, on the part of all its votaries, in certain great and eternal principles, which, if always acted upon, would beyond all doubt sometimes make great artists and always good men.

The principle which artists now have mainly to contend for is that of TRUTH; forgotten, trodden under foot, despised, and hated for ages: this must be their watchword. If they be architects, let them remember how vitally necessary it is to any permanent success in even the smallest of their works; or sculptors, let them recollect how vain and unsatisfactory has been their abandonment of truth in their attempted revival among us of what in classic times were—what they no longer are—real representations and natural works of art; if painters, let them remember how all-important a return to first principles and truth in the delineation of nature and natural forms is to them, if they are ever to create a school of art by which they may be remembered in another age.

George Edmund Street (1824-1881).

84. THE GIRL'S EDUCATION

. . I learnt the collects and the catechism,
The creeds, from Athanasius back to Nice,
The Articles, the Tracts *against* the times,
(By no means Buonaventure's "Prick of Love,")
And various popular synopses of
Inhuman doctrines never taught by John,
Because she liked instructed piety.
I learnt my complement of classic French
(Kept pure of Balzac and neologism)
And German also, since she liked a range
Of liberal education,—tongues, not books.
I learnt a little algebra, a little
Of the mathematics,—brushed with extreme flounce
The circle of the sciences, because
She misliked women who are frivolous.
I learnt the royal genealogies
Of Oviedo, the internal laws
Of the Burmese empire,—by how many feet
Mount Chimborazo outsoars Teneriffe,
What navigable river joins itself
To Lara, and what census of the year five
Was taken by Klagenfurt,—because she liked
A general insight into useful facts.
I learnt much music,—such as would have been
As quite impossible in Johnson's day
As still it might be wished—fine sleights of hand
And unimagined fingering, shuffling off
The hearer's soul through hurricanes of notes
To a noisy Tophet; and I drew . . . costumes

From French engravings, nereids neatly draped,
(With smirks of simmering godship): I washed in
Landscapes from nature (rather say, washed out).
I danced the polka and Cellarius,
Spun glass, stuffed birds, and modelled flowers in wax,
Because she liked accomplishments in girls.
I read a score of books on womanhood
To prove, if women do not think at all,
They may teach thinking (to a maiden-aunt
Or else the author)—books that boldly assert
Their right of comprehending husband's talk
When not too deep, and even of answering
With pretty "may it please you," or "so it is,"—
Their rapid insight and fine aptitude,
Particular worth and general missionariness,
As long as they keep quiet by the fire
And never say "no" when the world says "ay,"
For that is fatal,—their angelic reach
Of virtue, chiefly used to sit and darn,
And fatten household sinners,—their, in brief,
Potential faculty in everything
Of abdicating power in it: she owned
She liked a woman to be womanly,
And English women, she thanked God and sighed,
(Some people always sigh in thanking God)
Were models to the universe. . .

                    Elizabeth Barrett Browning (1806-1861).

85. QUEEN VICTORIA SINGS

QUEEN VICTORIA did not regard art, letters or music as in any
way springing from national character: they were something
quite apart, elegant decorations resembling a scarf or a bracelet,
and in no way expressive of the soul of the country.   But a
pretty taste and competent execution were part of the education
of a young lady, . . . she had her drawing lessons from Mr. Lear,
she learned to etch with considerable technical skill, and
Mendelssohn taught her singing.   She was very proud of this:

once, when quite an old woman, she suddenly made the portentous announcement to Alick Yorke who was in waiting, that after lunch he and she would sing duets. Someone sat down at the piano to play the accompaniment, and the Queen propped up on the table between the two vocalists, a copy of Gilbert and Sullivan's opera *Patience*, and found the place. She said, "Now, Mr. Yorke, you begin," and Mr. Yorke obediently sang to the Queen, "Prithee, pretty maiden, will you marry me?" He got through his verse fairly well, and then the Queen in a very clear soft voice sang, "Gentle Sir, although to marry I'm inclined." She was much pleased with herself, and stopped in the middle of her verse to say, "You know, Mr. Yorke, I was taught singing by Mendelssohn."

E. F. Benson (1867-1940).

86. THE ENGLISHMAN IN ITALY

. . My father was an austere Englishman,
  Who, after a dry life-time spent at home
  In college-learning, law, and parish talk,
  Was flooded with a passion unaware,
  His whole provisioned and complacent past
  Drowned out from him that moment. As he stood
  In Florence, where he had come to spend a month
  And note the secret of Da Vinci's drains,
  He musing somewhat absently perhaps
  Some English question . . . whether men should pay
  The unpopular but necessary tax
  With left or right hand—in the alien sun
  In that great square of the Santissima
  There drifted past him (scarcely marked enough
  To move his comfortable island scorn)
  A train of priestly banners, cross and psalm,
  The white-veiled rose-crowned maidens holding up
  Tall tapers, weighty for such wrists, aslant
  To the blue luminous tremor of the air,
  And letting drop the white wax as they went
  To eat the bishop's wafer at the church;

From which long trail of chanting priests and girls,
A face flashed like a cymbal on his face
And shook with silent clangour brain and heart,
Transfiguring him to music. Thus, even thus,
He too received his sacramental gift
With eucharistic meanings; for he loved. . .
                    Elizabeth Barrett Browning (1806-1861).

87. MORNING NEAR SALISBURY

. . I woke at three; for I was bid
    To breakfast with the Dean at nine,
And thence to Church. My curtain slid,
    I found the dawning Sunday fine;
And could not rest, so rose. The air
    Was dark and sharp; the roosted birds
Cheep'd, "Here am I, Sweet; are you there?"
    On Avon's misty flats the herds
Expected, comfortless, the day,
    Which slowly fired the clouds above;
The cock scream'd, somewhere far away;
    In sleep the matrimonial dove
Was crooning; no wind waked the wood,
    Nor moved the midnight river-damps,
Nor thrill'd the poplar; quiet stood
    The chestnut with its thousand lamps;
The moon shone yet, but weak and drear,
    And seem'd to watch, with bated breath,
The landscape, all made sharp and clear
    By stillness, as a face by death. . .
                    Coventry Patmore (1823-1896).

88. AFTER THE WEDDING

. . Whirl'd off at last, for speech I sought,
    To keep shy Love in countenance;
But, whilst I vainly tax'd my thought,
    Her voice deliver'd mine from trance:

"Look, is not this a pretty shawl,
　　Aunt's parting gift." "She's always kind,"
"The new wing spoils Sir John's old Hall:
　　You'll see it, if you pull the blind."

I drew the silk: in heaven the night
　　Was dawning; lovely Venus shone,
In languishment of tearful light,
　　Swath'd by the red breath of the sun. . .
　　　　　　　　　Coventry Patmore (1823-1896).

89. THROUGH THE COUNTRY HOUSE WINDOW

. . I had a little chamber in the house,
As green as any privet-hedge a bird
Might choose to build in, though the nest itself
Could show but dead-brown sticks and straws; the walls
Were green, the carpet was pure green, the straight
Small bed was curtained greenly, and the folds
Hung green about the window which let in
The out-door world with all its greenery.
You could not push your head out and escape
A dash of dawn-dew from the honeysuckle,
But so you were baptized into the grace
And privilege of seeing. . .
　　　　　　　　　　First the lime,
(I had enough there, of the lime, be sure,—
My morning-dream was often hummed away
By the bees in it;) past the lime, the lawn,
Which, after sweeping broadly round the house,
Went trickling through the shrubberies in a stream
Of tender turf, and wore and lost itself
Among the acacias, over which you saw
The irregular line of elms by the deep lane
Which stopped the grounds and dammed the overflow
Of arbutus and laurel. Out of sight
The lane was; sunk so deep, no foreign tramp
Nor drover of wild ponies out of Wales
Could guess if lady's hall or tenant's lodge

Dispensed such odours,—though his stick well-crooked
Might reach the lowest trail of blossoming briar
Which dipped upon the wall.   Behind the elms,
And through their tops, you saw the folded hills
Striped up and down with hedges, (burly oaks
Projecting from the line to show themselves)
Through which my cousin Romney's chimneys smoked
As still as when a silent mouth in frost
Breathes, showing where the woodlands hid Leigh Hall;
While, far above, a jut of table-land,
A promontory without water, stretched,—
You could not catch it if the days were thick,
Or took it for a cloud; but, otherwise
The vigorous sun would catch it up at eve
And use it for an anvil till he had filled
The shelves of heaven with burning thunderbolts,
Protesting against night and darkness:—then,
When all his setting trouble was resolved
To a trance of passive glory, you might see
In apparition on the golden sky
(Alas, my Giotto's background!) the sheep run
Along the fine clear outline, small as mice
That run along a witch's scarlet thread.

Not a grand nature.   Not my chestnut-woods
Of Vallombrosa, cleaving by the spurs
To the precipices.   Not my headlong leaps
Of waters, that cry out for joy or fear
In leaping through the palpitating pines,
Like a white soul tossed out to eternity
With thrills of time upon it.   Not indeed
My multitudinous mountains, sitting in
The magic circle, with the mutual touch
Electric, panting from their full deep hearts
Beneath the influent heavens, and waiting for
Communion and commission.   Italy
Is one thing, England one.

                            On English ground
You understand the letter,—ere the fall

How Adam lived in a garden. All the fields
Are tied up fast with hedges, nosegay-like;
The hills are crumpled plains, the plains parterres,
The trees, round, woolly, ready to be clipped,
And if you seek for any wilderness
You find, at best, a park. A nature tamed
And grown domestic like a barn-door fowl,
Which does not awe you with its claws and beak
Nor tempt you to an eyrie too high up,
But which, in cackling, sets you thinking of
Your eggs to-morrow at breakfast, in the pause
Of finer meditation. . .

Elizabeth Barrett Browning (1806-1861).

90. READING *WUTHERING HEIGHTS*

Jan. 8, 1856.—As to *Wuthering Heights* I can't find in my heart
to criticise the book. If I were walking with you over those
empurpled fells for an autumn day, startling the moor sheep
and the lapwing with passionate talk, I could not criticise what
I said or what you said. It would become sacred. The re-
membrance of it would make my heart swell and the tears
come to my eyes in the midst of the stern, hard life of the city.
And yet, if I could see it to be a duty, I should greatly enjoy
shutting myself up in a lone farmhouse for three days in winter
to write a criticism on it. It is a wild, wailing, moorland wind,
full of that unutterable love and anguish and mystery and
passion which form the substratum of high natures. Turner
has a landscape which is *it*. It *is* those wild hills, and a storm is
wuthering over them, and the molten lightning is licking the
heather, and nobody knows it but the one solitary soul, which
he has not put there, who is watching it from a window in the
waste.

But there is a very solemn and peaceful perception of a truth
most powerful just now to my mind, even while I am giving
inwardly a full unrestrained tribute of sympathy and admiration to it, and the mind that conceived it, viz. that the real,
eternal, the true, the abiding, does not lie in these grandeurs

and swelling emotions, and entrancing passions in any measure. They are, indeed, noble lineaments of our nature, but that by which we *live* is different.

Heathcliff is quite impossible, and therefore, so far, feeble. He is no bogie to me at all. Catherine is far more fearful, because quite possible. Heathcliff is an impalpable nightmare, and I put him beside the man who followed me in a dream with a loaded horse pistol, among the rafters of Lincoln Cathedral, holding a dark lantern.

James Smetham (1821-1889).

91. MEADOW-SWEET

. . And even while she spoke, I saw where James
Made toward us, like a wader in the surf,
Beyond the brook, waist-deep in meadow-sweet. . .
Alfred Tennyson (1809-1892).

92. THE BUDS

. . The June was in me, with its multitudes
Of nightingales all singing in the dark,
And rosebuds reddening where the calyx split. . .
Elizabeth Barrett Browning (1806-1861).

93. LINES OF BEAUTY

Look for pleasure at the line of beauty, and other curves of charming grace in the wind-blown stems of grass, and bowing barley or wheat; in the water-shaken bulrush, in the leaves of plants, and in the petals of flowers; in the outlines of birds, and even their feathers and eggs; in the flowing lines of the greyhound, the horse and cat, and other animals; in the shell of the mollusc, and in the wings and markings of insects; in the swell of the downy cheek, the rounded chin, the flowing bendings of the pole and back, and the outswelling and in-winding lines from the head to the leg of woman stepping

onward in the pride of youthful grace; and tell us whether
nature does not show us graceful curves enough to win us
from ugliness, even in a porringer?

William Barnes (1800-1886).

94. PEERING INTO DETAIL

. . Sanguine he was: a but less vivid hue
Than of that islet in the chestnut-bloom
Flamed in his cheek. . .

Alfred Tennyson (1809-1892).

95. SNOWDROP AND CELANDINE

A SNOWDROP was to me, as to Wordsworth, part of the Sermon
on the Mount; but I never should have written sonnets to the
celandine, because it is of a coarse yellow, and imperfect form.

John Ruskin (1819-1900).

96. THE SEA WORM

YOU see it? That black, shiny, knotted lump among the gravel,
small enough to be taken up in a dessert-spoon. Look now, as
it is raised, and its coils drawn out! Three feet—six—nine,
at least; with a capability of seemingly endless expansion; a
slimy tape of living caoutchouc some eighth of an inch in
diameter, a dark chocolate-black, with paler longitudinal lines.
Is it alive? It hangs, helpless and motionless, a mere velvet
string across the hand. Ask the neighbouring Annelids, and
the fry of the rock fishes, or put it in a vase, at home, and see.
It lies motionless, trailing itself among the gravel; you cannot
tell where it begins or ends: it may be a dead strip of seaweed,
Himanthalia lorea or *Chorda filum*; or even a tarred string.
So thinks the little fish, who plays over and over it, till he
touches at last what is too surely a head. In an instant a bell-
shaped sucker mouth has fastened to his side. In another instant, from one lip, a concave double proboscis, just like a tapir's
(another instance of the repetition of forms), has clasped him

like a finger; and now begins the struggle: but in vain. He is being "played" with such a fishing line as the skill of a Wilson or a Stoddart never could invent; a living line, with elasticity beyond that of the most delicate fly-rod, which follows every lunge, shortening and lengthening, slipping and turning round every piece of gravel and stem of seaweed, with a tiring drag such as no Highland wrist or step could ever bring to bear on salmon or on trout. The victim is tired now; and slowly, yet dexterously, his blind assailant is feeling and shifting along his side, till he reaches one end of him; and then the black lips expand, and slowly and surely the curved finger begins packing him end-foremost down into the gullet, where he sinks, inch by inch, till the swelling which marks his place is lost among the coils, and he is probably macerated to a pulp long before he has reached the opposite extremity of his cave of doom. Once safe down, the black murderer slowly contracts into a knotted heap, and lies, like a boa with a stag inside him, motionless and blest.   *Charles Kingsley* (1819-1875).

97. FITNESS

IN all these beautiful things [i.e. *in a landscape*] there is fitness —fitness of water to irrigate growth, and to run for all lips to the sea; fitness of land to take and send onward the stream; fitness of strength to weight, as of the stem to the head of a tree; fitness of elasticity to force, as that of the poplar, and the bough whose very name is bending, and the bulrush and grass to the wind; fitness of protection to life, as in the armed holly and thorn, and the bush, or ditch-guarded epilobium; and a harmony of the whole with the good of man.

                         William Barnes (1800-1886).

98. TWO WORDPAINTERS

i. THE CASTLE IN DECAY

. . Then rode Geraint into the castle court,
    His charger trampling many a prickly star
    Of sprouted thistle on the broken stones.

He look'd and saw that all was ruinous.
Here stood a shatter'd archway plumed with fern;
And here had fall'n a great part of a tower,
Whole, like a crag that tumbles from the cliff,
And like a crag was gay with wilding flowers:
And high above a piece of turret stair,
Worn by the feet that now were silent, wound
Bare to the sun, and monstrous ivy-stems
Claspt the gray walls with hairy-fibred arms,
And suck'd the joining of the stones, and look'd
A knot, beneath, of snakes, aloft, a grove. . .

Alfred Tennyson (1809-1892).

ii. THE MADREPORE, OR DEVONSHIRE CUP-CORAL

LET it, after being torn from the rock, recover its equanimity;
then you will see a pellucid gelatinous flesh emerging from
between the plates, and little exquisitely formed and coloured
tentacula, with white clubbed tips fringing the sides of the
cup-shaped cavity in the centre, across which stretches the
oval disc marked with a star of some rich and brilliant colour,
surrounding the central mouth, a slit with wide crenated lips,
like the orifice of one of those elegant cowrie shells which we
put upon our mantelpieces. The mouth is always more or
less prominent, and can be protruded and expanded to an
astonishing extent. The space surrounding the lips is commonly fawn colour, or rich chestnut-brown; the star or
vandyked circle rich red, pale vermilion, and sometimes the
most brilliant emerald green, as brilliant as the gorget of a
humming-bird.

P. H. Gosse, F.R.S. (1810-1888).

99. ANTIQUE MODERNISM: THE POINTED ARCH

MY own feeling is, that, as in the pointed arch we have not
only the most beautiful, but at the same time incomparably
the most convenient feature in construction which ever has

been, or which, I firmly believe, ever can be invented, we
should not be true artists if we neglected to use it.

I hold firmly the doctrine that no architect has any right
whatever to neglect to avail himself of every improvement in
construction which the growing intelligence of this mechanical
age can afford him; but this doctrine in no way hinders the
constant employment of the pointed arch; on the contrary, it
makes it necessary, because it is at once the most beautiful and
the most economical way of doing the work we have to be done.

George Edmund Street (1824-1881).

100. THE JUDGEMENT OF THE DAY

. . Every age
Appears to souls who live in 't (ask Carlyle)
Most unheroic. Ours, for instance, ours:
The thinkers scout it, and the poets abound
Who scorn to touch it with a finger-tip:
A pewter age,—mixed metal, silver-washed:
An age of scum, spooned off the richer past,
An age of patches for old gaberdines,
An age of mere transition, meaning nought
Except that what succeeds must shame it quite
If God please. That's wrong thinking, to my mind,
And wrong thoughts make poor poems.

Every age,
Through being beheld too close, is ill-discerned
By those who have not lived past it. We'll suppose
Mount Athos carved, as Alexander schemed,
To some colossal statue of a man.
The peasants, gathering brushwood in her ear,
Had guessed as little as the browsing goats
Of form or feature of humanity
Up there,—in fact, had travelled five miles off
Or ere the giant image broke on them,
Full human profile, nose and chin distinct,
Mouth, muttering rhythms of silence up the sky
And fed at evening with the blood of suns;

Grand torso,—hand, that flung perpetually
The largesse of a silver river down
To all the country pastures.   'Tis even thus
With times we live in,—evermore too great
To be apprehended near.
                                    But poets should
Exert a double vision; should have eyes
To see near things as comprehensively
As if afar they took their point of sight,
And distant things as intimately deep
As if they touched them.   Let us strive for this.
I do distrust the poet who discerns
No character or glory in his times,
And trundles back his soul five hundred years,
Past moat and drawbridge, into a castle-court,
To sing—oh, not of lizard or of toad
Alive i' the ditch there,—'twere excusable,
But of some black chief, half knight, half sheep-lifter,
Some beauteous dame, half chattel and half queen,
As dead as must be, for the greater part,
The poems made on their chivalric bones;
And that's no wonder: death inherits death.

Nay, if there's room for poets in this world
A little overgrown, (I think there is)
Their sole work is to represent the age,
Their age, not Charlemagne's,—this live, throbbing age,
That brawls, cheats, maddens, calculates, aspires,
And spends more passion, more heroic heat,
Betwixt the mirrors of its drawing-rooms,
Than Roland with his knights at Roncesvalles.
To flinch from modern varnish, coat or flounce,
Cry out for togas and the picturesque,
Is fatal,—foolish too.   King Arthur's self
Was commonplace to Lady Guenever;
And Camelot to minstrels seemed as flat
As Fleet Street to our poets. . .

                         Elizabeth Barrett Browning (1806-1861).

101. ITALY

. . What I love best in all the world
Is a castle, precipice-encurled,
In a gash of the wind-grieved Apennine
Or look for me, old fellow of mine,
(If I get my head from out the mouth
O' the grave, and loose my spirit's bands,
And come again to the land of lands)—
In a sea-side house to the farther South,
Where the baked cicala dies of drouth,
And one sharp tree—'tis a cypress—stands,
By the many hundred years red-rusted,
Rough iron-spiked, ripe fruit-o'ercrusted,
My sentinel to guard the sands
To the water's edge.   For, what expands
Before the house, but the great opaque
Blue breadth of sea without a break?
While, in the house, for ever crumbles
Some fragment of the frescoed walls,
From blisters where a scorpion sprawls.
A girl bare-footed brings, and tumbles
Down on the pavement, green-flesh melons,
And says there's news to-day—the king
Was shot at, touched in the liver-wing,
Goes with his Bourbon arm in a sling:
—She hopes they have not caught the felons. . .
Robert Browning (1812-1889).

102. LIMERICKS

i

ON THE PAINTER VAL PRINSEP

THERE is a creator called God
Whose creations are some of them odd.
I maintain, and I shall, the creation of Val
Reflects little credit on God.

ii

ON THE SAME

THERE is a big artist named Val,
The roughs' and the prizefighters' pal:
The mind of a groom, and the head of a broom,
Were nature's endowments to Val.

iii

ON WHISTLER

THERE'S a combative artist named Whistler
Who is, like his own hog's-hairs, a bristler:
A tube of white lead and a punch on the head
Offer varied attractions to Whistler.

iv

ON ROBERT BUCHANAN, WHO ATTACKED HIM UNDER THE PSEUDONYM OF "THOMAS MAITLAND"

As a critic the poet Buchanan
Thinks "Pseudo" much safer than "Anon."
Into Maitland he's shrunk, yet the smell of the skunk
Guides the shuddering nose to Buchanan.

v

ON THE TWO AGNEWS

THERE are dealers in pictures named Agnew
Whose soft soap would make an old rag new:
The Father of Lies, with his tail to his eyes,
Cries—"Go to it, Tom Agnew, Bill Agnew!"
                    D. G. Rossetti (1828-1882).

103. LIMERICKS

i

THERE was an old man of the Dargle
Who purchased six barrels of Gargle;

For he said, "I'll sit still, and will roll them down hill,
For the fish in the depths of the Dargle."

ii

THERE was an old man of Port Grigor,
Whose actions were noted for vigour;
He stood on his head, till his waistcoat turned red,
That eclectic old man of Port Grigor.

iii

THERE was an old man whose despair
Induced him to purchase a hare:
Whereon one fine day, he rode wholly away,
Which partly assuaged his despair.

iv

THERE was an old person of Bar,
Who passed all her life in a jar,
Which she painted pea-green, to appear more serene,
That placid old person of Bar.

Edward Lear (1812-1888).

104. A LIGHT WOMAN

I

So far as our story approaches the end,
    Which do you pity the most of us three?—
My friend, or the mistress of my friend
    With her wanton eyes, or me?

II

My friend was already too good to lose,
    And seemed in the way of improvement yet,
When she crossed his path with her hunting-noose
    And over him drew her net.

D*

III

When I saw him tangled in her toils,
  A shame, said I, if she adds just him
To her nine-and-ninety other spoils,
  The hundredth, for a whim!

IV

And before my friend be wholly hers,
  How easy to prove to him, I said,
An eagle's the game her pride prefers,
  Though she snaps at a wren instead!

V

So, I gave her eyes my own eyes to take,
  My hand sought hers as in earnest need,
And round she turned for my noble sake,
  And gave me herself indeed.

VI

The eagle am I, with my fame in the world,
  The wren is he, with his maiden face.
—You look away and your lip is curled?
  Patience, a moment's space!

VII

For see, my friend goes shaking and white;
  He eyes me as the basilisk:
I have turned, it appears, his day to night,
  Eclipsing his sun's disk.

VIII

And I did it, he thinks, as a very thief:
  "Though I love her—that, he comprehends—
One should master one's passions, (love, in chief)
  And be loyal to one's friends!"

IX

And she,—she lies in my hand as tame
  As a pear late basking over a wall;
Just a touch to try and off it came;
  'Tis mine,—can I let it fall?

X

With no mind to eat it, that's the worst!
  Were it thrown in the road, would the case assist?
'Twas quenching a dozen blue-flies' thirst
  When I gave its stalk a twist.

XI

And I,—what I seem to my friend, you see:
  What I soon shall seem to his love, you guess:
What I seem to myself, do you ask of me?
  No hero, I confess.

XII

'Tis an awkward thing to play with souls,
  And matter enough to save one's own:
Yet think of my friend, and the burning coals
  He played with for bits of stone!

XIII

One likes to show the truth for the truth;
  That the woman was light is very true:
But suppose she says,—Never mind that youth!
  What wrong have I done to you?

XIV

Well, any how, here the story stays,
  So far at least as I understand;
And, Robert Browning, you writer of plays,
  Here's a subject made to your hand!

                              Robert Browning (1812-1889).

105. MODERN PAINTERS

OWING to the attention being wholly concentrated upon the moral element in man, the optical sensibility of English painters is blunted and unhinged. I do not think that paintings more displeasing to the eye have ever been produced. It is hard to imagine more crude effects, more exaggerated and violent colouring, more extreme and glaring dissonances, a falser and more abrupt commingling of tones. In Hunt's "Two Gentlemen of Verona," blue-tinted trees stand forth against the brown earth and scarlet clothes; "Christ the Light of the World" is set in a greenish-yellow atmosphere, resembling that perceived on ascending to the surface of turbid water after a plunge. In Millais' "Daughters of Noah leaving the Ark," the violet of the dress, and the manner in which it is relieved by its surroundings, is a thing to be seen. In Crowe's "Pope presented to Dryden" are light blue waistcoats and red velvet coats, while the accessories are brought into full and harsh relief, apparently for a wager. Mulready's "Bathers" seem to be made of porcelain. In the "Eve of St. Agnes" of Millais, a lady in a low-bodied evening dress is represented through the medium of a studied effect of twilight, as having the appearance of a corpse-like green, and the chamber is of the same hue. On every hand there are landscapes in which blood-red poppies are set in grass of the tint of a green parrot; apple trees in blossom, whereof the staring white of the petals against the dark branches is painful to the sight; a green churchyard in the sunlight, where each blade of grass shows its brightness like the blade of a penknife; sunsets which might certainly be taken for displays of fireworks. Indeed, the condition of their retina is peculiar. In order to comprehend this, recourse must be had to analogies, and they may be found in twenty details of daily life, in the red and violet, the lees of wine, the raw-green tints with which their children's books are coloured, in the flaunting and overdone dresses of their women, in the aspect of their meadows, their flowers, their landscapes beheld under a sudden gleam of sunshine. Perhaps it must be admitted that in every country the external appearances of things educate the eye, that its customs form its tastes, that there is a secret

affinity between the arrangement of its artificial decorations
and the colours of its natural sights. Here, in fact, the brilliancy,
the freshness, the opulence of the style of dress recall the
splendours, the youthfulness, the magnificence, the contrasts
and appearances of the vegetation. Resemblances may be
detected between their mauve and violet silks and the changing
colours of the distances and the clouds, between their gauze
scarfs, their fleecy lace shawls, and the pale or splendid haze
of their horizons. Yet a number of effects which are harmonious in nature, are displeasing when painted; they are
unfit for representation on canvas, at least they should not be
reproduced in all their nakedness. In the latter state they
produce discord, in default of the surroundings with which they
harmonise. For Nature has many resources at her disposal
which are wanting in painting—among others, the full sun,
real light, the sparkle of daylight on water, the scintillation of
sunbeams upon a green leaf. These are the supreme values
which dominate all the others, and relieve them of their ex-
cessive crudeness; deprived of this atmosphere, the others
produce as unpleasant an effect as a chord from which the
leading note is omitted. They must, therefore, be transposed
in order to be expressed. No painter, no artist, is a pure copyist.
He invents, even while he confines himself to translating; for
that which Nature executes through the medium of one system
of means and values, he is obliged to render by another system
of values and means. Herein is the mistake of contemporary
English painters. They are faithful, but literally so. After
seeing their country, it is obvious that the majority of their
effects are truthful. This picture really represents a piece of
English turf vivified by a recent shower. This other one
represents the white morning sky; the glittering sands at low
water; the bright green or violet hue of undulating waves.
This one represents the ears of corn against the pale-yellow
hue of the sheaves, the ruddy purple heaths under the sun on a
lonely common. On reflection the exactitude of all this cannot
be denied; better still, we recall that the sight of the real
landscape gave pleasure, and we experience surprise at feeling
dissatisfied in presence of the painted landscape. This is
because the translation is nothing but a transcription. It is

because, desiring to be faithful in one thing, they have misrepresented the whole. With the patience of fastidious workmen, they have put on canvas one by one the unmodified sensations of their eyes. Meanwhile they meditated, moralised, following as poets the soft or sad emotions which the real landscape awakened in their souls. Between the workman and the poet the artist has had no place. Their patience commands applause. We feel that we should be touched in the presence of the original; their copy, however, is but a memorandum, and we gladly turn away from it because it is ugly.

Hippolyte Taine (1828-1893).

106. SHAMEFUL DEATH

THERE were four of us about that bed;
　The mass-priest knelt at the side,
I and his mother stood at the head,
　Over his feet lay the bride;
We were quite sure that he was dead,
　Though his eyes were open wide.

He did not die in the night,
　He did not die in the day,
But in the morning twilight
　His spirit pass'd away,
When neither sun nor moon was bright,
　And the trees were merely grey.

He was not slain with the sword,
　Knight's axe, or the knightly spear,
Yet spoke he never a word
　After he came in here;
I cut away the cord
　From the neck of my brother dear.

He did not strike one blow,
　For the recreants came behind,

In a place where the hornbeams grow,
   A path right hard to find,
For the hornbeam boughs swing so,
   That the twilight makes it blind.

They lighted a great torch then,
   When his arms were pinion'd fast,
Sir John the knight of the Fen,
   Sir Guy of the Dolorous Blast,
With knights threescore and ten,
   Hung brave Lord Hugh at last.

I am threescore and ten,
   And my hair is all turn'd grey,
But I met Sir John of the Fen
   Long ago on a summer day,
And am glad to think of the moment when
   I took his life away.

I am threescore and ten,
   And my strength is mostly pass'd,
But long ago I and my men,
   When the sky was overcast,
And the smoke roll'd over the reeds of the fen,
   Slew Guy of the Dolorous Blast.

And now, knights all of you,
   I pray you pray for Sir Hugh,
A good knight and a true,
   And for Alice, his wife, pray too.
                 William Morris (1834-1896).

107. RIDING TOGETHER

FOR many, many days together
   The wind blew steady from the East;
For many days hot grew the weather,
   About the time of our Lady's Feast.

For many days we rode together,
   Yet met we neither friend nor foe;
Hotter and clearer grew the weather,
   Steadily did the East wind blow.

We saw the trees in the hot, bright weather,
   Clear-cut, with shadows very black,
As freely we rode on together
   With helms unlaced and bridles slack.

And often, as we rode together,
   We, looking down the green-bank'd stream,
Saw flowers in the sunny weather,
   And saw the bubble-making bream.

And in the night lay down together,
   And hung above our heads the rood,
Or watch'd night-long in the dewy weather,
   The while the moon did watch the wood.

Our spears stood bright and thick together,
   Straight out the banners stream'd behind,
As we gallop'd on in the sunny weather,
   With faces turn'd towards the wind.

Down sank our threescore spears together,
   As thick we saw the pagans ride;
His eager face in the clear fresh weather,
   Shone out that last time by my side.

Up the sweep of the bridge we dash'd together,
   It rock'd to the crash of the meeting spears,
Down rain'd the buds of the dear spring weather,
   The elm-tree flowers fell like tears.

There, as we roll'd and writhed together,
   I threw my arms above my head,
For close by my side, in the lovely weather,
   I saw him reel and fall back dead.

I and the slayer met together,
  He waited the death-stroke there in his place,
With thoughts of death, in the lovely weather,
  Gapingly mazed at my madden'd face.

Madly I fought as we fought together;
  In vain: the little Christian band
The pagans drown'd, as in stormy weather,
  The river drowns low-lying land.

They bound my blood-stain'd hands together,
  They bound his corpse to nod by my side:
Then on we rode, in the bright March weather,
  With clash of cymbals did we ride.

We ride no more, no more together;
  My prison-bars are thick and strong,
I take no heed of any weather,
  The sweet Saints grant I live not long.
                    William Morris (1834-1896).

108. TWO PICTURES

. . What's in the *Times*?—a scold
    At the Emperor deep and cold;
        He has taken a bride
        To his gruesome side,
    That's as fair as himself is bold:
        There they sit ermine-stoled,
    And she powders her hair with gold.

    Fancy the Pampas' sheen!
    Miles and miles of gold and green
        Where the sunflowers blow
        In a solid glow,
    And—to break now and then the screen—
        Black neck and eyeballs keen,
    Up a wild horse leaps between. . .
                    Robert Browning (1812-1889).

109. EVOLUTION: THE DEVELOPMENT
THEORY MATURES

AUTHORS of the highest eminence seem to be fully satisfied with the view that each species has been independently created. To my mind it accords better with what we know of the laws impressed on matter by the Creator, that the production and extinction of the past and present inhabitants of the world should have been due to secondary causes, like those determining the birth and death of the individual. When I view all beings not as special creations, but as the lineal descendants of some few beings which lived long before the first bed of the Cambrian system was deposited, they seem to me to become ennobled. Judging from the past, we may safely infer that not one living species will transmit its unaltered likeness to a distant futurity. And of the species now living very few will transmit progeny of any kind to a far distant futurity; for the manner in which all organic beings are grouped, shows that the greater number of species in each genus, and all the species in many genera, have left no descendants, but have become utterly extinct. We can so far take a prophetic glance into futurity as to foretell that it will be the common and widely-spread species, belonging to the larger and dominant groups within each class, which will ultimately prevail and procreate new and dominant species. As all the living forms of life are the lineal descendants of those which lived long before the Cambrian epoch, we may feel certain that the ordinary succession by generation has never once been broken, and that no cataclysm has desolated the whole world. Hence we may look with some confidence to a secure future of great length. And as natural selection works solely by and for the good of each being, all corporeal and mental endowments will tend to progress towards perfection.

It is interesting to contemplate a tangled bank, clothed with many plants of many kinds, with birds singing on the bushes, with various insects flitting about, and with worms crawling through the damp earth, and to reflect that these elaborately constructed forms, so different from each other, and dependent

upon each other in so complex a manner, have all been produced
by laws acting around us. These laws, taken in the largest
sense, being Growth with Reproduction; Inheritance which is
almost implied by reproduction; Variability from the indirect
and direct action of the condition of life, and from use and disuse:
a Ratio of Increase so high as to lead to a Struggle for Life, and
as a consequence to Natural Selection, entailing Divergence of
Character and the Extinction of less-improved forms. Thus,
from the war of nature, from famine and death, the most
exalted object which we are capable of conceiving, namely, the
production of the higher animals, directly follows. There is
grandeur in this view of life, with its several powers, having
been originally breathed by the Creator into a few forms or
into one; and that, whilst this planet has gone cycling on
according to the fixed law of gravity, from so simple a beginning
endless forms most beautiful and most wonderful have been,
and are being evolved.

Charles Darwin (1809-1882).

110. EVOLUTION AND PROGRESS

OUR race's progress and perfectibility is a dream, because
revelation contradicts it.

J. H. Newman (1801-1890).

111. THE BLUE CLOSET

THE DAMOZELS

LADY ALICE, Lady Louise,
Between the wash of the tumbling seas
We are ready to sing, if so ye please;
So lay your long hands on the keys;
                    Sing, "*Laudate pueri.*"

And ever the great bell overhead
Boom'd in the wind a knell for the dead,
Though no one toll'd it, a knell for the dead.

LADY LOUISE

Sister, let the measure swell
Not too loud; for you sing not well
If you drown the faint boom of the bell;
     He is weary, so am I.

And ever the chevron overhead
Flapp'd on the banner of the dead ;
(Was he asleep, or was he dead ?)

LADY ALICE

Alice the Queen, and Louise the Queen,
Two damozels wearing purple and green,
Four lone ladies dwelling here
From day to day and year to year;
And there is none to let us go;
To break the locks of the doors below,
Or shovel away the heaped-up snow;
And when we die no man will know
That we are dead; but they give us leave,
Once every year on Christmas-eve,
To sing in the Closet Blue one song;
And we should be so long, so long,
If we dared, in singing; for dream on dream,
They float on in a happy stream;
Float from the gold strings, float from the keys,
Float from the open'd lips of Louise;
But, alas! the sea-salt oozes through
The chinks of the tiles of the Closet Blue;

And ever the great bell overhead
Booms in the wind a knell for the dead,
The wind plays on it a knell for the dead.

    (They sing all together.)

How long ago was it, how long ago,
He came to this tower with hands full of snow?

"Kneel down, O love Louise, kneel down," he said,
And sprinkled the dusty snow over my head.

He watch'd the snow melting, it ran through my hair,
Ran over my shoulder, white shoulders and bare.

"I cannot weep for thee, poor love Louise,
For my tears are all hidden deep under the seas;

"In a gold and blue casket she keeps all my tears,
But my eyes are no longer blue, as in old years;

"Yea, they grow grey with time, grow small and dry,
I am so feeble now, would I might die."

And in truth the great bell overhead
Left off his pealing for the dead,
Perchance, because the wind was dead.

Will he come back again, or is he dead?
O! is he sleeping, my scarf round his head?

Or did they strangle him as he lay there,
With the long scarlet scarf I used to wear?

Only I pray thee, Lord, let him come here!
Both his soul and his body to me are most dear.

Dear Lord, that loves me, I wait to receive
Either body or spirit this wild Christmas-eve.

Through the floor shot up a lily red,
With a patch of earth from the land of the dead
For he was strong in the land of the dead.

What matter that his cheeks were pale,
  His kind kiss'd lips all grey?
"O, love Louise, have you waited long?"
  "O, my lord Arthur, yea."

What if his hair that brush'd her cheek
    Was stiff with frozen rime?
His eyes were grown quite blue again,
    As in the happy time.

"O, love Louise, this is the key
    Of the happy golden land!
O, sisters, cross the bridge with me,
    My eyes are full of sand.
What matter that I cannot see,
    If ye take me by the hand?"

And ever the great bell overhead,
And the tumbling seas mourn'd for the dead ;
For their song ceased, and they were dead.

                William Morris (1834-1896).

112. THE NATURAL SELECTION OF BEAUTY

WITH respect to the belief that organic beings have been created beautiful for the delight of man,—a belief which it has been pronounced is subversive of my whole theory,—I may first remark that the sense of beauty obviously depends on the nature of the mind, irrespective of any real quality in the admired object; and that the idea of what is beautiful, is not innate or unalterable. We see this, for instance, in the men of different races admiring an entirely different standard of beauty in their women. If beautiful objects had been created solely for man's gratification, it ought to be shown that before man appeared, there was less beauty on the face of the earth than since he came on the stage. Were the beautiful volute and cone shells of the Eocene epoch, and the gracefully sculptured ammonites of the Secondary period, created that man might ages afterwards admire them in his cabinet? Few objects are more beautiful than the minute siliceous cases of the diatomaceae: were these created that they might be examined and admired under the higher powers of the microscope? The beauty in this latter case, and in many others, is apparently wholly due to symmetry of growth. Flowers rank amongst the most beautiful productions of nature; but they have been rendered conspicuous in contrast with the green leaves, and in consequence at the same time beautiful, so that they may be easily observed by insects. I have come to this conclusion from finding it an invariable rule that when a flower is fertilised by the wind it never has a gaily-coloured corolla. Several plants habitually produce two kinds of flowers; one kind open and coloured so as to attract insects; the other closed, not coloured, destitute of nectar, and never visited by insects. Hence we may conclude that, if insects had not been developed on the face of the earth, our plants would not have been decked with beautiful flowers, but would have produced only such poor flowers as we see on our fir, oak, nut and ash trees, on grasses, spinach, docks, and nettles, which are all fertilised through the agency of the wind. A similar line of argument holds good with fruits; that a ripe strawberry or cherry is as pleasing to the eye as to the palate,—that the gaily-coloured fruit of the spindle-wood tree and the scarlet berries of the holly are beautiful objects,—will be admitted by every one. But this beauty serves merely as a guide to birds and beasts, in order that the fruit may be devoured and the manured seeds disseminated: I infer that this is the case from having as yet found no exception to the rule that seeds are always thus disseminated when embedded within a fruit of any kind (that is within a fleshy or pulpy envelope), if it be coloured of any brilliant tint, or rendered conspicuous by being white or black.

On the other hand, I willingly admit that a great number of male animals, as all our most gorgeous birds, some fishes, reptiles, and mammals, and a host of magnificently coloured butterflies, have been rendered beautiful for beauty's sake; but this has been effected through sexual selection, that is, by the more beautiful males having been continually preferred by the females, and not for the delight of man. So it is with the music of birds. We may infer from all this that a nearly similar taste for beautiful colours and for musical sounds runs through a large part of the animal kingdom. When the female is as beautifully coloured as the male, which is not rarely the case with birds and butterflies, the cause apparently lies in the colours acquired through sexual selection having been transmitted to both sexes, instead of to the males alone. How the sense of beauty in its simplest form—that is, the reception of a peculiar kind of pleasure from certain colours, forms, and sounds—was first developed in the mind of man and of the lower animals, is a very obscure subject. The same sort of difficulty is presented, if we enquire how it is that certain flavours and odours give pleasure, and others displeasure. Habit in all these cases appears to have come to a certain extent into play; but there must be some fundamental cause in the constitution of the nervous system in each species.

Charles Darwin (1809-1882).

PART THREE: PAST INTO PRESENT

And many a wink they wunk, and shook
Their heads, but furthermore they took
     Ⓞ miserie!*

No note: it was a way they had,
In Camelot, when folks went mad. . .
     Ⓞ miserie!*

            George du Maurier.

The fly-wheel with a mellow murmur turn'd.
            Charles Tennyson Turner.

113. THE BURIAL HOUR

"At eve should be the time," they said,
"To close their brother's narrow bed:"
  'Tis at that pleasant hour of day
  The labourer treads his homeward way.

His work was o'er, his toil was done,
And therefore, with the set of sun,
  To wait the wages of the dead
  We laid our hireling in his bed.

Robert Stephen Hawker (1803-1875).

114. ORIGINAL SIN

To consider the world in its length and breadth, its various
history, the many races of man, their starts, their fortunes,
their mutual alienation, their conflicts; and then their ways,
habits, governments, forms of worship; their enterprises, their
aimless courses, their random achievements and acquirements,
the impotent conclusion of long-standing facts, the tokens, so
faint and broken, of a superintending design, the blind evolution
of what turn out to be great powers or truths, the progress of
things, as if from unreasoning elements, not towards final
causes, the greatness and littleness of man, his far-reaching
aims, his short duration, the curtain hung over his futurity, the
disappointments of life, the defeat of good, the success of evil,
physical pain, mental anguish, the prevalence and intensity of
sin, the pervading idolatries, the corruptions, the dreary hopeless irreligion, that condition of the whole race, so fearfully yet
exactly described in the Apostle's words, "having no hope and
without God in the world,"—all this is a vision to dizzy and
appal; and inflicts upon the mind the sense of a profound
mystery, which is absolutely beyond human solution.

What shall be said to this heart-piercing, reason-bewildering fact? I can only answer, that either there is no Creator, or this living society of men is in a true sense discarded from His presence. Did I see a boy of good make and mind, with the tokens on him of a refined nature, cast upon the world without provision, unable to say whence he came, his birth-place or his family connexions, I should conclude that there was some mystery connected with his history, and that he was one, of whom, from one cause or other, his parents were ashamed. Thus only should I be able to account for the contrast between the promise and the condition of his being. And so I argue about the world;—*if* there be a God, *since* there is a God, the human race is implicated in some terrible aboriginal calamity. It is out of joint with the purposes of its Creator. This is a fact, a fact as true as the fact of its existence; and thus the doctrine of what is theologically called original sin becomes to me almost as certain as that the world exists, and as the existence of God.

J. H. Newman (1801-1890).

115. LITTLE PHOEBE

Or THE SECOND GATHERING OF THE SEA-SHELLS

THE rain had pour'd all day, but clear'd at night,
When, with her little basket on her arm,
She left the door-step of that seaside farm;
The weeping tamarisk glisten'd in the light,
And chanticleer's green feathers softly waved
Against the dying sunshine. Forth she fared,
Our host's sweet child, his Phoebe golden-hair'd,
To gather shells, wherewith the beach was paved;
At dusk, she took the homeward path that led
Beneath yon dark-blue ridge, when, sad to tell,
On her fair head the gloomy Lias fell,
Crumbled by storms,—they found her bruised and dead:
Her basket-store was scatter'd by the fall,
But loving hands replaced and kept them all.

Charles Tennyson Turner (1808-1879).

116. DREAM

I

WITH camel's hair I clothed my skin,
  I fed my mouth with honey wild;
And set me scarlet wool to spin,
  And all my breast with hyssop filled;
Upon my brow and cheeks and chin
  A bird's blood spilled.

I took a broken reed to hold,
  I took a sponge of gall to press;
I took weak water-weeds to fold
  About my sacrificial dress.

I took the grasses of the field,
  The flax was bolled upon my crine;
And ivy thorn and wild grapes healed
  To make good wine.

I took my scrip of manna sweet,
  My cruse of water did I bless;
I took the white dove by the feet,
  And flew into the wilderness.

II

The tiger came and played;
Uprose the lion in his mane;
The jackal's tawny nose
And sanguine dripping tongue
Out of the desert rose
And plunged its sands among;
The bear came striding o'er the desert plain.

Uprose the horn and eyes
And quivering flank of the great unicorn,

And galloped round and round;
Uprose the gleaming claw
Of the leviathan, and wound
In steadfast march did draw
Its course away beyond the desert's bourn.

I stood within a maze
Woven round about me by a magic art,
And ordered circle-wise:
The bear more near did trend,
And with two fiery eyes,
And with a wolfish head,
Did close the circle round in every part.

III

With scarlet corded horn,
With frail wrecked knees and stumbling pace,
The scapegoat came:
His eyes took flesh and spirit dread in flame
At once, and he died looking towards my face.

R. W. Dixon (1833-1900).

117. THE MURDERER SIPÓ

i

THERE is something in a tropical forest akin to the ocean in its
effects on the mind. Man feels so completely his insignificance
there, and the vastness of nature. A naturalist cannot help
reflecting on the vegetable forces manifested on so grand a
scale around him. A German traveller, Burmeister, has said
that the contemplation of a Brazilian forest produced on him
a painful impression, on account of the vegetation displaying a
spirit of restless selfishness, eager emulation, and craftiness.
He thought the softness, earnestness, and repose of European
woodland scenery were far more pleasing, and that these

formed one of the causes of the superior moral character of
European nations.

In these tropical forests each plant and tree seems to be
striving to outvie its fellow, struggling upwards towards light
and air—branch and leaf and stem—regardless of its neighbours.
Parasitic plants are seen fastening with firm grip on others,
making use of them with reckless indifference as instruments
for their own advancement. Live and let live is clearly not
the maxim taught in these wildernesses. There is one kind of
parasitic tree, very common near Pará, which exhibits this
feature in a very prominent manner. It is called the Sipó
Matador, or the Murderer Liana. . . . I observed many specimens. The base of its stem would be unable to bear the weight
of the upper growth; it is obliged therefore to support itself
on a tree of another species. In this it is not essentially different
from other climbing trees and plants, but the way the Matador
sets about it is peculiar, and produces certainly a disagreeable
impression. It springs up close to the tree on which it intends
to fix itself, and the wood of its stem grows by spreading itself
like a plastic mould over one side of the trunk of its supporter.
It then puts forth from each side an arm-like branch, which
grows rapidly, and looks as though a stream of sap were flowing
and hardening as it went. This adheres closely to the trunk of
the victim, and the two arms meet on the opposite side and
blend together. These arms are put forth at somewhat regular
intervals in mounting upwards, and the victim, when its
strangler is full grown, becomes tightly clasped by a number
of inflexible rings. These rings gradually grow larger as the
Murderer flourishes, rearing its crown of foliage to the sky
mingled with that of its neighbour, and in course of time they
kill it by stopping the flow of its sap. The strange spectacle
then remains of the selfish parasite clasping in its arms the
lifeless and decaying body of its victim, which had been a help
to its own growth. Its ends have been served—it has flowered
and fruited, reproduced and disseminated its kind; and now
when the dead trunk moulders away, its own end approaches;
its support is gone, and itself also falls.

The Murderer Sipó merely exhibits, in a more conspicuous
manner than usual, the struggle which necessarily exists

amongst vegetable forms in these crowded forests, where individual is competing with individual and species with species, all striving to reach light and air in order to unfold their leaves and perfect their organs of fructification. All species entail in their successful struggles the injury or destruction of many of their neighbours or supporters, but the process is not in others so speaking to the eye as it is in the case of the Matador. . .

ii

I think there is plenty, in tropical nature, to counteract any unpleasant impression which the reckless energy of the vegetation might produce. There is the incomparable beauty and variety of the foliage, the vivid colours, the richness and exuberance everywhere displayed, which make, in my opinion, the richest woodland scenery in Northern Europe a sterile desert in comparison. But it is especially the enjoyment of life manifested by individual existences which compensates for the destruction and pain caused by the inevitable competition. Although this competition is nowhere more active, and the dangers to which each individual is exposed nowhere more numerous, yet nowhere is this enjoyment more vividly displayed. If vegetation had feeling, its vigorous and rapid growth, uninterrupted by the cold sleep of winter, would, one would think, be productive of pleasure to its individuals. In animals the mutual competition may be greater, the predaceous species more constantly on the alert, than in temperate climates: but there is at the same time no severe periodical struggle with inclement seasons. In sunny nooks, and at certain seasons, the trees and the air are gay with birds and insects, all in the full enjoyment of existence; the warmth, the sunlight, and the abundance of food producing their results in the animation and sportiveness of the beings congregated together. We ought not to leave out of sight, too, the sexual decorations— the brilliant colours and ornamentation of the males, which, although existing in the fauna of all climates, reach a higher degree of perfection in the tropics than elsewhere. This seems to point to the pleasures of the pairing seasons.

H. W. Bates, F.R.S. (1825-1892).

118. THE MUSIC OF THE SPHERES

. . He that but once too nearly hears
The music of forfended spheres,
Is thenceforth lonely, and for all
His days like one who treads the Wall
Of China, and, on this hand, sees
Cities and their civilities,
And, on the other, lions. . .

Coventry Patmore (1823-1896).

119. DESPAIR

I FIND myself by a black spring and cold,
    Which slowly bursts from this rock's heavy head,
Like drops of sweat wrung from our God of old,
            And plashes dead
Into a basin hollowed from the mould.

I trace this fountain rolling deeply down—
    Dark is the night, my pathway ruinous—
Here foam the muddy billows thick and brown,
            Then issue thus
Into a lake where all the world might drown.

I mark the mountains stand about and brood—
    The lake and they together, God, remain,
As black and deep and steep as walls of mud
            On some vast plain
Block out and brood upon a swimming drain.

I mark a woman on the farther shore
    Walk ghost-like; her I shriek to with my might;
Ghost-like she walketh ever more and more;
            Her face how white!
How small between us seems the Infinite!

E

I call her, but she ever tacks and veers
   Like some wan sail that sails in the salt seas
Unheeding all the shore's strained eyes and ears;
        Must this not cease?
Ah! hear my cry, dear soul, and give me peace.

I call her; never may she heed or note:
   Is this the end? Just Judge, this place is cursed!
Each breath I draw within my beating throat
        Doth make and burst
Bubbles of blood. Death, death! Death last and first.
          R. W. Dixon (1833-1900).

120. THE WRECK

ONE morning I can remember well, how we watched from the
Hartland Cliffs a great barque, which came drifting and rolling
in before the western gale, while we followed her up the coast,
parsons and sportsmen, farmers and Preventive men, with the
Manby's mortar lumbering behind us in a cart, through stone
gaps and track-ways, from headland to headland.—The maddening excitement of expectation as she ran wildly towards the
cliffs at our feet, and then sheered off again inexplicably;—her
foremast and bowsprit, I recollect, were gone short off by the
deck; a few rags of sail fluttered from her main and mizzen.
But with all straining of eyes and glasses, we could discern no
sign of man on board. Well I recollect the mingled disappointment and admiration of the Preventive men, as a fresh set of
salvors appeared in view, in the form of a boat's crew of Clovelly
fishermen; how we watched breathlessly the little black speck
crawling and struggling up in the teeth of the gale, under the
shelter of the land, till, when the ship had rounded a point
into smoother water, she seized on her like some tiny spider
on a huge unwieldy fly; and then how one still smaller black
speck showed aloft on the mainyard, and another—and then
the desperate efforts to get the topsail set—and how we saw it
tear out of their hands again, and again, and again, and almost
fancied we could hear the thunder of its flappings above the
roar of the gale, and the mountains of surf which made the

rocks ring beneath our feet;—and how we stood silent, shuddering, expecting every moment to see whirled into the sea from
the plunging yards one of those same tiny black specks, in each
one of which was a living human soul, with sad women praying
for him at home! And then how they tried to get her head
round to the wind, and disappeared instantly in a cloud of
white spray—and let her head fall back again—and jammed
it round again—and at last let her drive helplessly up the bay,
while we kept pace with her along the cliffs; and how at last,
when she had been mastered and fairly taken in tow, and was
within two miles of the pier, and all hearts were merry with
the hopes of a prize which would make them rich, perhaps, for
years to come—one-third, I suppose, of the whole value of her
cargo—how she broke loose from them at the last moment,
and rushed frantically in upon those huge rocks below us,
leaping great banks of slate at the blow of each breaker, tearing
off masses of ironstone which lie there to this day to tell the
tale, till she drove up high and dry against the cliff, and lay,
like an enormous stranded whale, grinding and crashing herself
to pieces against the walls of her adamantine cage. And well I
recollect the sad records of the log-book which was left on
board the deserted ship; how she had been waterlogged for
weeks and weeks, buoyed up by her timber cargo, the crew
clinging in the tops, and crawling down, when they dared, for
putrid biscuit-dust and drops of water, till the water was
washed overboard and gone; and then notice after notice,
"On this day such an one died," "On this day such an one was
washed away"—the log kept up to the last, even when there
was only that to tell, by the stern business-like merchant
skipper, whoever he was; and how at last, when there was
neither food nor water, the strong man's heart seemed to have
quailed, or perhaps risen, into a prayer jotted down in the log
—"The Lord have mercy on us!"—and then a blank of several
pages, and, scribbled with a famine-shaken hand, "Remember
thy Creator in the days of thy youth";—and so the log and
the ship were left to the rats which covered the deck when our
men boarded her. And well I remember the last act of that
tragedy; for a ship has really, as sailors feel, a personality,
almost a life and soul of her own; and as long as her timbers

hold together, all is not over. You can hardly call her a corpse, though the human beings who inhabited her, and were her soul, may have fled into the far eternities; and so we felt that night as we came down along the woodland road, with the north-west wind hurling dead branches and showers of crisp oak-leaves about our heads; till suddenly, as we staggered out of the wood, we came upon such a piece of chiaroscuro as would have baffled Correggio, or Rembrandt himself. Under a wall was a long tent of sails and spars, filled with Preventive men, fishermen, Lloyd's underwriters, lying about in every variety of strange attitude and costume; while candles, stuck in bayonet-handles in the wall, poured out a wild glare over shaggy faces and glittering weapons, and piles of timber, and rusty iron cable, that glowed red-hot in the light, and then streamed up the glen towards us through the salty misty air in long fans of light, sending fiery bars over the brown transparent oak foliage and the sad beds of withered autumn flowers, and glorifying the wild flakes of foam, as they rushed across the light-stream, into troops of tiny silver angels, that vanished into the night and hid themselves among the woods from the fierce spirit of the storm. And then, just where the glare of the lights and watch-fires was most brilliant, there too the black shadows of the cliff had placed the point of intensest darkness, lightening gradually upwards right and left, between the two great jaws of the glen, into a chaos of gray mist, where the eye could discern no form of sea or cloud, but a perpetual shifting and quivering as if the whole atmosphere was writhing with agony in the clutches of the wind.

The ship was breaking up; and we sat by her like hopeless physicians by a deathbed-side, to watch the last struggle,—and "the effects of the deceased." I recollect our literally warping ourselves down to the beach, holding on by rocks and posts. There was a saddened awe-struck silence, even upon the gentleman from Lloyd's with the pen behind his ear. A sudden turn of the clouds let in a wild gleam of moonshine upon the white leaping heads of the breakers, and on the pyramid of the Black-church Rock, which stands in summer in such calm grandeur gazing down on the smiling bay, with the white sand of Braunton and the red cliffs of Portledge shining through

its two vast arches; and against a slab of rock on the right, for
years afterwards discoloured with her paint, lay the ship, rising
slowly on every surge, to drop again with a piteous crash as
the wave fell back from the cliff, and dragged the roaring
pebbles back with it under the coming wall of foam. You
have heard of ships at the last moment crying aloud like living
things in agony? I heard it then, as the stumps of her masts
rocked and reeled in her, and every plank and joint strained
and screamed with the dreadful tension.

A horrible image—a human being shrieking on the rack,
rose up before me at those strange semi-human cries, and
would not be put away—and I tried to turn, and yet my eyes
were riveted on the black mass, which seemed vainly to implore
the help of man against the stern ministers of the Omnipotent.

Still she seemed to linger in the death-struggle, and we turned
at last away; when, lo! a wave huger than all before it, rushed
up the boulders towards us.—We had just time to save ourselves.—A dull, thunderous groan, as if a mountain had
collapsed, rose above the roar of the tempest; and we all turned
with an instinctive knowledge of what had happened, just in
time to see the huge mass melt away into the boiling white,
and vanish for evermore. And then the very raving of the
wind seemed hushed with awe; the very breakers plunged
more silently towards the shore, with something of a sullen
compunction; and as we stood and strained our eyes into the
gloom, one black plank after another crawled up out of the
darkness upon the head of the coming surge, and threw itself
at our feet like the corpse of a drowning man, too spent to
struggle more.   *Charles Kingsley* (1819-1875).

121. LOVE

. . A cast of bees, a slowly moving wain,
    The scent of bean-flowers wafted up a dell,
  Blue pigeons wheeling over fields of grain,
    Or bleat of folded lamb, would please her well;
  Or cooing of the early coted dove;—
  She sauntering mused of these; I, following, mused of
        love. . .   *Jean Ingelow* (1820-1897).

122. THE PARTING

. . "O let me trouble her no more with sighs!
    Heart-healing comes by distance, and with time:
Then let me wander, and enrich mine eyes
    With the green forests of a softer clime,
Or list by night at sea the wind's low stave
And long monotonous rockings of the wave.

"Through open solitudes, unbounded meads,
    Where, wading on breast-high in yellow bloom,
Untamed of man, the shy white llama feeds—
    There would I journey and forget my doom;
Or far, O far as sunrise I would see
The level prairie stretch away from me!

"Or I would sail upon the tropic seas,
    Where fathom long and blood-red dulses grow,
Droop from the rock and waver in the breeze,
    Lashing the tide to foam; while calm below
The muddy mandrakes throng those waters warm,
 And purple, gold, and green, the living blossoms swarm. . ."
                       Jean Ingelow (1820-1897).

123. TOMMY'S DEAD

You may give over plough, boys,
You may take the gear to the stead,
All the sweat o' your brow, boys,
Will never get beer and bread.
The seed's waste, I know, boys,
There's not a blade will grow, boys,
'Tis cropped out, I trow, boys,
And Tommy's dead.

Send the colt to the fair, boys,
He's going blind, as I said,
My old eyes can't bear, boys,
To see him in the shed:

The cow's dry and spare, boys,
She's neither here nor there, boys,
I doubt she's badly bred;
Stop the mill to-morn, boys,
There'll be no more corn, boys,
Neither white nor red;
There's no sign of grass, boys,
You may sell the goat and the ass, boys,
The land's not what it was, boys,
And the beasts must be fed:
You may turn Peg away, boys,
You may pay off old Ned,
We've had a dull day, boys,
And Tommy's dead.

Move my chair on the floor, boys,
Let me turn my head:
She's standing there in the door, boys,
Your sister Winifred!
Take her away from me, boys,
Your sister Winifred!
Move me round in my place, boys,
Let me turn my head,
Take her away from me, boys,
As she lay on her death-bed,
The bones of her thin face, boys,
As she lay on her death-bed!
I don't know how it be, boys,
When all's done and said,
But I see her looking at me, boys,
Wherever I turn my head;
Out of the big oak-tree, boys,
Out of the garden-bed,
And the lily as pale as she, boys,
And the rose that used to be red.
There's something not right, boys,
But I think it's not in my head,
I've kept my precious sight, boys—
The Lord be hallowed!

Outside and in
The ground is cold to my tread,
The hills are wizen and thin,
The sky is shrivelled and shred,
The hedges down by the loan
I can count them bone by bone,
The leaves are open and spread,
But I see the teeth of the land,
And hands like a dead man's hand,
And the eyes of a dead man's head.
There's nothing but cinders and sand,
The rat and the mouse have fed,
And the summer's empty and cold;
Over valley and wold
Wherever I turn my head
There's a mildew and a mould,
The sun's going out over head,
And I'm very old,
And Tommy's dead.

What am I staying for, boys,
You're all born and bred,
'Tis fifty years and more, boys,
Since wife and I were wed,
And she's gone before, boys,
And Tommy's dead.

She was always sweet, boys,
Upon his curly head,
She knew she'd never see 't, boys,
And she stole off to bed;
I've been sitting up alone, boys,
For he'd come home, he said,
But it's time I was gone, boys,
For Tommy's dead.

Put the shutters up, boys,
Bring out the beer and bread,

Make haste and sup, boys,
For my eyes are heavy as lead;
There's something wrong i' the cup, boys,
There's something ill wi' the bread,
I don't care to sup, boys,
And Tommy's dead.

I'm not right, I doubt, boys,
I've such a sleepy head,
I shall never more be stout, boys,
You may carry me to bed.
What are you about, boys,
The prayers are all said,
The fire's raked out, boys,
And Tommy's dead.

The stairs are too steep, boys,
You may carry me to the head,
The night's dark and deep, boys,
Your mother's long in bed,
'Tis time to go to sleep, boys,
And Tommy's dead.

I'm not used to kiss, boys,
You may shake my hand instead.
All things go amiss, boys,
You may lay me where she is, boys,
And I'll rest my old head:
'Tis a poor world, this, boys,
And Tommy's dead.
                              Sydney Dobell (1824-1874).

124. LOVE IN DEATH

. . Yes; love requires the focal space
    Of recollection or of hope,
    Ere it can measure its own scope.
    Too soon, too soon comes Death to show
    We love more deeply, than we know!

E*

The rain, that fell upon the height
Too gently to be call'd delight,
Within the dark vale reappears
As a wild cataract of tears;
And love in life should strive to see
Sometimes what love in death would be!
Easier to love, we so should find,
It is than to be just and kind. . .

Coventry Patmore (1823-1896).

125. THE ARTIST ON PENMAENMAWR

THAT first September day was blue and warm,
Flushing the shaly flanks of Penmaenmawr;
While youths and maidens, in the lucid calm
Exulting, bathed or bask'd from hour to hour;
What colour-passion did the artist feel!
While evermore the jarring trains went by,
Now, as for evermore, in fancy's eye,
Smutch'd with the cruel fires of Abergele;
Then fell the dark o'er the great crags and downs,
And all the night-struck mountain seem'd to say,
"Farewell! these happy skies, this peerless day!
And these fair seas—and fairer still than they,
The white-arm'd girls in dark blue bathing-gowns,
Among the snowy gulls and summer spray."

Charles Tennyson Turner (1808-1879).

126. THE OLD CHARTIST

I

WHATE'ER I be, old England is my dam!
So there's my answer to the judges, clear
I'm nothing of a fox, nor of a lamb;
I don't know how to bleat nor how to leer:

I'm for the nation!
That's why you see me by the wayside here,
Returning home from transportation.

II

It's Summer in her bath this morn, I think.
I'm fresh as dew, and chirpy as the birds:
And just for joy to see old England wink
    Thro' leaves again, I could harangue the herds:
        Isn't it something
    To speak out like a man when you've got words,
      And prove you're not a stupid dumb thing?

III

They shipp'd me off for it; I'm here again.
Old England is my dam, whate'er I be!
Says I, I'll tramp it home, and see the grain:
    If you see well, you're king of what you see:
        Eyesight is having,
    If you're not given, I said, to gluttony.
      Such talk to ignorance sounds as raving.

IV

You dear old brook, that from his Grace's park
    Come bounding! on you run near my old town:
My lord can't lock the water; nor the lark,
    Unless he kills him, can my lord keep down.
        Up, is the song-note!
I've tried it, too:—for comfort and renown,
    I rather pitch'd upon the wrong note.

V

I'm not ashamed: Not beaten's still my boast:
    Again I'll rouse the people up to strike.
But home's where different politics jar most.
    Respectability the women like.

This form, or that form,—
The Government may be a hungry pike,
But don't you mount a Chartist platform!

VI

Well, well! Not beaten—spite of them, I shout;
And my estate is suffering for the Cause.—
Now, what is yon brown water-rat about,
Who washes his old poll with busy paws?
What does he mean by 't?
It's like defying all our natural laws,
For him to hope that he'll get clean by 't.

VII

His seat is on a mud-bank, and his trade
Is dirt:—he's quite contemptible; and yet
The fellow's all as anxious as a maid
To show a decent dress, and dry the wet.
Now it's his whisker,
And now his nose, and ear: he seems to get
Each moment at the motion brisker!

VIII

To see him squat like little chaps at school,
I could let fly a laugh with all my might.
He peers, hangs both his fore-paws:—bless that fool,
He's bobbing at his frill now!—what a sight!
Licking the dish up,
As if he thought to pass from black to white,
Like parson into lawny bishop.

IX

The elms and yellow reed-flags in the sun
Look on quite grave:—the sunlight flecks his side;
And links of bindweed-flowers round him run,
And shine up doubled with him in the tide.

I'm nearly splitting,
But nature seems like seconding his pride
And thinks that his behaviour's fitting.

X

That isle o' mud looks baking dry with gold,
His needle-muzzle still works out and in.
It really is a wonder to behold,
And makes me feel the bristles of my chin;
Judged by appearance,
I fancy of the two I'm nearer Sin,
And might as well commence a clearance.

XI

And that's what my fine daughter said:—she meant:
Pray, hold your tongue, and wear a Sunday face.
Her husband, the young linendraper, spent
Much argument thereon:—I'm their disgrace.
Bother the couple!
I feel superior to a chap whose place
Commands him to be neat and supple.

XII

But if I go and say to my old hen:
I'll mend the gentry's boots, and keep discreet,
Until they grow *too* violent,—why, then,
A warmer welcome I might chance to meet:
Warmer and better.
And if she fancies her old cock is beat,
And drops upon her knees—so let her!

XIII

She suffered for me:—woman, you'll observe,
Don't suffer for a Cause, but for a man.
When I was in the dock she show'd her nerve:
I saw beneath her shawl my old tea-can

Trembling . . . she brought it
To screw me for my work: she'd loath'd my plan,
And therefore doubly kind I thought it.

XIV

I've never lost the taste for that same tea:
That liquor on my logic floats like oil,
When I state facts, and fellows disagree.
For human creatures all are in a coil:
All may want pardon.
I see a day when every pot will boil
Harmonious in one great Tea-garden!

XV

We wait before the setting of the Dandy's day,
Before that time!—He's furbishing his dress,—
He *will* be ready for it!—and I say,
That yon old dandy rat amid the cress,—
Thanks to hard labour!—
If cleanliness is next to godliness,
The old fat fellow's heaven's neighbour!

XVI

You teach me a fine lesson, my old boy!
I've looked on my superiors far too long,
And small has been my profit as my joy.
You've done the right while I've denounced the wrong.
Prosper me later!
Like you I will despise the sniggering throng,
And please myself and my Creator.

XVII

I'll bring the linendraper and his wife
Some day to see you; taking off my hat.
Should they ask why, I'll answer: in my life
I never found so true a democrat.

Base occupation
Can't rob you of your own esteem, old rat!
I'll preach you to the British nation.
                        George Meredith (1828-1909).

127. WHITE AND BLUE

. . Or where below the clear blue sky
    The snow-white linen hung to dry. . .
                    William Barnes (1800-1886).

128. BRAZILIAN BUTTERFLIES

As the waters retreated from the beach, vast numbers of
sulphur-yellow and orange-coloured butterflies congregated on
the moist sand. The greater portion of them belonged to the
genus Callidryas. They assembled in densely packed masses,
sometimes two or three yards in circumference, their wings all
held in an upright position, so that the beach looked as though
variegated with beds of crocuses.
                    H. W. Bates, F.R.S. (1825-1892).

129. *From* "LAURENCE BLOOMFIELD IN IRELAND"

i. *A Landscape*

AMONG those mountain-skirts a league away
Lough Braccan spread, with many a silver bay
And islet green; a dark cliff, tall and bold,
Half-muffled in its cloak of ivy old,
Bastion'd the southern brink, beside a glen
Where birch and hazel hid the badger's den,
And through the moist ferns and firm hollies play'd
A rapid rivulet from light to shade.
Above the glen, and wood, and cliff, was seen,
Majestically simple and serene,

Like some great soul above the various crowd,
A purple mountain-top, at times in cloud
Or mist, as in celestial veils of thought,
Abstracted heavenward.

                    Creeps a little boat,
Along the path of evening's golden smile,
To where the shatter'd castle on its isle
May seem a broad-wing'd ship; two massive tow'rs
Lifted against the yellow light that pours
On half the lough and sloping fields,—half-laid,
Creek, bush, and crag, within the mountain shade.
Dark bramble-leaves now show a curling fringe,
And sallies wear the first autumnal tinge;
With speckled plumes high wave the crowded reeds,
Amongst whose watery stems the mallard feeds.
Full many a time, on deep Lough Braccan's wave,
Has Neal inveigled from its liquid cave,
With youthful comrades, in a fragile keel,
The pike, the perch, the trout, the twisting eel;
Alone, and musingly, he glides to-day,
Has fish'd an hour in vain, and coil'd his line away.

   The coble beach'd at lonely Innisree,
High at a rifted window, musing free
On ancient sky and water, freshly fair,
A poet's or a painter's rich despair,
And on the fame of olden times, which threw
Across the firm world a transcendent hue,
No more with petty toils and cares dismay'd,
The young man watch'd that glowing landscape fade.

   South-westward, where th' autumnal sun went down,
A lake-reflected headland heaved its crown
Of darkling trees, and, knew you where to search,
The hoary ruins of a little church,
That mingled there with human skulls and bones
The mossy downfall of its sculptured stones;
While, like one poem scatheless and sublime
Amid the vast forgetfulness of Time,

Slender and tall a Round Tower's pointed crest
Rose dimly black against the gorgeous west. . . .

ii. *The Eviction*

.. In early morning twilight, raw and chill,
Damp vapours brooding on the barren hill,
Through miles of mire in steady grave array
Three-score well-arm'd police pursue their way;
Each tall and bearded man a rifle swings,
And under each greatcoat a bayonet clings;
The Sheriff on his sturdy cob astride
Talks with the Chief, who marches by their side,
And, creeping on behind them, Paudeen Dhu
Pretends his needful duty much to rue.
Six big-boned labourers, clad in common frieze,
Walk in the midst, the Sheriff's staunch allies;
Six crowbar-men, from distant county brought,—
Orange, and glorying in their work, 'tis thought,
But wrongly,—churls of Catholics are they,
And merely hired at half-a-crown a day.

The Hamlet clustering on its hill is seen,
A score of petty homesteads, dark and mean;
Poor always, not despairing until now;
Long used, as well as poverty knows how,
With life's oppressive trifles to contend,
This day will bring its history to an end.
Moveless and grim against the cottage walls
Lean a few silent men: but some one calls
Far off; and then a child without a stitch
Runs out of doors, flies back with piercing screech,
And soon from house to house is heard the cry
Of female sorrow, swelling loud and high,
Which makes the men blaspheme between their teeth.
Meanwhile, o'er fence and watery field beneath,
The little army moves through drizzling rain;
A "Crowbar" leads the Sheriff's nag; the lane

Is enter'd, and their plashing tramp draws near;
One instant, outcry holds its breath to hear;
"Halt!"—at the doors they form in double line,
And ranks of polish'd rifles wetly shine.

The Sheriff's painful duty must be done;
He begs for quiet—and the work's begun.
The strong stand ready; now appear the rest,
Girl, matron, grandsire, baby on the breast,
And Rosy's thin face on a pallet borne;
A motley concourse, feeble and forlorn.
One old man, tears upon his wrinkled cheek,
Stands trembling on a threshold, tries to speak,
But in defect of any word for this,
Mutely upon the doorpost prints a kiss,
Then passes out for ever. Through the crowd
The children run bewilder'd, wailing loud;
Where needed most, the men combine their aid;
And, last of all, is Oona forth convey'd,
Reclined in her accustom'd strawen chair,
Her aged eyelids closed, her thick white hair
Escaping from her cap; she feels the chill,
Looks round and murmurs, then again is still.

Now bring the remnants of each household fire;
On the wet ground the hissing coals expire;
And Paudeen Dhu, with meekly dismal face,
Receives the full possession of the place.

Whereon the Sheriff, "We have legal hold.
Return to shelter with the sick and old.
Time shall be given; and there are carts below
If any to the workhouse choose to go."
A young man makes him answer, grave and clear,
"We're thankful to you! but there's no one here
Going back into them houses: do your part.
Nor we won't trouble Pigot's horse and cart."
At which name, rushing into th' open space,
A woman flings her hood from off her face,

Falls on her knees upon the miry ground,
Lifts hands and eyes, and voice of thrilling sound,—
"Vengeance of God Almighty fall on you,
James Pigot!—may the poor man's curse pursue,
The widow's and the orphan's curse, I pray,
Hang heavy round you at your dying day!"
Breathless and fix'd one moment stands the crowd
To hear this malediction fierce and loud.

  Meanwhile (our neighbour Neal is busy there)
On steady poles be lifted Oona's chair,
Well-heap'd with borrow'd mantles; gently bear
The sick girl in her litter, bed and all; .
Whilst others hug the children weak and small
In careful arms, or hoist them pick-a-back;
And, 'midst the unrelenting clink and thwack
Of iron bar on stone, let creep away
The sad procession from that hill-side gray,
Through the slow-falling rain.   In three hours more
You find, where Ballytullagh stood before,
Mere shatter'd walls, and doors with useless latch,
And firesides buried under fallen thatch. . .

iii. *The Murder of James Pigot the Agent*

To Newbridge House the pretty bye-way goes,
'Tween scarlet-berried hawthorn and wild rose,
Rowan and woodbine; the dark-fruited briar
Bends to its bordering grass, through which aspire
The yellow hawk-weed and blue scabious-ball;
Grass full of grasshoppers, and flies, and small
Innumerable things.   You sometimes hear
A distant voice, or warbling near and clear
Poor-Robin's plaintive melody, at one
With the mild glory of the sinking sun,
Which now, completing this autumnal day,
Looks from the great world's end with parting ray,
O'er all the golden landscape with its sheaves,
And through the curtain of the wayside leaves.

Across the road a new-cut holly lay.
Doyle must alight to drag it from their way.
Through Pigot's heart and brain a sudden gush
Whirl'd all his life to fever: mad thoughts rush
Around their burning prison: "I am caught!"—
And hasty fingers his revolver sought.
One terrible moment—courage all drawn dry
To earthquake-ebb—and ere the wave pour high
Returning, from the hedge beside him broke
Two sharp explosions, two white puffs of smoke;
The mare leap'd round, and gallop'd off pell-mell,
But heavily to earth her master fell.

No longer Mrs. Pigot bears to wait;
She sends a horseman by the lower gate;
Who rides not far. A man came running fast;
'Twas bailiff Doyle, pale, breathless, all aghast;
"He's shot! they've killed him!"—and the servants found,
Three furlongs distant, prostrate on the ground
Amidst a pool of blood, James Pigot's form,
A dreadful burden, lifeless, though still warm.

James Pigot's race is run: and shall we call
This man a victim, or a criminal?
Or one who with men's natures coarsely dealt,
Drew out their evil, and its fury felt?
He did so; but not his alone the blame.
Elsewhere he might in peace have lived the same,
And breathed away at last a quiet breath,
No worse than most men in his life and death.
But where the subtle powers of Circumstance,
Multiplex operations that advance
Out of the boundless Bygone World, and make
The Present with the flitting forms they take,
Are in an evil seethe like wizard's pot,
Who stirs the same, 'tis now and then his lot
To catch the spurted venom. Where one dies,
Hundreds escape; and danger ever tries
To wear a mask of innocence; no less,
They cook and finger a strong poison-mess.

Fair-evening as it was, no friendly hand
Lifted the dead; the people chose to stand
Far-off, or take the fields, or else turn back,
But not to follow on the murderers' track;
Not one made haste to give policemen word;
By special message first the news was heard.

For many weeks from every wall and gate
Stared "MURDER" and "REWARD" in letters great,
Two Hundred Pounds the Lord Lieutenant's bribe,
One Thousand which the gentry round subscribe,
But all in vain; for, his employer dead,
The Spy took mortal fear to heart, and fled.
Few even dared to read the bills, and they
Walk'd off in silence; if they said their say,
'Twas said with caution and in secrecy.
A huge converging crowd of low and high
Had swell'd the costly funeral, and flow'd
In solemn pomp, outstretch'd along the road.
The native press was vocal, and the *Times*
Anew said something old on Irish crimes.

And meanwhile, bringing softly night and day,
The round Earth roll'd on her appointed way,
With dead and living, 'mid the starry quire,
Brimm'd with material and celestial fire,
And to and fro, with emmets' briskness, ran
The shifting, multifarious brood of Man.

William Allingham (1824-1889).

130. MILL, LIBERTY, AND SHELLEY

[*John Stuart Mill is with Lord and Lady Amberley, the
parents of Bertrand Russell, who was Mill's godchild.*]

Wednesday, *September* 28, 1870. . . . After dinner Mr. Mill
read us Shelley's Ode to Liberty & he got quite excited &
moved over it rocking backwards & forwards & nearly choking
with emotion; he said himself: "it is almost too much for me."

From *The Amberley Papers.*

131. HEAVEN-HAVEN

A NUN TAKES THE VEIL

I HAVE desired to go
   Where springs not fail,
To fields where flies no sharp and sided hail
   And a few lilies blow.

And I have asked to be
   Where no storms come,
Where the green swell is in the havens dumb,
   And out of the swing of the sea.
         Gerard Manley Hopkins (1844-1889).

132. MERCY

EARTH, sad earth, thou roamest
   Through the day and night;
Weary with the darkness,
   Weary with the light.

Clouds of hanging judgment,
   And the cloud that weeps for me,
Swell above the mountain,
   Strive above the sea.

But, sad earth, thou knowest
   All my love for thee;
Therefore thou dost welcome
   The cloud that weeps for me.
         R. W. Dixon (1833-1900).

133. LEAVING BRAZIL

DURING this last night on the Pará river a crowd of unusual thoughts occupied my mind. Recollections of English climate, scenery, and modes of life came to me with a vividness I had never before experienced during the eleven years of my absence. Pictures of startling clearness rose up of the gloomy winters, the long grey twilights, murky atmosphere, elongated shadows, chilly springs, and sloppy summers; of factory chimneys and crowds of grimy operatives, rung to work in early mornings by factory bells; of union workhouses, confined rooms, artificial cares, and slavish conventionalities. To live again amidst these dull scenes I was quitting a country of perpetual summer, where my life had been spent like that of three-fourths of the people in gipsy fashion, on the endless streams or in the boundless forests. I was leaving the equator, where the well-balanced forces of nature maintained a land-surface and climate that seemed to be typical of mundane order and beauty, to sail towards the North Pole, where lay my home under crepuscular skies somewhere about fifty-two degrees of latitude. It was natural to feel a little dismayed at the prospect of so great a change; but now, after three years of renewed experience of England, I find how incomparably superior is civilised life, where feelings, tastes, and intellect find abundant nourishment, to the spiritual sterility of half-savage existence, even if it were passed in the garden of Eden. What has struck me powerfully is the immeasurably greater diversity and interest of human character and social conditions in a single civilised nation, than in equatorial South America, where three distinct races of man live together. The superiority of the bleak north to tropical regions, however, is only in its social aspect; for I hold to the opinion that, although humanity can reach an advanced state of culture only by battling with the inclemencies of nature in high latitudes, it is under the equator alone that the perfect race of the future will attain to complete fruition of man's beautiful heritage, the earth.

H. W. Bates, F.R.S. (1825-1892).

134. DUTY AND GEORGE ELIOT

I REMEMBER how, at Cambridge, I walked with her once in the Fellows' Garden of Trinity, on an evening of rainy May; and she, stirred somewhat beyond her wont, and taking as her text the three words which have been used so often as the inspiring trumpet-calls of men,—the words God, Immortality, Duty,—pronounced, with terrible earnestness, how inconceivable was the first, how unbelievable the second, and yet how peremptory and absolute the third. Never, perhaps, have sterner accents affirmed the sovereignty of impersonal and unrecompensing Law. I listened, and night fell; her grave, majestic countenance turned toward me like a Sibyl's in the gloom; it was as though she withdrew from my grasp, one by one, the two scrolls of promise, and left me the third scroll only, awful with inevitable fates. And when we stood at length and parted, amid that columnar circuit of the forest-trees, beneath the last twilight of starless skies, I seemed to be gazing, like Titus at Jerusalem, on vacant seats and empty halls,—on a sanctuary with no Presence to hallow it, and heaven left lonely of a God.   *F. W. H. Myers* (1843-1901).

135. ON THE CLIFF

I

I LEANED on the turf,
I looked at a rock
Left dry by the surf;
For the turf, to call it grass were to mock:
Dead to the roots, so deep was done
The work of the summer sun.

II

And the rock lay flat
As an anvil's face:
No iron like that!
Baked dry; of a weed, of a shell, no trace:
Sunshine outside, but ice at the core,
Death's altar by the lone shore.

III

On the turf, sprang gay
With his films of blue,
No cricket, I'll say,
But a warhorse, barded and chamfroned too,
The gift of a quixote-mage to his knight,
Real fairy, with wings all right.

IV

On the rock, they scorch
Like a drop of fire
From a brandished torch,
Fall two red fans of a butterfly:
No turf, no rock: in their ugly stead,
See, wonderful, blue and red!

V

Is it not so
With the minds of men?
The level and low,
The burnt and bare, in themselves; but then
With such a blue and red grace, not theirs,—
Love settling unawares!

Robert Browning (1812-1889).

136. ON THE ECLIPSE OF THE MOON OF OCTOBER 1865

ONE little noise of life remain'd—I heard
The train pause in the distance, then rush by,
Brawling and hushing, like some busy fly
That murmurs and then settles; nothing stirr'd
Beside. The shadow of our travelling earth
Hung on the silver moon, which mutely went
Through that grand process, without token sent,
Or any sign to call a gazer forth,

Had I not chanced to see; dumb was the vault
Of heaven, and dumb the fields—no zephyr swept
The forest walks, or through the coppice crept;
Nor other sound the stillness did assault,
Save that faint-brawling railway's move and halt;
So perfect was the silence Nature kept.

> *Charles Tennyson Turner* (1808-1879).

137. THE LAST WORD

CREEP into thy narrow bed,
Creep, and let no more be said!
Vain thy onset! all stands fast;
Thou thyself must break at last.

Let the long contention cease!
Geese are swans, and swans are geese.
Let them have it how they will!
Thou are tired; best be still!

They out-talk'd thee, hiss'd thee, tore thee.
Better men fared thus before thee;
Fired their ringing shot and pass'd,
Hotly charged—and broke at last.

Charge once more, then, and be dumb!
Let the victors, when they come,
When the forts of folly fall,
Find thy body by the wall.

> *Matthew Arnold* (1822-1888).

138. THE GIRLS AND THE SWANS

. . Where greyheaded withies do leän by the feäce
O' greylighted waters, a-slacknèn their peäce,
An' only the maïdens an' swans be in white,
Like snow on grey moss in the mid-winter's light. . .

> *William Barnes* (1800-1886).

139. THE STEAM THRESHING-MACHINE

With the Straw Carrier

FLUSH with the pond the lurid furnace burn'd
At eve, while smoke and vapour fill'd the yard;
The gloomy winter sky was dimly starr'd,
The fly-wheel with a mellow murmur turn'd;
While, ever rising on its mystic stair
In the dim light, from secret chambers borne,
The straw of harvest, sever'd from the corn,
Climb'd, and fell over, in the murky air.
I thought of mind and matter, will and law,
And then of him, who set his stately seal
Of Roman words on all the forms he saw
Of old-world husbandry: *I* could but feel
With what a rich precision *he* would draw
The endless ladder, and the booming wheel!

Charles Tennyson Turner (1808-1879).

140. PRIVATE FORTUNES

MY English friends confirm what I had guessed about the large number and the vastness of the private fortunes. "Take a cab from Sydenham; for five miles you will pass houses which indicate an annual outlay of £1,500 and upwards." According to the official statistics of 1841, there are one million of servants to sixteen millions of inhabitants. The liberal professions are much better remunerated than on the Continent. I know a musician at Leipzig of first-class talent; he receives 3s. a lesson at the Academy of Leipzig, 6s. in the city, and one guinea in London. The visit of a doctor who is not celebrated costs 4s. or 9s. in Paris, and a guinea here. With us a professor at the College of France receives £300, at the Sorbonne £480, at the School of Medicine £400. A professor at Oxford, a head of a house, has often from £1,000 to £3,000. Tennyson, who writes little, is said to make £5,000 a year. The Head Master

of Eton has a salary of £6,080, of Harrow £6,280, of Rugby
£2,960; many of the masters in these establishments have
salaries from £1,200 to £1,240—one of them at Harrow has
£2,220. The Bishop of London has £10,000 a year, the Arch-
bishop of York has £15,000. An article is paid for at the rate
of £8 the sheet in the *Revue des Deux Mondes*, and £20 in the
English Quarterlies. The *Times* has paid £100 for a certain
article. Thackeray, the novelist, has made £160 in twenty-four
hours through the medium of two lectures, the one being
delivered in Brighton, the other in London; from the magazine
to which he contributed his novels he received £2,000 a year,
and £10 a page in addition; this magazine had 100,000 sub-
scribers; he estimated his own yearly earnings at £4,800.

Hippolyte Taine (1828-1893).

141. THE EVENING COMES

THE evening comes, the field is still.
The tinkle of the thirsty rill,
Unheard all day, ascends again;
Deserted is the new-reap'd grain,
Silent the sheaves! the ringing wain,
The reaper's cry, the dogs' alarms,
All housed within the sleeping farms!
The business of the day is done,
The last belated gleaner gone.
And from the thyme upon the height,
And from the elder-blossom white
And pale dog-roses in the hedge,
And from the mint-plant in the sedge,
In puffs of balm the night-air blows
The perfume which the day forgoes.
And on the pure horizon far,
See, pulsing with the first-born star,
The liquid sky above the hill!
The evening comes, the field is still. . .

Matthew Arnold (1822-1888).

142. ARISE, O WINDS!

Arise, O winds, and drive away
   The curling fog by mound and nook,
For we to-day would see you play
   Along the lightly-sparkling brook.
         By brook and brake,
         O winds, awake.

Arise! but do not mar our way
   With clouds of dust to blind our eyes,
For we would look this holiday
   On all the charms of land and skies.
         By hill and lake,
         O winds, awake.

O winds, blow on! but do not fly
   With dark'ning clouds of sudden show'rs,
For we would pass the fields all dry
   Among the heads of summer flow'rs.
         Sweep hill and plain,
         But not with rain.

And come to-night to clear away
   The clouds that o'er the moon may pass,
For we may wish to see you play
   By moonshades on the beech-side grass.
         So make, we pray,
         A happy day.
               William Barnes (1800-1886).

143. A NIGHT SONG, No. 1

Oh! do you wake, or do you sleep
   With window to the full-moon'd sky?
Oh! have you lost, or do you keep
   A thought of all the day gone by?
Or are you dead to all you knew
Of life, the while I live to you?

May air, o'er wallside roses brought,
   Of charming gardens give you dreams;
May rustling leaves beguile your thought
   With dreams of walks by falling streams.
And on your lids be light that yields
Bright dream-clouds over daisied fields.

Our meeting hour of yesterday
   To me, now deep in waning night,
Seems all a glory pass'd away
   Beyond a year-time's longsome flight
Though night seems far too short to weigh
Your words and deeds of yesterday. . .

                William Barnes (1800-1886).

144. A NIGHT SONG, No. 2

Be it midnight, be it dawning,
   Do the clouds hold up, or weep;
Be it moonlight, be it sunshine,
   Is no care to folk asleep.
So I linger not to tell you
   How the midnight moon may soar;
But if one thing be your business,
   'Tis that love is at the door.

Whether leafy is the chestnut,
   Or its chilly twigs be bare;
Whether dewy, whether frosty
   Be the grass, is not your care.
So forget until the morning,
   Land below, and sky above;
But it should be worth your knowing,
   That before your gate is love. . .

                William Barnes (1800-1886).

145. BATS IN BED

THE first few nights I was much troubled by bats. The room where I slept had not been used for many months, and the roof was open to the tiles and rafters. The first night I slept soundly, and did not perceive anything unusual; but on the next I was aroused about midnight by the rushing noise made by vast hosts of bats sweeping about the room. The air was alive with them; they had put out the lamp, and when I relighted it the place appeared blackened with the impish multitudes which were whirling round and round. After I had laid about well with a stick for a few minutes they disappeared amongst the tiles, but when all was still again they returned, and once more extinguished the light. I took no further notice of them, and went to sleep. The next night several got into my hammock; I seized them as they were crawling over me, and dashed them against the wall. The next morning I found a wound, evidently caused by a bat, on my hip. This was rather unpleasant, so I set to work with the negroes and tried to exterminate them. I shot a great many as they hung from the rafters, and the negroes having mounted with ladders to the roof outside, routed out from beneath the eaves many hundreds of them, including young broods.

H. W. Bates, F.R.S. (1825-1892).

146. NATURAL HISTORY LIMERICKS

i

THERE was an old person in black,
A Grasshopper jumped on his back;
When it chirped in his ear, he was smitten with fear,
That helpless old person in black.

ii

THERE was an old person of Rye,
Who went up to town on a fly;
But they said, "If you cough, you are safe to fall off!
You abstemious old person of Rye!"

iii

THERE was an old person of Jodd,
Whose ways were perplexing and odd;
She purchased a whistle, and sate on a thistle,
And squeaked to the people of Jodd.

iv

THERE was an old person of Skye,
Who danced with a Bluebottle fly:
They buzz'd a sweet tune, to the light of the moon,
And entranced all the people of Skye.

v

THERE was an old person of Crowle,
Who lived in the nest of an owl;
When they screamed in the nest, he screamed out
    with the rest,
That depressing old person of Crowle.

vi

THERE was an old person of Bromley,
Whose ways were not cheerful or comely;
He sate in the dust, eating spiders and crust,
That unpleasing old person of Bromley.

Edward Lear (1812-1888).

147. NATURE

As the word is now commonly used it excludes nature's most
interesting productions—the works of man. Nature is usually
taken to mean mountains, rivers, clouds and undomesticated
animals and plants. I am not indifferent to this half of nature,
but it interests me much less than the other half.

Samuel Butler (1835-1902).

148. BRINGING THESE THINGS IN

Tuesday, December 24, 1867. Irish landscape—"I saw wonderful things there—twenty different showers at once on a great expanse—a vast yellow cloud with a little bit of rainbow stuck on one corner" (Tennyson swept his arm round for the cloud and then gave a nick in the air with his thumb for the bit of rainbow)—"I wish I could bring these things in!"

Recorded by *William Allingham* (1824-1889).

149. POETRY

THE future of poetry is immense, because in poetry, where it is worthy of its high destinies, our race, as time goes on, will find an ever surer and surer stay. There is not a creed which is not shaken, not an accredited dogma which is not shown to be questionable, not a received tradition which does not threaten to dissolve. Our religion has materialised itself in the fact, in the supposed fact; it has attached its emotion to the fact, and now the fact is failing it. But for poetry the idea is everything.

Matthew Arnold (1822-1888).

150. LILAC AND PEACOCKS

Friday, May 18, 1866. Farringford. Walked with Tennyson among the trees and lawns. Tennyson said, "White lilac used to be my favourite flower."

Allingham: "It is something like a white peacock."

Then I told him what Browning said to me about a passage in the "Princess"—"Tennyson's taken to white peacocks! I always intended to use them. The Pope has a number of white peacocks."

Recorded by *William Allingham* (1824-1889).

F

151. ENOCH ARDEN'S ISLAND

. . The mountain wooded to the peak, the lawns
And winding glades high up like ways to Heaven,
The slender coco's drooping crown of plumes,
The lightning flash of insect and of bird,
The lustre of the long convolvuluses
That coil'd around the stately stems, and ran
Ev'n to the limit of the land, the glows
And glories of the broad belt of the world,
All these he saw; but what he fain had seen
He could not see, the kindly human face,
Nor ever hear a kindly voice, but heard
The myriad shriek of wheeling ocean-fowl,
The league-long roller thundering on the reef,
The moving whisper of huge trees that branch'd
And blossom'd in the zenith, or the sweep
Of some precipitous rivulet to the wave,
As down the shore he ranged, or all day long
Sat often in the seaward-gazing gorge,
A shipwreck'd sailor, waiting for a sail:
No sail from day to day, but every day
The sunrise broken into scarlet shafts
Among the palms and ferns and precipices;
The blaze upon the waters to the east;
The blaze upon his island overhead;
The blaze upon the waters to the west;
Then the great stars that globed themselves in Heaven,
The hollower-bellowing ocean, and again
The scarlet shafts of sunrise—but no sail. . .

Alfred Tennyson (1809-1892).

152. THE ROUGE OF ORNATE LITERATURE

(*Bagehot reviews " Enoch Arden"*)

i

A BRIDGE completes a river landscape; if of the old and many-
arched sort, it regulates by a long series of defined forms the
vague outline of wood and river, which before had nothing to

measure it; if of the new scientific sort, it introduces still more strictly a geometrical element; it stiffens the scenery which was before too soft, too delicate, too vegetable. Just such is the effect of pure style in literary art. It calms by conciseness; while the ornate style leaves on the mind a mist of beauty, an excess of fascination, a complication of charm, the pure style leaves behind it the simple, defined, measured idea, as it is, and by itself. That which is chaste chastens; there is a poised energy—a state half thrill, half tranquillity—which pure art gives, which no other can give; a pleasure justified as well as felt; an ennobled satisfaction at what ought to satisfy us, and must ennoble us.

Ornate art is to pure art what a painted statue is to an unpainted. It is impossible to deny that a touch of colour does bring out certain parts; does convey certain expressions; does heighten certain features, but it leaves on the work as a whole, a want, as we say, "of something"; a want of that inseparable chasteness which clings to simple sculpture, an impairing predominance of alluring details which impairs our satisfaction with our own satisfaction; which makes us doubt whether a higher being than ourselves will be satisfied even though we are. In the very same manner, though the rouge of ornate literature excites our eye, it also impairs our confidence. . .

ii

Whatever may be made of Enoch's "Ocean spoil in ocean-smelling osier," of the "portal-warding lion-whelp, and the peacock yew-tree," every one knows that in himself Enoch could not have been charming. People who sell fish about the country (and that is what he did, though Mr. Tennyson won't speak out, and wraps it up) never are beautiful. As Enoch was and must be coarse, in itself the poem must depend for a charm on a "gay confusion"—on a splendid accumulation of impossible accessories. . . . He has endeavoured to describe an exceptional sailor, at an exceptionally refined port, performing a graceful act, an act of relinquishment. And with this task before him, his profound taste taught him that ornate art was a necessary medium—was the sole effectual instrument—for his purpose. It was necessary for him if possible to abstract the mind from reality, to induce us *not* to conceive or think of sailors as they are while we are reading of his sailors, but to think of what a person who did not know, might fancy sailors to be. . .

iii

Nothing, too, can be more splendid than the description of the tropics as Mr. Tennyson delineates them, but a sailor would not have felt the tropics in that manner. The beauties of Nature would not have so much occupied him. He would have known little of the scarlet shafts of sunrise and nothing of the long convolvuluses. As in Robinson Crusoe, his own petty contrivances and his small ailments would have been the principal subject to him. "For three years," he might have said, "my back was bad; and then I put two pegs into a piece of driftwood and so made a chair; and after that it pleased God to send me a chill." In real life his piety would scarcely have gone beyond that. . . . Rude people are impressed by what is beautiful—deeply impressed—though they could not describe what they see or what they feel. But what is absurd in Mr. Tennyson's description—absurd when we abstract it from the gorgeous additions and ornaments with which Mr. Tennyson distracts us—is, that his hero feels nothing else but these great splendours.

iv

It is singularly characteristic of this age that the poems which rise to the surface should be examples of ornate art, and grotesque art, not of pure art. We live in the realm of the *half* educated. The number of readers grows daily, but the quality of readers does not improve rapidly. The middle class is scattered, heedless; it is well-meaning, but aimless; wishing to be wise, but ignorant how to be wise. The aristocracy of England never was a literary aristocracy, never even in the days of its full power, of its unquestioned predominance, did it guide—did it even seriously try to guide—the taste of England. Without guidance young men, and tired men, are thrown amongst a mass of books; they have to choose which they like; many of them would much like to improve their culture, to chasten their taste, if they knew how. But left to themselves, they take not pure art, but showy art. . . . A dressy literature, an exaggerated literature seem to be fated to us. These are our curses as other times had theirs.

Walter Bagehot (1826-1877).

153. ENGLAND IN NOVEMBER

. . the chill
November dawns and dewy-glooming downs,
The gentle shower, the smell of dying leaves,
And the low moan of leaden-colour'd seas. . .

Alfred Tennyson (1809-1892).

154. CLOUDS

A-RIDÈN slow, at lofty height,
   Wer' clouds, a-blown along the sky,
O' purple blue, an' pink, an' white,
   In pack an' pile, a-reächèn high,
A-shiftèn off, as they did goo,
   Their sheäpes, from new, ageän to new.

An' zome like rocks an' tow'rs o' stwone,
   Or hills or woods, a-reächèn wide;
An' zome like roads, wi' doust a-blown,
   A-glitt'rèn white up off their zide,
A-comèn bright, ageän to feäde
   In sheäpes a-meäde to be unmeäde. . .

William Barnes (1800-1886).

155. THE BROKEN JUG

JENNY AND JOHN

JENNY.   As if you coudden leave the jug alwone!
      Now you've a-smack'd my jug,
      Now you've a-whack'd my jug,
      Now you've a-crack'd my jug
         Ageän the stwone.

JOHN. Why he must be a-crack'd unknown to you,
        Zoo don't belie the stwone,
        He scarce went nigh the stwone;
        He just went by the stwone,
           An' broke in two.

JENNY. He, crack'd avore! no, he wer sound enough,
        Vrom back to lip, wer sound,
        To stand or tip wer sound,
        To hold or dip wer sound,
           Don't talk such stuff.

JOHN. How high then do the price o'n reach?
        I'd buy zome mwore, so good;
        I'd buy a score, so good;
        I'd buy a store, so good,
           At twopence each.

JENNY. Indeed! with stwonen jugs a-zwold so dear.
                     (*Slaps him.*)

        No, there's a tap, vor lies;
        An' there's a slap, vor lies;
        An' there's a rap, vor lies,
           About your ear.

JOHN. Oh! there be pretty hands! a little dear.

                      William Barnes (1800-1886).

156. NEUTRAL TONES

WE stood by a pond that winter day,
And the sun was white, as though chidden of God,
And a few leaves lay on the starving sod;
    —They had fallen from an ash, and were gray.

Your eyes on me were as eyes that rove
Over tedious riddles of years ago;
And some words played between us to and fro
    On which lost the more by our love.

The smile on your mouth was the deadest thing
Alive enough to have strength to die;
And a grin of bitterness swept thereby
    Like an ominous bird a-wing. . .

Since then, keen lessons that love deceives,
And wrings with wrong, have shaped to me
Your face, and the God-curst sun, and a tree
    And a pond edged with grayish leaves.

1867.   *Thomas Hardy* (1840-1928).

157. THE NIGHTINGALE

"FROM nine o'clock till morning light
  The copse was never more than grey.
  The darkness did not close that night
    But day passed into day.
  And soon I saw it shewing new
  Beyond the hurst with such a hue
  As silken garden-poppies do.

"A crimson East, that bids for rain.
  So from the dawn was ill begun
  The day that brought my lasting pain
    And put away my sun.
  But watching while the colour grew
  I only feared the wet for you
  Bound for the harbour and your crew.

"I did not mean to sleep, but found
  I had slept a little and was chill.
  And I could hear the tiniest sound,
    The morning was so still—
  The bats' wings lisping as they flew
  And water draining through and through
  The wood: but not a dove would coo.

"You know you said the nightingale
  In all our western shires was rare,
That more he shuns our special dale
    Or never lodges there:
And I had thought so hitherto—
Up till that morning's fall of dew,
And now I wish that it were true.

"For he began at once and shook
  My head to hear. He might have strung
A row of ripples in the brook,
    So forcibly he sung,
The mist upon the leaves have strewed,
And danced the balls of dew that stood
In acres all above the wood.

"I thought the air must cut and strain
  The windpipe when he sucked his breath
And when he turned it back again
    The music must be death.
With not a thing to make me fear,
A singing bird in morning clear
To me was terrible to hear.

"Yet as he changed his mighty stops
  Betweens I heard the water still
All down the stair-way of the copse
    And churning in the mill.
But that sweet sound which I preferred,
Your passing steps, I never heard
For warbling of the warbling bird."

Thus Frances sighed at home, while Luke
Made headway in the frothy deep.
She listened how the sea-gust shook
    And then lay back to sleep.
While he was washing from on deck
She pillowing low her lily neck
Timed her sad visions with his wreck.
                    Gerard Manley Hopkins (1844-1889).

158. SORROW ON THE SEA

("*There is sorrow on the sea ; it cannot be quiet.*"
Jeremiah xlix. 23.)

THE moon-drawn Deep, sad, endless font of tears,
Rests never—rests not under mildest suns,
And under softest moonbeams never sleeps.
She sorrowed at her birth, she sorrows still:
Her eyes weep ever, and her quivering lip,
Restless with sorrow, whitens round the world:
Now loud, now low, now silent is her voice;
But still she mourns. In mute midwinter's frost
Where spiked Auroras crackle in the air,
Sullen and dumb, with white unfooted snows
Wrapt over her, she lies and waits till suns
Of the brief summer crack the icebergs' roots,
While unsealed straits explode, and breaking floes
Heave on black wakening waters round the ship
Whose ribs were clasped all winter in the arms
Of tightening glaciers; then she swells and pants,
And struggles with her weight of turbulent woe,
And welters round the narwhale's wounded sides,
Joining her voice to that loud-sounding horn
Through which his heart's blood spouts into the air;
Or moans, or thunders as the toppling spires
And breaking arches of the ice temples fall.

Oct. 4, 1868.   *James Smetham* (1821-1889).

159. SHOOTING A MONKEY

WHEN in the deepest part of the ravine we heard a rustling sound in the trees overhead, and Manoel soon pointed out a Coaitá to me. There was something human-like in its appearance, as the lean, dark, shaggy creature moved deliberately amongst the branches at a great height. I fired, but unfortunately only wounded it in the belly. It fell with a crash, headlong, about twenty or thirty feet, and then caught a

F*

bough with its tail, which grasped it instantaneously, and then the animal remained suspended in mid-air. Before I could reload it recovered itself, and mounted nimbly to the topmost branches, out of the reach of a fowling-piece, where we could perceive the poor thing apparently probing the wound with its fingers. Coaitás are more frequently kept in a tame state than any other kind of monkey. The Indians are very fond of them as pets, and the women often suckle them when young at their breasts.

H. W. Bates, F.R.S. (1825-1892).

160. AFTER DEATH

THE four boards of the coffin lid
Heard all the dead man did.

The first curse was in his mouth,
Made of grave's mould and deadly drouth.

The next curse was in his head,
Made of God's work discomfited.

The next curse was in his hands,
Made out of two grave-bands.

The next curse was in his feet,
Made out of a grave-sheet.

"I had fair coins red and white,
And my name was as great light;

"I had fair clothes green and red,
And strong gold bound round my head.

"But no meat comes in my mouth,
Now I fare as the worm doth;

"And no gold binds in my hair,
Now I fare as the blind fare.

" My live thews were of great strength,
  Now am I waxen a span's length;

" My live sides were full of lust,
  Now are they dried with dust."

The first board spake and said:
"Is it best eating flesh or bread?"

The second answered it:
"Is wine or honey more sweet?"

The third board spake and said:
"Is red gold worth a girl's gold head?"

The fourth made answer thus:
"All these things are as one with us."

The dead man asked of them:
"Is the green land stained brown with flame?

" Have they hewn my son for beasts to eat,
  And my wife's body for beasts' meat?

" Have they boiled my maid in a brass pan,
  And built a gallows to hang my man?"

The boards said to him:
"This is a lewd thing that ye deem.

" Your wife has gotten a golden bed,
  All the sheets are sewn with red.

" Your son has gotten a coat of silk,
  The sleeves are soft as curded milk.

" Your maid has gotten a kirtle new,
  All the skirt has braids of blue.

" Your man has gotten both ring and glove,
    Wrought well for eyes to love."

The dead man answered thus :
"What good gift shall God give us?"

The boards answered him anon :
"Flesh to feed hell's worm upon."
                        A. C. Swinburne (1837-1909).

161. ART AND THE TRUTH

. . So, British Public, who may like me yet,
(Marry and amen!) learn one lesson hence
Of many which whatever lives should teach:
This lesson, that our human speech is naught,
Our human testimony false, our fame
And human estimation words and wind.
Why take the artistic way to prove so much?
Because, it is the glory and good of Art,
That Art remains the one way possible
Of speaking truth, to mouths like mine at least.
How look a brother in the face and say
"Thy right is wrong, eyes hast thou yet art blind,
Thine ears are stuffed and stopped, despite their length:
And, oh, the foolishness thou countest faith!"
Say this as silverly as tongue can troll—
The anger of the man may be endured,
The shrug, the disappointed eyes of him
Are not so bad to bear—but here's the plague
That all this trouble comes of telling truth,
Which truth, by when it reaches him, looks false,
Seems to be just the thing it would supplant,
Nor recognizable by whom it left:
While falsehood would have done the work of truth.
But Art,—wherein man nowise speaks to men,
Only to mankind,—Art may tell a truth
Obliquely, do the thing shall breed the thought,

Nor wrong the thought, missing the mediate word.
So may you paint your picture, twice show truth,
Beyond mere imagery on the wall,—
So, note by note, bring music from your mind,
Deeper than ever e'en Beethoven dived,—
So write a book shall mean beyond the facts,
Suffice the eye and save the soul beside. . .

Robert Browning (1812-1889).

162. O LYRIC LOVE

O LYRIC Love, half angel and half bird
And all a wonder and a wild desire,—
Boldest of hearts that ever braved the sun,
Took sanctuary within the holier blue,
And sang a kindred soul out to his face,—
Yet human at the red-ripe of the heart—
When the first summons from the darkling earth
Reached thee amid thy chambers, blanched their blue,
And bared them of the glory—to drop down,
To toil for man, to suffer or to die,—
This is the same voice: can thy soul know change?
Hail them, and hearken from the realms of help!
Never may I commence my song, my due
To God who best taught song by gift of thee,
Except with bent head and beseeching hand—
That still, despite the distance and the dark,
What was, again may be; some interchange
Of grace, some splendour once thy very thought,
Some benediction anciently thy smile:
—Never conclude, but raising hand and head
Thither where eyes, that cannot reach, yet yearn
For all hope, all sustainment, all reward,
Their utmost up and on,—so blessing back
In those thy realms of help, that heaven thy home,
Some whiteness which, I judge, thy face makes proud,
Some wanness where, I think, thy foot may fall! . . .

Robert Browning (1812-1889).

163. THE KING'S DAUGHTER

WE were ten maidens in the green corn,
  Small red leaves in the mill-water:
Fairer maidens never were born,
  Apples of gold for the king's daughter.

We were ten maidens by a well-head,
  Small white birds in the mill-water:
Sweeter maidens never were wed,
  Rings of red for the king's daughter.

The first to spin, the second to sing,
  Seeds of wheat in the mill-water;
The third may was a goodly thing,
  White bread and brown for the king's daughter.

The fourth to sew and the fifth to play,
  Fair green weed in the mill-water;
The sixth may was a goodly may,
  White wine and red for the king's daughter.

The seventh to woo, the eighth to wed,
  Fair thin reeds in the mill-water;
The ninth had gold work on her head,
  Honey in the comb for the king's daughter.

The ninth had gold work round her hair,
  Fallen flowers in the mill-water;
The tenth may was goodly and fair,
  Golden gloves for the king's daughter.

We were ten maidens in a field green,
  Fallen fruit in the mill-water;
Fairer maidens never have been,
  Golden sleeves for the king's daughter.

By there comes the king's young son,
 A little wind in the mill-water;
"Out of ten maidens ye'll grant me one,"
 A crown of red for the king's daughter.

"Out of ten mays ye'll give me the best,"
 A little rain in the mill-water;
A bed of yellow straw for all the rest,
 A bed of gold for the king's daughter.

He's ta'en out the goodliest,
 Rain that rains in the mill-water;
A comb of yellow shell for all the rest,
 A comb of gold for the king's daughter.

He's made her bed to the goodliest,
 Wind and hail in the mill-water;
A grass girdle for all the rest,
 A girdle of arms for the king's daughter.

He's set his heart to the goodliest,
 Snow that snows in the mill-water;
Nine little kisses for all the rest,
 An hundredfold for the king's daughter.

He's ta'en his leave of the goodliest,
 Broken boats in the mill-water;
Golden gifts for all the rest,
 Sorrow of heart for the king's daughter.

"Ye'll make a grave for my fair body,"
 Running rain in the mill-water;
"And ye'll streek my brother at the side of me,"
 The pains of hell for the king's daughter.
      A. C. Swinburne (1837-1909).

164. A Legend of Camelot

Part 1

TALL Braunighrindas left her bed
At cock-crow, with an aching head.
　　O miserie!

"I yearn to suffer and to do,"
　She cried, "ere sunset, something new
　　O miserie!

"To do and suffer, ere I die,
　I care not what.　I know not why.
　　O miserie!

"Some quest I crave to undertake,
　Or burden bear, or trouble make."
　　O miserie!

She shook her hair about her form
In waves of colour bright and warm.
　　O miserie!

It rolled and writhed, and reached the floor:
A silver wedding-ring she wore.
　　O miserie!

She left her tower, and wandered down
Into the High Street of the town.
　　O miserie!

Her pale feet glimmered, in and out,
Like tombstones as she went about.
　　O miserie!

From right to left and left to right;
And blue veins streakt her instep white;
　　O miserie!

And folks did ask her in the street
"How fared it with her long pale feet?"
>O miserie!

And blinkt, as though 'twere hard to bear
The red heat of her blazing hair!
>O miserie!

Sir Galahad and Sir Launcelot
Came hand-in-hand down Camelot;
>O miserie!

Sir Gauwaine followèd close behind;
A weight hung heavy on his mind.
>O miserie!

"Who knows this damsel burning bright,"
Quoth Launcelot, "like a northern light?"
>O miserie!

Quoth Sir Gauwaine : "*I* know her not!"
"Who quoth you *did*?" quoth Launcelot.
>O miserie!

"'Tis Braunighrindas," quoth Sir Bors
(Just then returning from the wars).
>O miserie!

Then quoth the pure Sir Galahad:
"She seems, methinks, but lightly clad!
>O miserie!

"The winds blow somewhat chill to-day;
Moreover, what would Arthur say?"
>O miserie!

She thrust her chin towards Galahad
Full many an inch beyond her head. . . .
>O miserie!

But when she noted Sir Gauwaine
She wept, and drew it in again!
    O miserie!

She wept: "How beautiful am I!"
He shook the poplars with a sigh.
    O miserie!

Sir Launcelot was standing near;
Him kist he thrice behind the ear.
    O miserie!

"Ah me!" sighed Launcelot where he stood,
"I cannot fathom it!" . . . (who could?)
    O miserie!

Hard by his wares a weaver wove,
And weaving with a will, he throve;
    O miserie!

Him beckoned Galahad, and said,—
"Gaunt Braunighrindas wants your aid. . . .
    O miserie!

"Behold the wild growth on her nape!
Good weaver, weave it into shape!"
    O miserie!

The weaver straightway to his loom
Did lead her, whilst the knights made room;
    O miserie!

And wove her locks, both web and woof,
And made them wind and waterproof;
    O miserie!

Then with his shears he opened wide
An arm-hole neat on either side,
    O miserie!

And bound her with his handkerchief
Right round the middle like a sheaf.
　　　𝕺 miserie!

"Are you content, knight?" quoth 𝔖ir 𝔅ors
　To 𝔊alaℏad; quoth he, "Of course!"
　　　𝕺 miserie!

"Ah, me! those locks," quoth 𝔖ir 𝔊auwaine,
"Will never know the comb again!"
　　　𝕺 miserie!

The bold 𝔖ir 𝔏auncelot quoth he nought;
So (haply) all the more he thought.
　　　𝕺 miserie!

Part 2

A one-eyed Eastern passed, who sold,
And bought, and bartered garments old;
　　　𝕺 miserie!

His yellow garb did show the thread,
A triple head-dress crowned his head;
　　　𝕺 miserie!

And, ever and anon, his throat,
Thick-bearded, gave a solemn note;
　　　𝕺 miserie!

The knights were gathered in a knot;
Rapt in a trance, they heard him not;
　　　𝕺 miserie!

Before them 𝔅raunighrindas stood
In native growth of gown and hood;
　　　𝕺 miserie!

Fresh from a cunning weaver's hand,
She looked, not gaudy, but so grand!
    𝔒 miserie!

Not gaudy, gentles, but so neat!
For chaste and knightly eyes a treat!
    𝔒 miserie!

The Pilgrim eyed her shapely dress
With curious eye to business:
    𝔒 miserie!

Then whispered he to 𝔏auncelot,
"I'll give five shekels for the lot!"
    𝔒 miserie!

𝔊auwaine his battle-axe he drew. . . .
Once and again he clove him through!
    𝔒 miserie!

"No man of many words am I!"
Quoth he, and wope his weapon dry.
    𝔒 miserie!

A butcher caught the sounds and said,
"There go two cracks upon one head!"
    𝔒 miserie!

A baker whispered in his fun:
"Baker, more heads are cracked than one!"
    𝔒 miserie!

"The moon is up to many tricks!"
Quoth he who made the candlesticks! . . .
    𝔒 miserie!

Dead limp, the unbeliever lay
Athwart the flags and stopt the way. . . .
    𝔒 miserie!

The bold 𝔖𝔦𝔯 𝔏𝔞𝔲𝔫𝔠𝔢𝔩𝔬𝔱 mused a bit,
And smole a bitter smile at it.
    𝕺 miserie!

𝔊𝔞𝔲𝔴𝔞𝔦𝔫𝔢, he gave his orders brief:—
"*Manants : emportez-moi ce Juif!*"
    𝕺 miserie!

Some heard the knight not: they that heard
Made answer to him none, nor stirred.
    𝕺 miserie!

But 𝔅𝔯𝔞𝔲𝔫𝔦𝔤𝔥𝔯𝔦𝔫𝔡𝔞𝔰 was not dumb;
Her opportunity had come.
    𝕺 miserie!

Her accents tinkled ivory-sweet—
"*Je vays l'emporter tout de suite!*" . . .
    𝕺 miserie!

She bowed her body, slenderly,
And lifted him full tenderly:
    𝕺 miserie!

Full silverly her stretchèd throat
Intoned the wonted Hebrew note:
    𝕺 miserie!

Right broke-in-halfenly she bent;
Jew-laden on her way she went!
    𝕺 miserie!

The knights all left her one by one,
And leaving, cried in unison—
    𝕺 miserie!

"*Voyez ce vilain Juif qui pend
Par derrière et par devant!*" . . .
    𝕺 miserie!

Yet bearing it she journeyed forth,
Selecting north-north-east by north.
    O miserie!

The knights (most wisely) with one mouth,
Selected south-south-west by south.
    O miserie!

The butcher, baker, and the rest,
Said, "Let them go where they like best!"
    O miserie!

And many a wink they wunk, and shook
Their heads, but furthermore they took
    O miserie!

No note: it was a way they had,
In Camelot, when folks went mad. . . .
    O miserie!

Part 3

She bore her burden all that day
Half-faint; the unconverted clay
    O miserie!

A burden grew, beneath the sun,
In many a manner more than one.
    O miserie!

Half-faint the whitening road along
She bore it, singing (in her song)—
    O miserie!

" The locks you loved, *Gauwaine, Gauwaine,*
  Will never know the comb again ! . . .

The man you slew, *Gauwaine, Gauwaine,*
  Will never come to life again !

So when they do, *Gauwaine, Gauwaine,*
  Then take me back to town again ! " . . .

The shepherds gazed, but marvelled not;
They knew the ways of Camelot!
     O miserie!

She heeded neither man nor beast:
Her shadow lengthened toward the east.
     O miserie!

A little castle she drew nigh,
With seven towers twelve inches high. . . .
     O miserie!

A baby castle, all a-flame
With many a flower that hath no name.
     O miserie!

It had a little moat all round:
A little drawbridge too she found,
     O miserie!

On which there stood a stately maid,
Like her in radiant locks arrayed. . . .
     O miserie!

Save that her locks grew rank and wild,
By weaver's shuttle undefiled! . . .
     O miserie!

Who held her brush and comb, as if
Her faltering hands had waxèd stiff
     O miserie!

With baulkt endeavour! whence she sung
A chant, the burden whereof rung:
     O miserie!

" These hands have striven in vain
    To part
These locks that won Gauwaine
    His heart ! "

All breathless, Braunighrindas stopt
To listen, and her load she dropt,
  O miserie!

And rolled in wonder wild and blear
The whites of her eyes grown green with fear:
  O miserie!

"What is your name, young person, pray?"
"Knights call me Fidele-strynges-le-fay."
  O miserie!

"You wear a wedding-ring, I see!"
"I do . . . Gauwaine he gave it me. . . ."
  O miserie!

"Are you Gauwaine his wedded spouse?
Is this Gauwaine his . . . country-house?"
  O miserie!

"I am . . . it is . . . we are . . . Oh who,
That you should greet me thus, are you?"
  O miserie!

"I am ANOTHER! . . . since the morn
The fourth month of the year was born!"
  O miserie!

"What! that which followed when the last
Bleak night of bitter March had past?" . . .
  O miserie!

"The same." "*That day for both had done!*
And you, and he, and I are ONE!" . . .
  O miserie!

Then hand in hand, most woefully,
They went, the willows weeping nigh;
  O miserie!

Left hand in left was left to cling!
On each a silver wedding-ring.
    O miserie!

And having walkt a little space,
They halted, each one in her place:
    O miserie!

And chanted loud a wondrous plaint
Well chosen: wild, one-noted, quaint:
    O miserie!

" Heigho! the Wind and the Rain!
   The Moon's at the Full, 𝔊auwaine, 𝔊auwaine!

Heigho! the Wind and the Rain!
   On gold-hair woven, and gold-hair plain!

Heigho! the Wind and the Rain!
   Oh when shall we Three meet again! "

Atween the river and the wood,
Knee-deep 'mid whispering reeds they stood:
    O miserie!

The green earth oozing soft and dank
Beneath them, soakt and suckt and sank! . . .
    O miserie!

Yet soak-and-suck-and-sink or not,
They, chanting, craned towards Camelot. . . .
    O miserie!

Part 4

The pale wet moon did rise and ride,
O'er misty wolds and marshes wide.
    O miserie!

Sad earth slept underneath the yew,
Lapt in the death-sweat men call dew.
O miserie!

O raven ringlets, ringing wet!
O bright eye rolling black as jet!
O miserie!

O matted locks about the chin!
O towering head-piece, battered in!
O miserie!

Three hats that fit each other tight,
Are worth the helmet of a knight!
O miserie!

He rose all shapeless from the mud,
His yellow garb was stained with blood;
O miserie!

"Vat ish thish schwimming in mine head?
Thish turning round and round?" he said.
O miserie!

He took three paces through the night,
He saw red gold that glittered bright!
O miserie!

Two Royal Heads of Hair he saw!
And One was Woven, and One was Raw!
O miserie!

"O Sholomon! if there ain't a pair
Of dead young damsels shinking there!

"O Mosesh! what a precioush lot
Of beautiful red hair they've got!

"The prishe of it would compenshate
  Most handsome for my broken pate!

"How much their upper lipsh do pout!
  How very much their chins shtick out!

"How dreadful shtrange they shtare! They sheem
  Half to be dead, and half to dream!

"The Camelot peoplesh alvaysh try
  To look like that!   I vonder vy?

"Yet each hath got a lovely fashe!
  Good Father Jacob shend them grashe!

"O Jacob, blesh the lovely light,
  That lit the moon that shtruck the knight,
  That married the maid that carried the Jew,
  That shold (as he intensh to do)
  The golden locks and shilver rings
  Of 𝔅𝔯𝔞𝔲𝔫𝔦𝔤𝔥𝔯𝔦𝔫𝔡𝔢 and 𝔣𝔦𝔡𝔡𝔩𝔢𝔰𝔥𝔱𝔯𝔦𝔫𝔤𝔰!"
          𝔒 𝔪𝔦𝔰𝔢𝔯𝔦𝔢!

Thus having given thanks, he drew
His two-fold weapon cutting true;
          𝔒 𝔪𝔦𝔰𝔢𝔯𝔦𝔢!

And close he clipt, and clean and clear,
From crown and temple, nape and ear.
          𝔒 𝔪𝔦𝔰𝔢𝔯𝔦𝔢!

The wind in pity soughed and sighed!
The river beat the river side!
          𝔒 𝔪𝔦𝔰𝔢𝔯𝔦𝔢!

The willows wept to stand and see
The sweetest, softest heads that be,
          𝔒 𝔪𝔦𝔰𝔢𝔯𝔦𝔢!

In ghastliest baldness gleam dead-white,
And sink unhallowed out of sight!
     𝔒 miserie!

But, lo, you! Ere kind earth could fold
Their shame within its bosom cold,
     𝔒 miserie!

The moon had laught in mockery down,
And stampt a high-light on each crown!! . . .
     𝔒 miserie!

Thrice muttering deep his mystic note,
The stillness of the night he smote:
     𝔒 miserie!

Then, with a treasure hanging slack
From either shoulder adown his back,
     𝔒 miserie!

He, whistling in his whistle, strode,
Nor felt he faint upon the road!
     𝔒 miserie!

You may be sure that it was not
The road that leads to Camelot!
     𝔒 miserie!

Part 5

The castle weeds have grown so tall
Knights cannot see the red brick wall.
     𝔒 miserie!

The little drawbridge hangs awry,
The little flowery moat is dry!
     𝔒 miserie!

And the wind, it soughs and sighs alway
Through the grey willows, night and day!
    𝕺 miserie!

And ever more two willows there
Do weep, whose boughs are always bare:
    𝕺 miserie!

At all times weep they, in and out
Of season, turn and turn about!
    𝕺 miserie!

But, later, when the year doth fall,
And other willows, one and all,
    𝕺 miserie!

In yellowing and dishevelled leaf
Sway haggard with their autumn grief,
    𝕺 miserie!

Then do these leafless willows now
Put forth a rosebud from each bough!
    𝕺 miserie!

What time 𝕲auwaine, with spurless heels,
Barefoot (but not bare-headed) kneels
    𝕺 miserie!

Between! . . . as fits a bigamous knight
Twice widowed in a single night:
    𝕺 miserie!

And then, for that promiscuous way
Of axing Hebrews in broad day,
    𝕺 miserie!

He ever uttereth a note
Of Eastern origin remote. . . .
    𝕺 miserie!

A well-known monochord, that tells
Of one who, wandering, buys and sells!
  𝖮 miserie!

What time the knights and damsels fair,
Of 𝔄rthur's court come trooping there,
  𝖮 miserie!

They come in dresses of dark green,
Two damsels take a knight between:
  𝖮 miserie!

One sad and sallow knight is fixt
Dyspeptic damsels twain betwixt!
  𝖮 miserie!

They speak not, but their weary eyes
And wan white eyelids droop and rise
  𝖮 miserie!

With dim dead gaze of mystic woe!
They always take their pleasure so
  𝖮 miserie!

In Camelot. . . . It doth not lie
With us to ask, or answer, why!
  𝖮 miserie!

Yet, seeing them so fair and good,
Fain would we cheer them, if we could!
  𝖮 miserie!

And every time they find a bud,
They pluck it, and it bleeds red blood.
  𝖮 miserie!

And when they pluck a full blown rose,
And breathe the same, its colour goes!
  𝖮 miserie!

But with 𝔊auwaine alone at night,
The willows dance in their delight!
    O miserie!

The rosebuds wriggle in their bliss,
And lift them for his lips to kiss!
    O miserie!

And if he kiss a rose instead,
It blushes of a deeper red!
    O miserie!

And if he like it, let him be!
It makes no odds to you or me!
    O miserie!

O many-headed multitude,
Who read these rhymes that run so rude,
    O miserie!

Strive not to fathom their intent!
But say your prayers and rest content
    O miserie!

That, notwithstanding those two cracks
He got from 𝔊auwaine's battle-axe,
    O miserie!

The Hebrew had the best of it!
So, Gentles, let us rest a bit.
    O miserie!
          George du Maurier (1834-1896).

165. VENUS

BEFORE our lady came on earth
  Little there was of joy or mirth;
About the borders of the sea
  The sea-folk wandered heavily;
About the wintry river side
  The weary fishers would abide.

Alone within the weaving-room
The girls would sit before the loom,
And sing no song, and play no play;
Alone from dawn to hot mid-day,
From mid-day unto evening,
The men afield would work, nor sing,
'Mid weary thoughts of man and God,
Before thy feet the wet ways trod.

Unkissed the merchant bore his care,
Unkissed the knights went out to war,
Unkissed the mariner came home,
Unkissed the minstrel men did roam.

Or in the stream the maids would stare,
Nor know why they were made so fair;
Their yellow locks, their bosoms white,
Their limbs well wrought for all delight,
Seemed foolish things that waited death,
As hopeless as the flowers beneath
The weariness of unkissed feet:
No life was bitter then, or sweet.

Therefore, O Venus, well may we
Praise the green ridges of the sea
O'er which, upon a happy day,
Thou cam'st to take our shame away.
Well may we praise the curdling foam
Amidst the which thy feet did bloom,
Flowers of the gods; the yellow sand
They kissed atwixt the sea and land;
The bee-beset ripe-seeded grass,
Through which thy fine limbs first did pass;
The purple-dusted butterfly,
First blown against they quivering thigh;
The first red rose that touched thy side,
And over-blown and fainting died;
The flickering of the orange shade,
Where first in sleep thy limbs were laid;

The happy day's sweet life and death,
Whose air first caught thy balmy breath—
Yea, all these things well praised may be,
But with what words shall we praise thee—
O Venus, O thou love alive,
Born to give peace to souls that strive?

William Morris (1834-1896).

166. IN THE ORCHARD

(Provençal Burden)

Leave go my hands, let me catch breath and see;
Let the dew-fall drench either side of me;
  Clear apple-leaves are soft upon that moon
Seen sidelong like a blossom in the tree;
  Ah God, ah God, that day should be so soon.

The grass is thick and cool, it lets us lie.
Kissed upon either cheek and either eye,
  I turn to thee as some green afternoon
Turns toward sunset, and is loth to die;
  Ah God, ah God, that day should be so soon.

Lie closer, lean your face upon my side,
Feel where the dew fell that has hardly dried,
  Hear how the blood beats that went nigh to swoon;
The pleasure lives there when the sense has died;
  Ah God, ah God, that day should be so soon.

O my fair lord, I charge you leave me this:
Is it not sweeter than a follish kiss?
  Nay take it then, my flower, my first in June,
My rose, so like a tender mouth it is:
  Ah God, ah God, that day should be so soon.

G

Love, till dawn sunder night from day with fire,
Dividing my delight and my desire,
  The crescent life and love the plenilune,
Love me though dusk begin and dark retire;
    Ah God, ah God, that day should be so soon.

Ah, my heart fails, my blood draws back; I know,
When life runs over, life is near to go;
  And with the slain of love love's ways are strewn,
And with their blood, if love will have it so;
    Ah God, ah God, that day should be so soon.

Ah, do thy will now; slay me if thou wilt;
There is no building now the walls are built,
  No quarrying now the corner-stone is hewn,
No drinking now the vine's whole blood is spilt;
    Ah God, ah God, that day should be so soon.

Nay, slay me now; nay, for I will be slain;
Pluck thy red pleasure from the teeth of pain,
  Break down thy vine ere yet grape-gatherers prune,
Slay me ere day can slay desire again;
    Ah God, ah God, that day should be so soon.

Yea, with thy sweet lips, with thy sweet sword; yea,
Take life and all, for I will die, I say;
  Love, I gave love, is life a better boon?
For sweet night's sake I will not live till day;
    Ah God, ah God, that day should be so soon.

Nay, I will sleep then only; nay, but go.
Ah sweet, too sweet to me, my sweet, I know
  Love, sleep, and death go to the sweet same tune;
Hold my hair fast, and kiss me through it so.
    Ah God, ah God, that day should be so soon.

                                    A. C. Swinburne (1837-1909).

167. ROSES AND MOUNTAINS

Thursday, 9 *June*, 1870. In the night there came a cooler
wind and fair showers out of the west. The falling white
blossoms of the clematis drift in at the open window on the
fresh morning breeze. In the garden there are red roses, and
blue hills beyond. Last night the moon was shining in at my
west window through the lacing boughs of the mountain ash—
the moonbeams fell across the bed and I saw "the gusty shadow
sway" on the white bed curtain. Called at Cae Mawr at 3.30
and found Mr. and Mrs. Morrell playing croquet with his sister
and Miss Morrell of Moulsford who are staying in the house,
having returned with him on Tuesday. Joined them and we
had two merry games. The two eldest Miss Baskervilles came
in by the wicket gate whilst we were playing and we had tea
on the lawn. I staid to dinner. After dinner we had archery.

Francis Kilvert (1840-1879).

168. A PAINTING IN WORDS

. . So till the dusk that follow'd evensong
Rode on the two, reviler and reviled;
Then after one long slope was mounted, saw,
Bowl-shaped, thro' tops of many thousand pines
A gloomy-gladed hollow slowly sink
To westward—in the deeps whereof a mere,
Round as the red eye of an Eagle-owl,
Under the half-dead sunset glared; and shouts
Ascended, and there brake a servingman
Flying from out of the black wood, and crying,
"They have bound my lord to cast him in the mere."
Then Gareth, "Bound am I to right the wrong'd,
But straitlier bound am I to bide with thee."
And when the damsel spake contemptuously,
"Lead, and I follow," Gareth cried again,
"Follow, I lead!" so down among the pines
He plunged; and there, blackshadow'd nigh the mere,
And mid-thigh-deep in bulrushes and reed,
Saw six tall men haling a seventh along,

A stone about his neck to drown him in it.
Three with good blows he quieted, but three
Fled thro' the pines; and Gareth loosed the stone
From off his neck, then in the mere beside
Tumbled it; oilily bubbled up the mere.
Last, Gareth loosed his bonds and on free feet
Set him, a stalwart Baron, Arthur's friend. . .
                          Alfred Tennyson (1809-1892).

169. BY THE MILL IN SPRING

WITH wind to blow, and streams to flow,
To flow along the gravel stone,
The waves were bright, the cliffs were white,
Were white before the evening sun,
Where shaken sedge would softly sigh,
As we, with windblown locks, went by.

As lambs would swing their tails, and spring;
And spring about the ground chalk white;
The smoke was blue, above the yew;
The yew beside your house in sight;
And wind would sing with sullen sound,
Against the tree beside the mound;

Where down at mill, the wheel was still,
Was still, and dripp'd with glitt'ring tears,
With dusty poll, up lane would stroll,
The miller's man with mill-stunn'd ears;
While weakly-wailing wind would swim,
By ground with ivied elm-trees dim.

My work and way may fail or fay,
Or fay as days may freeze or glow,
I'll try to bear my toil or care,
Or care, with either friend or foe,
If, after all, the evening tide
May bring me peace, where I abide.
                          William Barnes (1800-1886).

170. CHRISTMAS SONG

OUTLANDERS, whence come ye last?
   The snow in the street and the wind on the door.
Through what green seas and great have ye passed?
   Minstrels and maids, stand forth on the floor.

From far away, O masters mine,
   The snow in the street and the wind on the door.
We come to bear you goodly wine,
   Minstrels and maids, stand forth on the floor.

From far away we come to you,
   The snow in the street and the wind on the door.
To tell of great tidings strange and true.
   Minstrels and maids, stand forth on the floor.

News, news of the Trinity,
   The snow in the street and the wind on the door.
And Mary and Joseph from over the sea!
   Minstrels and maids, stand forth on the floor.

For as we wandered far and wide,
   The snow in the street and the wind on the door.
What hap do ye deem there should us betide!
   Minstrels and maids, stand forth on the floor.

Under a bent when the night was deep,
   The snow in the street and the wind on the door.
There lay three shepherds tending their sheep.
   Minstrels and maids, stand forth on the floor.

"O ye shepherds, what have ye seen,
   The snow in the street and the wind on the door.
To slay your sorrow, and heal your teen?"
   Minstrels and maids, stand forth on the floor.

"In an ox-stall this night we saw,
  The snow in the street and the wind on the door.
A babe and a maid without a flaw.
  Minstrels and maids, stand forth on the floor.

"There was an old man there beside,
  The snow in the street and the wind on the door.
His hair was white and his hood was wide.
  Minstrels and maids, stand forth on the floor.

"And as we gazed this thing upon,
  The snow in the street and the wind on the door.
Those twain knelt down to the Little One.
  Minstrels and maids, stand forth on the floor.

"And a marvellous song we straight did hear,
  The snow in the street and the wind on the door.
That slew our sorrow and healed our care."
  Minstrels and maids, stand forth on the floor.

News of a fair and marvellous thing,
  The snow in the street and the wind on the door.
Nowell, nowell, nowell, we sing!
  Minstrels and maids, stand forth on the floor.
                              William Morris (1834-1896).

171. THE MOONLIT MORNING

Saturday, Easter Eve, 16 April, 1870. I awoke at 4.30 and
there was a glorious sight in the sky, one of the grand spectacles
of the universe. There was not a cloud in the deep wonderful
blue of the heavens. Along the eastern horizon there was a
clear deep intense glow neither scarlet nor crimson but a
mixture of both. This red glow was very narrow, almost like
a riband, and it suddenly shaded off into the deep blue. Opposite
in the west the full moon shining in all its brilliance was setting
upon the hill beyond the church steeple. Thus the glow in the
east bathed the church in a warm rich tinted light, while the

moon from the west was casting strong shadows. The moon
dropped quickly down behind the hill bright to the last, till
only her rim could be seen sparkling among the tops of the
orchards on the hill. The sun rose quickly and his rays struck
red upon the white walls of Pen Uan, but not so brilliantly as
in the winter sunrisings. I got up soon after 5 and set to work
on my Easter sermon, getting two hours for writing before
breakfast.   *Francis Kilvert* (1840-1879).

172. THE NEW LAWCOURTS AND THE CHINESE
STEAM-ENGINE

THE highest poetry must always express emotions excited by
the deepest convictions of the time. A modern Dante, if such
a person existed, could no longer compose a Divine Comedy,
when placed in the chilling medium of modern scepticism.
Descartes, says Pascal, tried to do without God, but was obliged
to retain him in order to give a fillip to start the machinery of
the universe. A God of this kind—a mere *roi fainéant*, a
constitutional king, secured from our sight by responsible
ministers in the shape of second causes—will hardly stir the
vehement passions which burst spontaneously into verse. The
psalms sung in his honour would be as languid as the feelings
he inspires. A God who is not allowed even to make a fly or
launch a thunderbolt will be worshipped in strains widely
different from those which celebrated the Ruler who clothed
the horse's neck with thunder, and whose voice shook the
wilderness. The prevalent conceptions of the day will somehow
permeate its poetry—if it has any—in spite of all that can be
done to keep them out. Shakespeare and Bacon were not
independent phenomena, brought together by an accidental
coincidence. They were rooted in the same soil, and the im-
pulse, though it led to different manifestations, was ultimately
derived from the same sources.

   This, of course, is a commonplace; but we have a device in
modern times for evading the apparent conclusion. We are, it
is said, pre-eminently an historical age; our special function is
the critical. We do not produce original thought, but live upon

examining and dressing up the accumulated inheritance of our ancestors. We want the simplicity and the freshness which was necessary to produce new forms of art or faith. Indeed when we come across regions in which such forms still linger, we are apt to spoil them by our touch. The native dress of India disappears in favour of Manchester prints, and perhaps native religions may be superseded in time by equally vulgar forms of European superstition. The remedy is to be found in that judicious spirit of revivalism which is now so popular. We must learn to cherish instead of destroying. Since Scott revealed to us the surprising fact that mediaeval knights and ladies were real human beings, instead of names in a book, and succeeded in impressing that fact upon the world at large, we have made surprising progress. We have been reviving all manner of things once supposed to be hopelessly dead. We have succeeded in building churches so carefully modelled after the old patterns, that William of Wykeham might rise from the dead and fancy that his old architects were at work. Nay, we have revived the men themselves. We have clergymen who succeed in accomplishing very fairly the surprising feat of living in two centuries at once; and the results are held to be infinitely refreshing and commendable. We have been just told, for example, that our new courts of law must be unimpeachable because there is not a window or a tower in them which might not have been built just as well six hundred years ago. Poets can affect an infantile lisp, and tell us legends of old times as naturally as if human beings at the present day had still a lively interest in them. We have undoubtedly obtained some very pretty results, and have a beautiful new set of toys, which we may persuade ourselves are almost capable of living and moving. There is only one objection to our complete success. The more skilfully we imitate obsolete modes of art or religion the more palpably dead they become. One of our modern imitations of an ancient church resembles its original as minutely as the Chinese imitation of a steam-engine, the only fault of which is that it won't work. The old building was the natural production of men working freely, by all means in their power, to give expression to their feelings: the new building is the work of men fettered by the self-imposed law that they will use the forms invented in an epoch permeated by different creeds, aspirations and emotions. A genuine revival could only be produced by reproducing all the intellectual and social conditions under which the old art arose; and in that case it would have a spontaneous resurrection. Till then we shall only see what we see now—spasmodic attempts to be pretty and picturesque, with infinite antiquarian labour, and yet, with all our products marked by that feebleness of constitution characteristic of any natural or artificial object forcibly transplanted to an uncongenial medium.·

In art, it may be said, there is room for such methods. There can be no reason why the poet or the painter should not help us to enter into the spirit of the past, and to contemplate with pleasure the picturesque and graceful forms from which all vitality has departed. Speaking frankly, indeed, art of this kind, whether it takes the shape of the careful historical romance or of·the pictorial representation, is apt to be rather oppressive. At best it is fitted for decorative purposes. The emotions to which it appeals are those with which we enter a museum, not those with which we enter a church. But, at any rate, an art which has become entirely parasitical must fall into decay.

Sir Leslie Stephen (1832-1904).

PART FOUR: STRANGE DYES

Any stirring of the senses, strange dyes, strange flowers, and curious odours, or work of the artist's hands. . .

Walter Pater.

Shake the pan violently till all the Amblongusses have become a pale purple colour.

Edward Lear.

Clouds, mists, and mountains are unimportant beside the wear on a threshold, or the print of a hand.

Thomas Hardy.

173. THE ULTIMATE AIM OF THE POET

THE ultimate aim of the poet should be to touch our hearts by showing his own, and not to exhibit his learning, or his fine taste, or his skill in mimicking the notes of his predecessors.

Sir Leslie Stephen (1832-1904).

174. A BALLADE OF EVOLUTION

IN the mud of the Cambrian main
    Did our earliest ancestor dive:
From a shapeless albuminous grain
    We mortals our being derive.
He could split himself up into five,
    Or roll himself round like a ball;
For the fittest will always survive,
    While the weakliest go to the wall.

As an active ascidian again
    Fresh forms he began to contrive,
Till he grew to a fish with a brain,
    And brought forth a mammal alive.
With his rivals he next had to strive
    To woo him a mate and a thrall;
So the handsomest managed to wive,
    While the ugliest went to the wall.

At length as an ape he was fain
    The nuts of the forest to rive,
Till he took to the low-lying plain,
    And proceeded his fellows to knive.
Thus did cannibal men first arrive
    One another to swallow and maul:
And the strongest continued to thrive,
    While the weakliest went to the wall.

Prince, in our civilised hive,
　　Now money's the measure of all;
And the wealthy in coaches can drive,
　　While the needier go to the wall.
　　　　　　　Grant Allen (1848-1899).

175. PERSONIFIED SCIENCE

SCIENCE is being daily more and more personified and anthropo-
morphised into a god.　By and by they will say that science
took our nature upon him, and sent down his only begotten son,
Charles Darwin, or Huxley, into the world so that those who
believe in him, etc.; and they will burn people for saying
that science, after all, is only an expression for our ignorance
of our own ignorance.
　　　　　　　Samuel Butler (1835-1902).

176. TO HOPE

A SONNET

FAIR Hope, that once, fair Hope, my prisoned heart
　　Delightedst with thy lustre, piercing night
With eyelet twinkle, now thy former part
　　Renew, with thy one beam my heart delight;
Starlike, not sunlike, not scattering the dark,
　　Spreading in prisons, thee I ask to shine;
Only to pierce, not scatter, with thy spark
　　As stars the night, such night wherein I pine.

Then move some space in heaven: but let thy beam
　　Solace me still: and I shall know and feel
Thy cluster near, the sisters of thy team,
　　Which in the night above our day do wheel:
Faith, love are there, where Hope on high doth glide,
Through further, fainter, in heaven's depth they ride.
　　　　　　　R. W. Dixon (1833-1900).

177. THE MOUNTAINEER WATCHES THE SUNRISE

EVERY traveller has occasionally done a sunrise, and a more lamentable proceeding than the ordinary view of a sunrise can hardly be imagined. You are cold, miserable, breakfastless; have risen shivering from a warm bed, and in your heart long only to creep into bed again. To the mountaineer all this is changed. He is beginning a day full of the anticipation of a pleasant excitement. He has, perhaps, been waiting anxiously for fine weather, to try conclusions with some huge giant not yet scaled. He moves out with something of the feeling with which a soldier goes to the assault of a fortress, but without the same probability of coming home in fragments; the danger is trifling enough to be merely exhilatory, and to give a pleasant tension to the nerves; his muscles feel firm and springy, and his stomach—no small advantage to the enjoyment of scenery —is in excellent order. He looks at the sparkling stars with keen satisfaction, prepared to enjoy a fine sunrise with all his faculties at their best, and with the added pleasure of a good omen for his day's work. Then a huge dark mass begins to mould itself slowly out of the darkness, the sky begins to form a background of deep purple, against which the outline becomes gradually more definite; one by one, the peaks catch the exquisite Alpine glow, lighting up in rapid succession, like a vast illumination; and when at last the steady sun settles upon them, and shows every rock and glacier, without even a delicate film of mist to obscure them, he feels his heart bound, and steps gaily out to the assault—just as the people on the Rigi are giving thanks that the show is over and that they may go to bed. Still grander is the sight when the mountaineer has already reached some lofty ridge, and, as the sun rises, stands between the day and the night—the valley still in deep sleep, with the mists lying between the folds of the hills, and the snow-peaks standing out clear and pale white just before the sun reaches them, whilst a broad band of orange light runs all around the vast horizon. The glory of sunsets is equally increased in the thin upper air. The grandest of all such sights that live in my memory is that of a sunset from the Aiguille du Goûté. The snow at our feet was glowing with rich light, and the shadows in our footsteps a vivid green by contrast. Beneath us was a vast horizontal floor of thin level mists suspended in mid air, spread like a canopy over the whole boundless landscape, and tinged with every hue of sunset. Through its rents and gaps we could see the lower mountains, the distant plains, and a fragment of the Lake of Geneva lying in a more sober purple. Above us rose the solemn mass of Mont Blanc in the richest glow of an Alpine sunset. The sense of lonely sublimity was almost oppressive, and although half of our party was suffering from sickness, I believe even the guides were moved to a sense of solemn beauty.

Sir Leslie Stephen (1832-1904).

178. THE FLESH-FLY AND THE BEE

A BEE upon a briar-rose hung
And wild with pleasure suck'd and kiss'd;
A flesh-fly near, with snout in dung,
Sneer'd, "What a Transcendentalist!"

Coventry Patmore (1823-1896).

179. TRUTH?

POETRY, like Painting, has improved immensely in truthfulness since its earliest days. The first poets deal only in a few stock aesthetic objects, to which they merely allude without special description. Roses are their only flowers, the lark their only bird: red gold, ladies gay, the green wood, the gallant steed, reappear in every ballad. There is a conventional epithet for every noun; the white-armed, the cloud-compelling, the laughter-loving, the grey-eyed; and these are always employed, however incongruous the context. The colours are almost as primitive and unshaded as those of the Egyptian paintings. Homer knows only three or four; the Attic poets enlarge the stock; Latin verse gets to some dozen; while the modern poet subdivides by all the known tints, by all the precious metals and stones, by all the flowers and leaves, by sky and sea and human features. . . . Indeed, unpopular as the opinion may be,

I do not hesitate to say that Poetry, as an imitative art, has
advanced as far above the Homeric level as Painting has above
the Egyptian. And I do not base this statement upon mere
individual taste, but upon a careful comparison of epithets,
descriptions, similes, and metaphors. The composers of the
early cycle were doubtless wonderful versifiers for their age;
but they belonged to *their* age, not to ours.

Grant Allen (1848-1899).

180. THE DARK BED

How fair a flower is sown
When Knowledge goes, with fearful tread,
To the dark bed
Of the divine Unknown!

Coventry Patmore (1823-1896).

181. POETRY AND SCIENCE

i

POETRY, then, I conceive, whatever be its metaphysical essence,
or however various may be its kinds, whether it more probably
belongs to action or to suffering, nay, whether it is more at
home with society or with nature, whether its spirit is seen
to best advantage in Homer or in Virgil, at any rate, is always
the antagonist to *science*. As science makes progress in any
subject-matter, poetry recedes from it. The two cannot stand
together; they belong respectively to two modes of viewing
things, which are contradictory of each other. Reason in-
vestigates, analyses, numbers, weighs, measures, ascertains,
locates, the objects of its contemplation, and thus gains a
scientific knowledge of them. Science results in system, which
is complex unity; poetry delights in the indefinite and various
as contrasted with unity, and in the simple as contrasted with
system. The aim of science is to get a hold of things, to grasp
them, to handle them, to comprehend them; that is (to use
the familiar term), to *master* them, or to be superior to them.
Its success lies in being able to draw a line round them, and

to tell where each of them is to be found within that circumference, and how each lies relatively to all the rest. Its mission
is to destroy ignorance, doubt, surmise, suspense, illusions,
fears, deceits, according to the "Felix qui potuit rerum cog-
noscere causas" of the Poet, whose whole passage, by the way,
may be taken as drawing out the contrast between the poetical
and the scientific. But as to the poetical, very different is the
frame of mind which is necessary for its perception. It demands,
as its primary condition, that we should not put ourselves above
the objects in which it resides, but at their feet; that we should
feel them to be above and beyond us, that we should look up
to them, and that, instead of fancying that we can comprehend
them, we should take for granted that we are surrounded and
comprehended by them ourselves. It implies that we understand them to be vast, impenetrable, inscrutable, mysterious;
so that at best we are only forming conjectures about them, not
conclusions, for the phenomena which they present admit of
many explanations, and we cannot know the true one. Poetry
does not address the reason, but the imagination and affections;
it leads to admiration, enthusiasm, devotion, love. The vague,
the uncertain, the irregular, the sudden are among its attributes
or sources. Hence it is that a child's mind is so full of poetry,
because he knows so little; and an old man of the world so
devoid of poetry, because his experience of facts is so wide.
Hence it is that nature is commonly more poetical than art, in
spite of Lord Byron, because it is less comprehensible and less
patient of definitions; history more poetical than philosophy;
the savage than the citizen; the knight-errant than the
brigadier-general; the winding bridle-path than the straight
railroad; the sailing vessel than the steamer; the ruin than
the spruce suburban box; the Turkish robe or Spanish doublet
than the French dress coat.

J. H. Newman (1801-1890).

ii

SCIENCE, the agile ape, may well
Up in his tree thus grin and grind his teeth
At us beneath,
The wearers of the bay and asphodel,

Laughing to be his butts,
And gathering up for use his ill-aim'd cocoa-nuts.
                              Coventry Patmore (1823-1896).

182. THE SCIENTIST

IF I may speak of the objects I have had more or less definitely
in view since I began the ascent of my hillock, they are briefly
these: To promote the increase of natural knowledge and to
forward the application of scientific methods of investigation
of all the problems of life to the best of my ability, in the conviction which has grown with my growth and strengthened
with my strength, that there is no alleviation for the sufferings
of mankind except veracity of thought and of action, and the
resolute facing of the world as it is when the garment of make-
believe by which pious hands have hidden its uglier features
is stripped off.

It is with this intent that I have subordinated any reasonable,
or unreasonable, ambition for scientific fame which I may
have permitted myself to entertain to other ends; to the
popularisation of science; to the development and organisation
of scientific education; to the endless series of battles and
skirmishes over evolution; and to untiring opposition to that
ecclesiastical spirit, that clericalism, which in England, as
everywhere else, and to whatever denomination it may belong,
is the deadly enemy of science.
                              T. H. Huxley (1825-1895).

183. THE MINDLESS HEAVENS

. . How the moon triumphs through the endless nights!
     How the stars throb and glitter as they wheel
  Their thick processions of supernal lights
     Around the blue vault obdurate as steel!
  And men regard with passionate awe and yearning
  The mighty marching and the golden burning,
     And think the heavens respond to what they feel.

Boats gliding like dark shadows of a dream,
   Are glorified from vision as they pass
The quivering moonbridge on the deep black stream;
   Cold windows kindle their dead glooms of glass
To restless crystals; cornice, dome, and column
Emerge from chaos in the splendour solemn;
   Like faëry lakes gleam lawns of dewy grass.

With such a living light these dead eyes shine,
   These eyes of sightless heaven, that as we gaze
We read a pity, tremulous, divine,
   Or cold majestic scorn in their pure rays:
Fond man! they are not haughty, are not tender;
There is no heart or mind in all their splendour,
   They thread mere puppets all their marvellous maze.

If we could near them with the flight unflown,
   We should but find them worlds as sad as this,
Or suns all self-consuming like our own
   Enringed by planet worlds as much amiss:
They wax and wane through fusion and confusion;
The spheres eternal are a grand illusion,
   The empyréan is a void abyss. . .

                 James Thomson (1834-1882).

184. TO MAKE AN AMBLONGUS PIE

TAKE 4 pounds (say $4\frac{1}{2}$ pounds) of fresh Amblongusses, and put them in a small pipkin.

Cover them with water and boil them for 8 hours incessantly, after which add 2 pints of new milk, and proceed to boil for 4 hours more.

When you have ascertained that the Amblongusses are quite soft, take them out and place them in a wide pan, taking care to shake them well previously.

Grate some nutmeg over the surface, and cover them care-

fully with powdered gingerbread, curry powder, and a sufficient
quantity of cayenne pepper.

Remove the pan into the next room, and place it on the
floor. Bring it back again, and let it simmer for three-quarters
of an hour. Shake the pan violently till all the Amblongusses
have become a pale purple colour.

Then, having prepared the paste, insert the whole carefully,
adding at the same time a small pigeon, 2 slices of beef, 4
cauliflowers, and any number of oysters.

Watch patiently till the crust begins to rise, and add a pinch
of salt from time to time.

Serve up in a clean dish, and throw the whole out of the
window as fast as possible.

Edward Lear (1812-1888).

185. AS I CAME THROUGH THE DESERT

. . As I came through the desert thus it was,
     As I came through the desert: All was black,
     In heaven no single star, on earth no track;
     A brooding hush without a stir or note,
     The air so thick it clotted in my throat;
     And thus for hours; then some enormous things
     Swooped past with savage cries and clanking wings:
              But I strode on austere;
              No hope could have no fear.

     As I came through the desert thus it was,
     As I came through the desert: Eyes of fire
     Glared at me throbbing with a starved desire;
     The hoarse and heavy and carnivorous breath
     Was hot upon me from deep jaws of death;
     Sharp claws, swift talons, fleshless fingers cold
     Plucked at me from the bushes, tried to hold:
              But I strode on austere;
              No hope could have no fear.

As I came through the desert thus it was,
As I came through the desert: Lo you, there,
That hillock burning with a brazen glare;
Those myriad dusky flames with points a-glow
Which writhed and hissed and darted to and fro;
A Sabbath of the Serpents, heaped pell-mell
For Devil's roll-call and some *fête* of Hell:
    Yet I strode on austere;
    No hope could have no fear.

As I came through the desert thus it was,
As I came through the desert: Meteors ran
And crossed their javelins on the black sky-span;
The zenith opened to a gulf of flame,
The dreadful thunderbolts jarred earth's fixed frame;
The ground all heaved in waves of fire that surged
And weltered round me sole there unsubmerged:
    Yet I strode on austere;
    No hope could have no fear.

As I came through the desert thus it was,
As I came through the desert: Air once more,
And I was close upon a wild sea-shore;
Enormous cliffs arose on either hand,
The deep tide thundered up a league-broad strand;
White foambelts seethed there, wan spray swept and flew;
The sky broke, moon and stars and clouds and blue:
    And I strode on austere;
    No hope could have no fear.

As I came through the desert thus it was,
As I came through the desert: On the left
The sun arose and crowned a broad crag-cleft;
There stopped and burned out black, except a rim,
A bleeding eyeless socket, red and dim;
Whereon the moon fell suddenly south-west,
And stood above the right-hand cliffs at rest :
    Still I strode on austere;
    No hope could have no fear.

As I came through the desert thus it was,
As I came through the desert: From the right
As shape came slowly with a ruddy light;
A woman with a red lamp in her hand,
Bareheaded and barefooted on that strand;
O desolation moving with such grace!
O anguish with such beauty in thy face!
       I fell as on my bier
       Hope travailed with such fear.

As I came through the desert thus it was,
As I came through the desert: I was twain,
Two selves distinct that cannot join again;
One stood apart and knew but could not stir,
And watched the other stark in swoon and her;
And she came on, and never turned aside,
Between such sun and moon and roaring tide:
       And as she came more near
       My soul grew mad with fear.

As I came through the desert thus it was,
As I came through the desert: Hell is mild
And piteous matched with that accursèd wild;
A large black sign was on her breast that bowed,
A broad black band ran down her snow-white shroud;
That lamp she held was her own burning heart,
Whose blood-drops trickled step by step apart:
       The mystery was clear;
       Mad rage had swallowed fear.

As I came through the desert thus it was,
As I came through the desert: By the sea
She knelt and bent above that senseless me;
Those lamp-drops fell upon my white brow there,
She tried to cleanse them with her tears and hair;
She murmured words of pity, love, and woe,
She heeded not the level rushing flow:
       And mad with rage and fear,
       I stood stonebound so near.

As I came through the desert thus it was,
As I came through the desert: When the tide
Swept up to her there kneeling by my side,
She clasped that corpse-like me, and they were borne
Away, and this vile me was left forlorn;
I know the whole sea cannot quench that heart,
Or cleanse that brow, or wash those two apart:
　　　　　They love; their doom is drear,
　　　　　Yet they nor hope nor fear;
　　　　　But I, what do I here? . .
　　　　　　　James Thomson (1834-1882).

186. RELIGION IN THE SEVENTIES

MOST contemporary teaching is the product of amiable senti-
mentalism and intellectual indolence. We shrink with effem-
inate dislike from all that is severe and melancholy in the old
creeds. Our ears are too polite to be shocked by the mention
of hell. We wrap ourselves in a complacent optimism; and
the only form of faith which seems to have no chance of revival
is that which endeavoured to look things boldly in the face,
and refused to evade the more awful consequences of theology.
Religion is to be an opiate instead of a stimulant. Christianity
is to mean nothing but the Sermon on the Mount; and its
historical basis and distinctive dogmas are to be withdrawn as
much as possible from view. We are told, in substance, that
if you take away from Christianity all the peculiarities by
which it is distinguished from other religions, there will remain
a very amiable system of morality; and this is put forward in
perfectly good faith as a sufficient reason for accepting it. The
residuum thus left is explained to be identical with the very
estimable doctrine dispersed through popular novelists and
the leaders of the *Daily Telegraph*. It will do very well for
comfortable middle-class people, who have no particular reason
to be discontented with the world, and are not apt to perplex
themselves with speculative difficulties. The learned writer
who has converted the Gospels into materials for a very pretty
French romance is generally stigmatised as an infidel; but his

method is substantially that of most popular preachers. Let us all be very amiable, turn away our eyes from the doubts which beset thinkers, and the evils which drive men to revolution, and we may manage to get along with a very comfortable, picturesque, and old-established belief.

Sir Leslie Stephen (1832-1904).

187. IN THE DESERT

HE found me in the desert, and then fell
In love with my exceeding loneliness.
Coventry Patmore (1823-1896).

188. STARS SWEEP AND QUESTION NOT

. . Stars sweep and question not.   This is enough
      That life and death and joy and woe abide;
And cause and sequence, and the course of time,
      And Being's ceaseless tide,

Which, ever changing, runs, linked like a river
      By ripples following ripples, fast or slow—
The same yet not the same—from far-off fountain
      To where its waters flow

Into the seas.   These, steaming to the Sun,
      Give the lost wavelets back in cloudy fleece
To trickle down the hills, and glide again;
      Having not pause or peace.

This is enough to know, the phantasms are;
      The Heavens, Earths, Worlds, and changes changing them,
A mighty whirling wheel of strife and stress
      Which none can stay or stem.

    Pray not! the Darkness will not brighten! Ask
      Nought from the Silence, for it cannot speak!
    Vex not your mournful minds with pious pains!
      Ah! Brothers, Sisters! seek

    Nought from the helpless gods by gift and hymn,
      Nor bribe with blood, nor feed with fruits and cakes;
    Within yourselves deliverance must be sought;
      Each man his prison makes. . .

                  Sir Edwin Arnold (1832-1904).

189. ISOLATION AMONG THE ALPS

LET us look round from this wonderful pinnacle in mid air, and note one or two of the most striking elements of the scenery.

You are, in the first place, perched on a cliff, whose presence is the more felt because it is unseen. Then you are in a region over which eternal silence is brooding. Not a sound ever comes there, except the occasional fall of a splintered fragment of rock, or a layer of snow; no stream is heard trickling, and the sounds of animal life are left thousands of feet below. The most that you can hear is some mysterious noise made by the wind eddying round the gigantic rocks; sometimes a strange flapping sound, as if an unearthly flag was shaking its invisible folds in the air. The enormous tract of country over which your view extends—most of it dim and almost dissolved into air by distance—intensifies the strange influence of the silence. You feel the force of the line I have quoted from Wordsworth—

    The sleep that is among the lonely hills.

None of the travellers whom you can see crawling at your feet has the least conception of what is meant by the silent solitudes of the High Alps. To you, it is like a return to the stir of active life, when, after hours of lonely wandering, you return to hear the tinkling of the cow-bells below; to them the same sound is the ultimate limit of the habitable world.

                  Sir Leslie Stephen (1832-1904).

190. THE LOVE OF MOUNTAINS:
ROUSSEAU TO RUSKIN

THE mountains, whose worship he [i.e. Rousseau] was the first to adumbrate, if not actually to institute, were the symbols of the great natural forces free from any stain of human interference. Greed and cruelty had not stained the pure waters of his lovely lake, or dimmed the light to which his vicar points as in the early morning it grazes the edge of the mighty mountain buttresses. Whatever symbolism may be found in the Alps, suggesting emotions of awe, wonder, and softened melancholy, came unstained by the association with the vices of a complex civilisation. If poets and critics have not quite analysed the precise nature of our modern love of mountain scenery, the sentiment may at least be illustrated by a modern parallel. The most eloquent writer who, in our day, has transferred to his pages the charm of Alpine beauties, shares in many ways Rousseau's antipathy for the social order. Mr. Ruskin would explain better than anyone why the love of the sublimest scenery should be associated with a profound conviction that all things are out of joint, and that society can only be regenerated by rejecting all the achievements upon which the ordinary optimist plumes himself. After all, it is not surprising that those who are most sick of man as he is should love the regions where man seems smallest.

Sir Leslie Stephen (1832-1904).

191. THE TWO OLD BACHELORS

Two old Bachelors were living in one house:
One caught a Muffin, the other caught a Mouse.
Said he who caught the Muffin to him who caught the Mouse,—
"This happens just in time! For we've nothing in the house,

"Save a tiny slice of lemon and a teaspoonful of honey,
And what to do for dinner—since we haven't any money?
And what can we expect if we haven't any dinner,
But to lose our teeth and eyelashes and keep on growing thinner?"

Said he who caught the Mouse to him who caught the Muffin,—
"We might cook this little Mouse, if we only had some Stuffin'!
If we had but Sage and Onion we could do extremely well,
But how to get that Stuffin' it is difficult to tell!"—

Those two old Bachelors ran quickly to the town
And asked for Sage and Onion as they wandered up and down;
They borrowed two large Onions, but no Sage was to be found
In the Shops, or in the Market, or in all the Gardens round.

But some one said,—"A hill there is, a little to the north,
And to its purpledicular top a narrow way leads forth;—
And there among the rugged rocks abides an ancient Sage,—
An earnest Man, who reads all day a most perplexing page.

"Climb up, and seize him by the toes!—all studious as he sits,—
And pull him down,—and chop him into endless little bits!
Then mix him with your Onion (cut up likewise into Scraps),—
When your Stuffin' will be ready—and very good: perhaps."

Those two old Bachelors without loss of time
The nearly purpledicular crags at once began to climb;
And at the top, among the rocks, all seated in a nook,
They saw that Sage, a-reading of a most enormous book.
"You earnest Sage!" aloud they cried, "your book you've
    read enough in!—
We wish to chop you into bits to mix you into Stuffin'!"

But that old Sage looked calmly up, and with his awful book,
At those two Bachelors' bald heads a certain aim he took;—
And over crag and precipice they rolled promiscuous down,—
At once they rolled, and never stopped in lane or field or town,—
And when they reached their house, they found (besides their
    want of Stuffin'),
The Mouse had fled;—and, previously, had eaten up the Muffin.

They left their home in silence by the once convivial door,
And from that hour those Bachelors were never heard of more.

                                        Edward Lear (1812-1888).

192. HUMPTY DUMPTY'S RECITATION

In winter, when the fields are white,
I sing this song for your delight—

In spring, when woods are getting green,
I'll try and tell you what I mean.

In summer, when the days are long,
Perhaps you'll understand the song:

In autumn, when the leaves are brown,
Take pen and ink, and write it down.

I sent a message to the fish:
I told them "This is what I wish."

The little fishes of the sea,
They sent an answer back to me.

The little fishes' answer was
"We cannot do it, Sir, because—"

I sent to them again to say
"It will be better to obey."

The fishes answered with a grin,
"Why, what a temper you are in!"

I told them once, I told them twice:
They would not listen to advice.

I took a kettle large and new,
Fit for the deed I had to do.

My heart went hop, my heart went thump;
I filled the kettle at the pump.

Then someone came to me and said
"The little fishes are in bed."

I said to him, I said it plain,
"Then you must wake them up again."

I said it very loud and clear;
I went and shouted in his ear.

But he was very stiff and proud;
He said "You needn't shout so loud!"

And he was very proud and stiff;
He said "I'd go and wake them, if—"

I took a corkscrew from the shelf:
I went to wake them up myself.

And when I found the door was locked,
I pulled and pushed and kicked and knocked.

And when I found the door was shut,
I tried to turn the handle, but—

Lewis Carroll (1832-1898).

193. THE NEW VESTMENTS

THERE lived an old man in the Kingdom of Tess,
Who invented a purely original dress;
And when it was perfectly made and complete,
He opened the door, and walked into the street.

By way of a hat he'd a loaf of Brown Bread,
In the middle of which he inserted his head;—
His Shirt was made up of no end of dead Mice,
The warmth of whose skins was quite fluffy and nice;—

His Drawers were of Rabbit-skins;—so were his Shoes;—
His Stockings were skins,—but it is not known whose;—
His Waistcoat and Trowsers were made of Pork Chops;—
His Buttons were Jujubes, and Chocolate Drops;—
His Coat was all Pancakes with Jam for a border,
And a girdle of Biscuits to keep it in order;
And he wore over all, as a screen from bad weather,
A Cloak of green Cabbage-leaves stitched all together.

He had walked a short way, when he heard a great noise,
Of all sorts of Beasticles, Birdlings, and Boys;—
And from every long street and dark lane in the town
Beasts, Birdles, and Boys in a tumult rushed down.
Two Cows and a Calf ate his Cabbage-leaf Cloak;—
Four Apes seized his Girdle, which vanished like smoke;—
Three Kids ate up half of his Pancaky Coat,—
And the tails were devoured by an ancient He Goat;—
An army of Dogs in a twinkling tore *up* his
Pork Waistcoat and Trowsers to give to their Puppies;—
And while they were growling and mumbling the Chops,
Ten Boys prigged the Jujubes and Chocolate Drops.—

He tried to run back to his house, but in vain,
For scores of fat Pigs came again and again;—
They rushed out of stables and hovels and doors,—
They tore off his Stockings, his Shoes, and his Drawers;—
And now from the housetops with screechings descend,
Striped, spotted, white, black, and gray cats without end,
They jumped on his shoulders and knocked off his Hat,—
When Crows, Ducks and Hens made a mincemeat of that;—
They speedily flew at his sleeves in a trice,
And utterly tore up his Shirt of dead Mice;—
They swallowed the last of his Shirt with a squall,—
Whereon he ran home with no clothes on at all.

And he said to himself as he bolted the door,
"I will not wear a similar dress any more,
Any more, any more, any more, never more!"

                                        Edward Lear (1812-1888).

194. INCIDENTS IN THE LIFE OF MY UNCLE ARLY

O MY agèd Uncle Arly!
Sitting on a heap of Barley
   Thro' the silent hours of night,—
Close beside a leafy thicket:—
On his nose there was a Cricket,—
In his hat a Railway-Ticket;—
   (But his shoes were far too tight).

Long ago, in youth, he squander'd
All his goods away, and wander'd
   To the Tiniskoop-hills afar.
There on golden sunsets blazing,
Every evening found him gazing,—
Singing—"Orb! you're quite amazing!
   How I wonder what you are!"

Like the ancient Medes and Persians,
Always by his own exertions
   He subsisted on those hills;—
Whiles,—by teaching children spelling,—
Or at times by merely yelling,—
Or at intervals by selling
   "Propter's Nicodemus Pills."

Later, in his morning rambles
He perceived the moving brambles
   Something square and white disclose;—
'Twas a First-class Railway-Ticket;
But, on stooping down to pick it
Off the ground,—a pea-green Cricket
   Settled on my uncle's Nose.

Never—never more,—oh! never,
Did that Cricket leave him ever,—
   Dawn or evening, day or night;—

Clinging as a constant treasure,—
Chirping with a cheerious measure,—
Wholly to my uncle's pleasure,—
    (Though his shoes were far too tight).

So for three-and-forty winters,
Till his shoes were worn to splinters,
    All those hills he wanders o'er,—
Sometimes silent;—sometimes yelling;—
Till he came to Borley-Melling,
Near his old ancestral dwelling;—
    (But his shoes were far too tight).

On a little heap of Barley
Died my agèd uncle Arly,
    And they buried him one night;—
Close beside the leafy thicket;—
There,—his hat and Railway-Ticket;—
There,—his ever-faithful Cricket;—
    (But his shoes were far too tight).

                        Edward Lear (1812-1888).

195. LIMERICK TOWN

THERE, I've got you, Philip Desmond, standing in the market-
    place,
'Mid the farmers and the corn sacks, and the hay in either
    space,
Near the fruit stalls, and the women knitting socks and selling
    lace.

There is High Street up the hillside, twenty shops on either
    side,
Queer, old-fashioned, dusky High Street, here so narrow, there
    so wide,
Whips and harness, saddles, sign-boards, hanging out in quiet
    pride.

                            H

Up and down the noisy highway, how the market people go!
Country girls in Turkey kerchiefs—poppies moving to and fro—
Frieze-clad fathers, great in buttons, brass and watch-seals all
    a-show.

Merry, merry are their voices, Philip Desmond, unto me,
Dear the mellow Munster accent, with its intermittent glee;
Dear the blue cloaks, and the grey coats, things I long have
    longed to see.

Even the curses, adjurations, in my senses sound like rhyme,
And the great, rough-throated laughter of that peasant in his
    prime,
Winking from the grassbound cart-shaft, brings me back the
    other time.

Not a soul, observe you, knows me, not a friend a hand will
    yield,
Would they know, if to the landmarks all around them I
    appealed?
Know me! If I died this minute, dig for me the Potter's
    field! . . .

Come, I want a storm of gossip, pleasant jests and ancient chat;
At that dusky doorway yonder my grandfather smoked and sat,
Tendrils of the wind-blown clover sticking in his broad-leafed
    hat.

There he sat and read the paper. Fancy I recall him now!
All the shadow of the house front slanting up from knee to
    brow;
Critic he of far convulsions, keen-eyed judge of sheep and
    cow. . . .

Hither, with my hand in her hand, came my mother many a
    day,
She, the old man's pet and darling, at his side or far away,
And her chair was near the window, half in square and half
    in bay.

Oh, my mother, my pure-hearted, dear to me as child and
    wife,
Ever earnest, ever toilsome in this quick, unresting strife,
Ever working out the mission of a silent, noble life, . . .

If I write this rhyming gossip all about the ancient street,
'Tis because the very footpaths were made blessed by your
    feet.
Dear, pale mother! writing of you, how my heart and pulses
    beat!

Beat and beat with warm convulsions, and my eyes are thick
    with tears,
And your low song by my cradle sounds again within my ears.
Here's the highway, which you trod once, I thrice filled with
    childish fears.

Rolled the waggons, swore the carters, outside in the crowded
    street,
Horses reared, and cattle stumbled, dogs barked high from loads
    of wheat;
But inside the room was pleasant, and the air with thyme was
    sweet.

Others now are in their places, honest folk who know us not;
Do I chafe at the transition? Philip, 'tis the common lot—
Do your duty, live your lifetime, say your prayers, and be
    forgot.

                John Francis O'Donnell (1837-1874).

196. AN EARLY MORNING

  . . Wet was the grass beneath our tread,
      Thick-dewed the bramble by the way;
   The lichen had a lovelier red,
      The elder-flower a fairer grey. . .

         John Francis O'Donnell (1837-1874).

197. A SINGLE SHARP IMPRESSION

At first sight experience seems to bury us under a flood of external objects, pressing upon us with a sharp importunate reality, calling us out of ourselves in a thousand forms of action. But when reflection begins to act upon those objects they are dissipated under its influence; the cohesive force is suspended like a trick of magic; each object is loosed into a group of impressions,—colour, odour, texture,—in the mind of the observer. And if we continue to dwell on this world, not of objects in the solidity with which language invests them, but of impressions unstable, flickering, inconsistent, which burn and are extinguished with our consciousness of them, it contracts still further; the whole scope of observation is dwarfed to the narrow chamber of the individual mind. Experience, already reduced to a swarm of impressions, is ringed round for each one of us by that thick wall of personality through which no real voice has ever pierced on its way to us, or from us to that which we can only conjecture to be without. Every one of these impressions is the impression of the individual in his isolation, each mind keeping as a solitary prisoner its own dream of a world.

Analysis goes a step further still, and tells us that those impressions of the individual to which, for each one of us, experience dwindles down, are in perpetual flight; that each of them is limited by time, and that as time is infinitely divisible, each of them is infinitely divisible also; all that is actual in it being a single moment, gone while we are trying to apprehend it, of which it may ever be more truly said that it has ceased to be than that it is. To such a tremulous wisp constantly reforming itself on the stream, to a single sharp impression, with a sense in it, a relic more or less fleeting, of such moments gone by, what is *real* in our life fines itself down. It is with the movement, the passage and dissolution of impressions, images, sensations, that analysis leaves off,—that continual vanishing away, that strange perpetual weaving and unweaving of ourselves.

Walter Pater (1839-1894).

198. THE SEA-POPPY

A POPPY grows upon the shore,
Bursts her twin cup in summer late:
Her leaves are glaucous-green and hoar,
Her petals yellow, delicate.

Oft to her cousins turns her thought,
In wonder if they care that she
Is fed with spray for dew, and caught
By every gale that sweeps the sea.

She has no lovers like the red,
That dances with the noble corn:
Her blossoms on the waves are shed,
Where she stands shivering and forlorn.

Robert Bridges (1844-1930).

199. CHRISTMAS IN LONDON

THE year lay dying in the east,
The Christmas chimes had swung and ceast,
The Christmas light died at the feast.

Down looked the moon, but looked no more
Upon the silent river shore,
Or on the hilltops faint and hoar,

Down into London's struggling gloom,
Down on the city of the Doom,
A scarf of cloud around her bloom.

Below the bridge the black ships lay,
The thin lamps gleamed from quay to quay,
The thin masts trembled in the grey. . .

John Francis O'Donnell (1837-1874).

200. SLOW FIELDS OF SUNSHINE

. . He looking landward from the brow of some great seacape's
    head,
Bray or Ben-Edar—sees beneath, in silent pageant grand,
Slow fields of sunshine spread o'er fields of rich, corn-
    bearing land;
Red glebe and meadow-margin green commingling to the
    view
With yellow stubble, browning woods, and upland tracts
    of blue;—
Then, sated with the pomp of fields, turns, seawards, to
    the verge
Where, mingling with the murmuring wash made by the
    far-down surge,
Come up the clangorous song of birds unseen, that, low
    beneath,
Poised off the rock, ply underfoot; and, 'mid the blossoming
    heath,
And mint-sweet herb that loves the ledge rare-air'd, at ease
    reclined,
Surveys the wide pale-heaving floor crisped by a curling
    wind;
With all its shifting, shadowy belts, and chasing scopes of
    green,
Sun-strown, foam-freckled, sail-embossed, and blackening
    squalls between,
And slant, cerulean-skirted showers that with a drowsy
    sound,
Heard inward, of ebullient waves, stalk all the horizon
    round;
And haply, being a citizen just 'scaped from some disease
That long has held him sick indoors, now, in the brine-fresh
    breeze,
Health-salted bathes; and says, the while he breathes
    reviving bliss,
"I am not good enough, oh God, nor pure enough for
    this!" . .

                         Sir Samuel Ferguson (1810-1886).

201. THE SEASIDE

In and Out of the Season

In summer-time it was a paradise
Of mountain, frith, and bay, and shining sand;
Our outward rowers sang towards the land,
Follow'd by waving hands and happy cries:
By the full flood the groups no longer roam;
And when, at ebb, the glistening beach grows wide,
No barefoot children race into the foam,
But passive jellies wait the turn of tide.
Like some forsaken lover, lingering there,
The boatman stands; the maidens trip no more
With loosen'd locks; far from the billows' roar
The Mauds and Maries knot their tresses fair,
Where not a foam-flake from th' enamour'd shore
Comes down the sea-wind on the golden hair.
Charles Tennyson Turner (1808-1879).

202. EGGS AND SERMONS

A great orator must use the language of his day; he cannot stop to pick and choose his words, and see that he has in every case the authority of Addison or Johnson's Dictionary. If preaching is bad at the present day, it is because it generally resembles an egg-dance, where the performer is afraid of coming into collision at every step with one of the Thirty-nine Articles. *Sir Leslie Stephen* (1832-1904).

203. FLOWERS

The blue wheat-acre is underneath
And the braided ear breaks out of the sheath,
The ear in milk, lush the sash,
And crush-silk poppies aflash,
The blood-gush blade-gash

Flame-rash rudred
Bud shelling or broad-shed
Tatter-tassel-tangled and dingle-a-dangled
Dandy-hung dainty head.

.   .   .   .   .

And down . . . the furrow dry
Sunspurge and oxeye
And lace-leaved lovely
Foam-tuft fumitory.

           Gerard Manley Hopkins (1844-1889).

204. THE CUCKOO

REPEAT that, repeat,
Cuckoo, bird, and open ear wells, heart-springs, delightfully
    sweet,
With a ballad, with a ballad, a rebound
Off trundled timber and scoops of the hillside ground,
    hollow hollow hollow ground:
The while landscape flushes on a sudden at a sound.

           Gerard Manley Hopkins (1844-1889).

205. A LETTER FROM A GIRL TO HER OWN OLD AGE

LISTEN, and when thy hand this paper presses,
O time-worn woman, think of her who blesses
What thy thin fingers touch, with her caresses.

O mother, for the weight of years that break thee!
O daughter, for slow Time must yet awake thee,
And from the changes of my heart must make thee.

O fainting traveller, morn is grey in heaven.
Dost thou remember how the clouds were driven?
And are they calm about the fall of even?

Pause near the ending of thy long migration,
For this one sudden hour of desolation
Appeals to one hour of thy meditation.

Suffer, O silent one, that I remind thee
Of the great hills that stormed the sky behind thee,
Of the wild winds of power that have resigned thee.

Know that the mournful plain where thou must wander
Is but a grey and silent world, but ponder
The misty mountains of the morning yonder.

Listen:—the mountain winds with rain were fretting,
And sudden gleams the mountain-tops besetting.
I cannot let thee fade to death, forgetting.

What part of this wild heart of mine I know not
Will follow with thee where the great winds blow not,
And where the young flowers of the mountain grow not.

         .   .   .   .   .   .

I have not writ this letter of divining
To make a glory of thy silent pining,
A triumph of thy mute and strange declining.

Only one youth, and the bright life is shrouded.
Only one morning, and the day was clouded.
And one old age with all regrets is crowded.

O hush, O hush! Thy tears my words are steeping.
O hush, hush, hush! So full, the fount of weeping?
Poor eyes, so quickly moved, so near to sleeping?

Pardon the girl; such strange desires beset her.
Poor woman, lay aside the mournful letter
That breaks thy heart; the one who wrote, forget her:

H*

The one who now thy faded features guesses,
With filial fingers thy grey hair caresses,
With morning tears thy mournful twilight blesses.

Alice Meynell (1847-1922).

206. WHISTLER versus RUSKIN: BURNE-JONES GIVES EVIDENCE

[*Ruskin's libel*: "For Mr. Whistler's own sake, no less than for the protection of the purchaser, Sir Coutts Lindsay ought not to have admitted works into the gallery in which the ill-educated conceit of the artist so nearly approached the aspect of wilful imposture. I have seen, and heard much, of cockney impudence before now; but never expected to hear a coxcomb ask two hundred guineas for flinging a pot of paint in the public's face."]

Evidence was then called on behalf of the defendant. . . . Mr. Edward Burne-Jones called. . . . "I am a painter, and have devoted about twenty years to the study. I have painted various works, including the 'Days of Creation' and 'Venus's Mirror,' both of which were exhibited at the Grosvenor Gallery in 1877. I have also exhibited 'Deferentia,' 'Fides,' 'St. George,' and 'Sybil.' I have one work 'Merlin and Vivian,' now being exhibited in Paris. In my opinion complete finish ought to be the object of all artists. A picture ought not to fall short of what has been for ages considered complete finish."

Mr. BOWEN (for the defendant): "Do you see any art quality in that nocturne, Mr. Jones?"

Mr. JONES: "Yes. . . . I must speak the truth, you know." . . . (*Emotion*)

Mr. BOWEN: . . . "Yes. Well, Mr. Jones, what quality do you see in it?"

Mr. JONES: "Colour. It has fine colour, and atmosphere."

Mr. BOWEN: "Ah. Well, do you consider detail and composition essential to a work of Art?"

Mr. JONES: "Most certainly I do."

Mr. BOWEN: "Then what detail and composition do you find in this nocturne?"

Mr. JONES: "Absolutely none."

Mr. BOWEN: "Do you think two hundred guineas a large price for that picture?"

Mr. JONES: "Yes. When you think of the amount of earnest work done for a smaller sum."

Examination continued: "Does it show the finish of a complete work of Art?"

"Not in any sense whatever. The picture representing a night scene on Battersea Bridge is good in colour, but bewildering in form; and it has no composition and detail. A day or a day and a half seems a reasonable time within which to paint it. It shows no finish—it is simply a sketch. The nocturne in black and gold has not the merit of the other two pictures, and it would be impossible to call it a serious work of art. Mr. Whistler's picture is only one of the thousand failures to paint night. The picture is not worth two hundred guineas."

From the report in " The Gentle Art of Making Enemies."

207. WITH THE DAWN

HUSBAND

WHY have you risen, to stand with naked feet
And thin robe stirring in the airs of night,
Looking from the casement?

WIFE

It is sweet
To view upon the broad sea, glimmering white,
Sails, in the low moonlight.

HUSBAND

I dream'd that you were lost to me afar,
And I had just recovered you once more.
Why linger you?—

WIFE

To watch that last large star
Sparkle our cradled child's calm slumber o'er.
Soft as the little wave that sweet and frore
Rises and sinks upon the sandy shore,—
 He breathes; and on his face there comes a smile,
 Just as the dawn's pale gold has touched, the while,
Yon faint cloud cradled on the distant deep.
 The calm sea-level turns from white to rose;
 And, as the space a richer glory grows,
The earliest bird sings faintly far away
 Upon the poplar by the ocean steep.

HUSBAND

Awake him not, O dear one, till 'tis day;
 To be alive, and suffer not, is sleep.

Thomas Caulfield Irwin.

208. THE BLEACHING AND THE FIRE

THE spiritualist is satisfied in seeing the sensuous elements escape from his conceptions; his interest grows, as the dyed garment bleaches in the keener air. But the artist steeps his thought again and again into the fire of colour.

Walter Pater (1839-1894).

209. THE SOUL

THE Soul
Sucking its life from the deep breasts of love.

Coventry Patmore (1823-1896).

210. ARBOR VITAE

WITH honeysuckle, over-sweet, festoon'd;
With bitter ivy bound;
Terraced with funguses unsound;
Deform'd with many a boss
And closed scar, o'ercushion'd deep with moss;
Bunch'd all about with pagan mistletoe;
And thick with nests of the hoarse bird
That talks, but understands not his own word;
Stands, and so stood a thousand years ago,
A single tree.
Thunder has done its worst among its twigs,
Where the great crest yet blackens, never pruned,
But in its heart, alway
Ready to push new verdurous boughs, whene'er
The rotting saplings near it fall and leave it air,
Is all antiquity and no decay.
Rich, though rejected by the forest-pigs,
Its fruit, beneath whose rough, concealing rind
They that will break it find
Heart-succouring savour of each several meat,
And kernell'd drink of brain-renewing power,
With bitter condiment and sour,
And sweet economy of sweet,
And odours that remind
Of haunts of childhood and a different day.
Beside this tree,
Praising no Gods nor blaming, sans a wish,
Sits, Tartar-like, the Time's civility,
And eats its dead-dog off a golden dish.
                    Coventry Patmore (1823-1896).

211. PAIN IN ALL LOVE

FROM the small life that loves with tooth and nail
To the thorn'd brow that makes the heavens pale.
                    Coventry Patmore (1823-1896).

212. ENTRIES IN A JOURNAL

A STORY has been told me of a doctor at Maiden Newton, who
attended a woman who could not pay him. He said he would
take the dead baby in payment. He had it, and it was kept on
his mantelpiece in a large glass jar in spirits, which stained the
body brown. The doctor, who was a young man, afterwards
married and used his wife badly, insisting on keeping the other
woman's dead baby on his mantelpiece.

1876.

I sometimes look upon all things in inanimate Nature as
pensive mutes.

1877.

September 28. An object or mark raised or made by man
on a scene is worth ten times any such formed by unconscious
Nature. Hence clouds, mists, and mountains are unimportant
beside the wear on a threshold, or the print of a hand.

1877.

Thomas Hardy (1840-1928).

213. *From* "THE LIGHT OF ASIA"

i

The Pleasure House of the young Buddha

. . Northwards soared
The stainless ramps of huge Himâla's wall
Ranged in white ranks against the blue—untrod,
Infinite, wonderful—whose uplands vast,
And lifted universe of crest and crag,
Shoulder and shelf, green slope and icy horn,
Riven ravine, and splintered precipice
Led climbing thought higher and higher, until
It seemed to stand in heaven and speak with gods.
Beneath the snows dark forests spread, sharp-laced
With leaping cataracts and veiled with clouds:
Lower grew rose-oaks and the great fir groves
Where echoed pheasant's call and panther's cry,

Clatter of wild sheep on the stones, and scream
Of circling eagles: under these the plain
Gleamed like a praying-carpet at the foot
Of those divinest altars. Fronting this
The builders set the bright pavilion up,
Fair-planted on the terraced hill, with towers
On either flank and pillared cloisters round.
Its beams were carved with stories of old time—
Radha and Krishna and the sylvan girls—
Sita and Hanuman and Draupadi;
And on the middle porch God Ganesha,
With disc and hook—to bring wisdom and wealth—
Propitious sate, wreathing his sidelong trunk.
By winding ways of garden and of court
The inner gate was reached, of marble wrought,
White, with pink veins; the lintel lazuli,
The threshold alabaster, and the doors
Sandal-wood, cut in pictured panelling;
Whereby to lofty halls and shadowy bowers
Passed the delighted foot, on stately stairs,
Through latticed galleries, 'neath painted roofs
And clustering columns, where cool fountains—fringed
With lotus and nelumbo—danced; and fish
Gleamed through their crystal, scarlet, gold, and blue.
Great-eyed gazelles in sunny alcoves browsed
The blown red roses; birds of rainbow wing
Fluttered among the palms; doves, green and grey,
Built their safe nests on gilded cornices;
Over the shining pavements peacocks drew
The splendours of their trains, sedately watched
By milk-white herons and the small house-owls.
The plum-necked parrots swung from fruit to fruit;
The yellow sunbirds whirred from bloom to bloom,
The timid lizards on the lattice basked
Fearless, the squirrels ran to feed from hand;
For all was peace: the shy black snake, that gives
Fortune to households, sunned his sleepy coils
Under the moon-flowers, where the musk-deer played,
And brown-eyed monkeys chattered to the crows.

And all this House of love was peopled fair
With sweet attendance, so that in each part
With lovely sights were gentle faces found,
Soft speech and willing service; each one glad
To gladden, pleased at pleasure, proud to obey;
Till gilded life beguiled, like a smooth stream
Banked by perpetual flow'rs, Yasôdhara
Queen of the enchanting Court.

ii

The young Buddha's gift to Yasôdhara

"Is there a gift for me?" she asked, and smiled.
"The gifts are gone," the Prince replied, "yet take
This for amends, dear sister, of whose grace
Our happy city boasts"; therewith he loosed
The emerald necklet from his throat, and clasped
Its green beads round her dark and silk-soft waist;
And their eyes mixed, and from the look sprang love.

iii

The Girls of the Pleasure House

Within—

Where the moon glittered through the lace-worked stone,
Lighting the walls of pearl-shell and the floors
Paved with veined marble—softly fell her beams
On such rare company of Indian girls,
It seemed some chamber sweet in Paradise
Where Devîs rested. All the chosen ones
Of Prince Siddârtha's pleasure-home were there,
The brightest and most faithful of the Court;
Each form so lovely in the peace of sleep,
That you had said "This is the pearl of all!"
Save that beside her or beyond her lay
Fairer and fairer, till the pleasured gaze
Roamed o'er that feast of beauty as it roams
From gem to gem in some great goldsmith-work,
Caught by each colour till the next is seen.

With careless grace they lay, their soft brown limbs
Part hidden, part revealed; their glossy hair
Bound back with gold or flowers, or flowing loose
In black waves down the shapely nape and neck.
Lulled into pleasant dreams by happy toils,
They slept, no wearier than jewelled birds
Which sing and love all day, then under wing
Fold head, till morn bids sing and love again.
Lamps of chased silver swinging from the roof
In silver chains, and fed with perfumed oils,
Made with the moonbeams tender lights and shades,
Whereby were seen the perfect lines of grace,
The bosom's placid heave, the soft stained palms
Drooping or clasped, the faces fair and dark,
The great arched brows, the parted lips, the teeth
Like pearls a merchant picks to make a string,
The satin-lidded eyes, with lashes dropped
Sweeping the delicate cheeks, the rounded wrists,
The smooth small feet with bells and bangles decked,
Tinkling low music where some sleeper moved,
Breaking her smiling dream of some new dance
Praised by the Prince, some magic ring to find,
Some fairy love-gift. Here one lay full-length
Her vina by her cheek, and in its strings
The little fingers still all interlaced
As when the last notes of her light song played
Those radiant eyes to sleep, and sealed her own.
Another slumbered folding in her arms
A desert-antelope, its slender head
Buried with black-sloped horns between her breasts,
Soft-nestling; it was eating—when both drowsed—
Red roses, and her loosening hand still held
A rose half-mumbled, while a rose-leaf curled
Between the deer's lips. Here two friends had dozed
Together, weaving môgra-buds, which bound
Their sister-sweetness in a starry chain,
Linking them limb to limb and heart to heart,
One pillowed on the blossoms, one on her.
Another, ere she slept, was stringing stones

To make a necklet—agate, onyx, sard,
Coral, and moonstone—round her wrist it gleamed
A coil of splendid colour, while she held,
Unthreaded yet, the bead to close it up—
Green turkis, carved with golden gods and scripts.
Lulled by the cadence of the garden stream,
Thus lay they on the clustered carpets, each
A girlish rose with shut leaves, waiting dawn
To open and make daylight beautiful.
This was the ante-chamber of the Prince;
But at the purdah's fringe the sweetest slept—
Gunga and Gotami—chief ministers
In that still House of love.

iv

Buddha and the Tigress

For aye so piteous was the Master's heart
To all that breathe this breath of fleeting life,
Yoked in one fellowship of joys and pains,
That it is written in the holy books
How, in an ancient age—when Buddha wore
A Brahman's form, dwelling upon the rock
Named Munda, by the village of Dâlidd—
Drought withered all the land: the young rice died
Ere it could hide a quail; in forest glades
A fierce sun sucked the pools; grasses and herbs
Sickened, and all the woodland creatures fled
Scattering for sustenance. At such a time,
Between the hot walls of a nullah, stretched
On naked stones, our Lord spied, as he passed,
A starving tigress. Hunger in her orbs
Glared with green flame; her dry tongue lolled a span
Beyond the gasping jaws and shrivelled jowl:
Her painted hide hung wrinkled on her ribs,
As when between the rafters sinks a thatch
Rotten with rains; and at the poor lean dugs
Two cubs, whining with famine, tugged and sucked,
Mumbling those milkless teats which rendered nought;

While she, their gaunt dam, licked full motherly
The clamorous twins, and gave her flank to them
With moaning throat, and love stronger than want,
Softening the first of that wild cry wherewith
She laid her famished muzzle to the sand
And roared a savage thunder-peal of woe.
Seeing which bitter strait, and heeding nought
Save the immense compassion of a Buddh,
Our Lord bethought: "There is no other way
To help this murderess of the woods but one.
By sunset these will die, having no meat:
There is no living heart will pity her,
Bloody with ravin, lean for lack of blood.
Lo! if I feed her, who shall lose but I,
And how can love lose doing of its kind
Even to the uttermost?" So saying, Buddh
Silently laid aside sandals and staff,
His sacred thread, turban, and cloth, and came
Forth from behind the milk-bush on the sand,
Saying, "Ho! mother, here is meat for thee!"
Whereat the perishing beast yelped hoarse and shrill,
Sprang from her cubs, and, hurling to the earth
That willing victim, had her feast of him
With all the crooked daggers of her claws
Rending his flesh, and all her yellow fangs
Bathed in his blood: the great cat's burning breath
Mixed with the last sigh of such fearless love.

v

Buddha (Prince Siddârtha) returns to his father's Kingdom

Then meekly bowed his head and spake our Lord
Before the people, "Surely I shall go!
It is my duty as it was my will;
Let no man miss to render reverence
To those who lend him life, whereby comes means
To live and die no more, but safe attain
Blissful Nirvâna, if ye keep the Law,
Purging past wrongs and adding nought thereto,

Complete in love and lovely charities.
Let the King know and let the Princess hear
I take the way forewith." This told, the folk
Of white Kapilavastu and its fields
Made ready for the entrance of their Prince.
At the south gate a bright pavilion rose
With flower-wreathed pillars, and the walls of silk
Wrought on their red and green with woven gold.
Also the roads were laid with scented boughs
Of neem and mango, and full mussuks shed
Sandal and jasmine on the dust; and flags
Fluttered; and on the day when he should come
It was ordained how many elephants—
With silver howdahs and their tusks gold-tipped—
Should wait beyond the ford, and where the drums
Should boom "Siddârtha cometh!" where the lords
Should light and worship, and the dancing girls
Where they should strew their flowers, with dance and song,
So that the steed he rode might tramp knee-deep
In rose and balsam, and the ways be fair;
While the town rang with music and high joy.
This was ordained, and all men's ears were pricked
Dawn after dawn to catch the first drum's beat
Announcing, "Now he cometh!"

                  But it fell—

Eager to be before—Yasôdhara
Rode in her litter to the city-walls
Where soared the bright pavilion. All around
A beauteous garden smiled—Nigrôdha named—
Shaded with bel-trees and the green-plumed dates,
New-trimmed and gay with winding walks and banks
Of fruits and flowers; for the southern road
Skirted its lawns, on this hand leaf and bloom,
On that the suburb-huts where base-borns dwelt
Outside the gates, a patient folk and poor,
Whose touch for Kshatriya and the priest of Brahm
Were sore defilement. Yet those, too, were quick
With expectation, rising ere the dawn
To peer along the road, to climb the trees

At far-off trumpet of some elephant,
Or stir of temple-drum; and when none came,
Busied with lowly chares to please the Prince;
Sweeping their door-stones, setting forth their flags,
Stringing the fluted fig-leaves into chains,
New furbishing the Lingam, decking new
Yesterday's faded arch of boughs, but aye
Questioning wayfarers if any noise
Be on the road of great Siddârtha. These
The Princess marked with lovely languid eyes,
Watching, as they, the southward plain, and bent
Like them to listen if the passers gave
News of the path. So fell it she beheld
One slow approaching with his head close shorn,
A yellow cloth over his shoulder cast,
Girt as the hermits are, and in his hand
An earthen bowl, shaped melonwise, the which
Meekly at each hut-door he held a space,
Taking the granted dole with gentle thanks
And all as gently passing where none gave.
Two followed him wearing the yellow robe,
But he who bore the bowl so lordly seemed,
So reverend, and with such a passage moved,
With so commanding presence filled the air,
With such sweet eyes of holiness smote all,
That, as they reached him alms the givers gazed
Awestruck upon his face, and some bent down
In worship, and some ran to fetch fresh gifts
Grieved to be poor; till slowly, group by group,
Children and men and women drew behind
Into his steps, whispering with covered lips,
"Who is he? who? when looked a Rishi thus?"
But as he came with quiet footfall on
Nigh the pavilion, lo! the silken door
Lifted, and, all unveiled, Yasôdhara
Stood in his path crying, "Siddârtha! Lord!"
With wide eyes streaming and with close-clasped hands,
Then sobbing fell upon his feet, and lay.

                              Sir Edwin Arnold (1832-1904).

214. SPRING

BLOW, summer wind, from yonder ocean blow
Along the wild sea banks and grasses drear,
And loamy shores, where mosses brown and sere
And pale pinks in the sandy ridges grow;
Float round yon promontory in the brine,
Whose stretching arm in deepest azure lies,
Where quiet browse the heavy-uddered kine
By rock and shining shallow, grey and clear;
And fill, this listless hour, the dreamy ear
With thy scarce toned and wordless harmonies:
For here with Nature will I rest, and please
My heart with sweetest fancies all the noon,
Until the limpid crescent of the moon
Lights the blue east above the evening trees.

Thomas Caulfield Irwin.

215. LOVE AND DEATH

WITHIN a wood I strayed at sunset hour,
The leaves were still and red upon the ground,
The trees themselves stood steadfast as a tower
That has survived a thousand things around,
The iris here and there in Autumn seed
Was brighter than in Spring; I saw no bird,
Nor noted breathing thing; all hushed indeed
Was this sad grove; whilst deep below I heard
The sea, with dull monotony of moan,
And saw the white foam die on marble strand;
Mountain and sky far up above looked lone,
Whilst by a brook, winged arrows in his hand,
Sat Love the imperishable one,—and near
The last grey mortal of the year.

J. W. Inchbold (1830-1888).

216. A SONG OF FAITH FORSWORN

TAKE back your suit.
It came when I was weary and distraught
With hunger.   Could I guess the fruit you brought?
I ate in mere desire of any food,
Nibbled its edge and nowhere found it good.
Take back your suit.

Take back your love,
It is a bird poached from my neighbour's wood:
Its wings are wet with tears, its beak with blood.
'Tis a strange fowl with feathers like a crow:
Death's raven, it may be, for all we know.
Take back your love.

Take back your gifts.
False is the hand that gave them; and the mind
That planned them, as a hawk spread in the wind
To poise and snatch the trembling mouse below
To ruin where it dares—and then to go.
Take back your gifts.

Take back your vows.
Elsewhere you trimmed and taught these lamps to burn;
You bring them stale and dim to serve my turn.
You lit those candles in another shrine,
Guttered and cold you offer them on mine.
Take back your vows.

Take back your words.
What is your love?   Leaves on a woodland plain,
Where some are running and where some remain:
What is your faith?   Straws on a mountain height,
Dancing like demons on Walpurgis night.
Take back your words.

Take back your lies.
Have them again: they wore a rainbow face,
Hollow with sin and leprous with disgrace;
Their tongue was like a mellow turret bell
To toll hearts burning into wide-lipped hell.
Take back your lies.

Take back your kiss.
Shall I be meek, and lend my lips again
To let this adder daub them with his stain?
Shall I turn cheek to answer, when I hate?
You kiss like Judas in the garden gate!
Take back your kiss.

Take back delight,
A paper boat launched on a heaving pool
To please a child, and folded by a fool;
The wild elms roared: it sailed—a yard or more.
Out went our ship but never came to shore.
Take back delight.

Take back your wreath.
Has it done service on a fairer brow?
Fresh, was it folded round her bosom snow?
Her cast-off weed my breast will never wear:
Your word is "love me." My reply "despair!"
Take back your wreath.

Lord de Tabley (1835-1895).

217. SPRING AND FALL:

To a young child

Márgarét, are you gríeving
Over Goldengrove unleaving?
Léaves, líke the things of man, you
With your fresh thoughts care for, can you?
Áh! ás the heart grows older
It will come to such sights colder

By and by, nor spare a sigh
Though worlds of wanwood leafmeal lie;
And yet you wíll weep and know why.
Now no matter, child, the name:
Sórrow's spríngs áre the same.
Nor mouth had, no nor mind, expressed
What heart heard of, ghost guessed:
It ís the blight man was born for,
It is Margaret you mourn for.

> *Gerard Manley Hopkins* (1844-1889).

218. DEATH AND VICTORY

HE wept, he wept: there came a wind
Out of the cloud heavy and blind:
  The angel of human thoughts had joy—
And water dropped from the cloud's hair,
The sun shone on the green leaves fair,
The wood-side sparkled everywhere.

He moaned: great pain weighed down his eyes;
His knees were bent, thick came his sighs:
  The angel of human wounds had joy—
The sad Earth was bemired with rain,
The ditches rose and stormed the plain,
The eddying wind blew round again.

He died: his head to earth was bowed,
Then sudden lifted to the cloud:
  The angel of broken wings had joy—
The sun grew strong in the thick air,
The rainbow fled; half heaven was bare,
The storm went off with wings aflare.

> *R. W. Dixon* (1833-1900).

219. THE DESIRE OF BEAUTY, THE LOVE OF ART FOR ART'S SAKE

WHILE all melts under our feet, we may well catch at any exquisite passion, or any contribution to knowledge that seems, by a lifted horizon, to set the spirit free for a moment, or any stirring of the senses, strange dyes, strange flowers, and curious odours, or work of the artist's hands, or the face of one's friend. Not to discriminate every moment some passionate attitude in those about us, and in the brilliance of their gifts some tragic dividing of forces on their ways, is on this short day of frost and sun, to sleep before evening. With this sense of the splendour of our experience and of its awful brevity, gathering all we are into one desperate effort to see and touch, we shall hardly have time to make theories about the things we see and touch. What we have to do is to be for ever curiously testing new opinions and courting new impressions, never acquiescing in a facile orthodoxy of Comte or of Hegel, or of our own. Theories, religious or philosophical ideas, as points of view, instruments of criticism, may help us to gather up what might otherwise pass unregarded by us. *La philosophie, c'est la microscope de la pensée.* The theory, or idea, or system, which requires of us the sacrifice of any part of this experience, in consideration of some interest into which we cannot enter, or some abstract morality we have not identified with ourselves, or what is only conventional, has no real claim upon us.

One of the most beautiful places in the writings of Rousseau is that in the sixth book of the *Confessions*, where he describes the awakening in him of the literary sense. An undefinable taint of death had always clung about him, and now in early manhood he believed himself stricken by mortal disease. He asked himself how he might make as much as possible of the interval that remained; and he was not biassed by anything in his previous life when he decided it must be by intellectual excitement, which he found in the clear, fresh writings of Voltaire. Well, we are all *condamnés*, as Victor Hugo says: *les hommes sont tous condamnés à morte avec des sursis indéfinis*: we have an interval, and then our place knows us no more. Some spend this interval in listlessness, some in high passions, the wisest in art and song. For our one chance is in expending that interval, in getting as many pulsations as possible into the given time. High passions give one this quickened sense of life, ecstasy and sorrow of love, political or religious enthusiasm, or the "enthusiasm of humanity." Only, be sure it is passion, that it does yield you this fruit of a quickened, multiplied consciousness. Of this wisdom, the poetic passion, the desire of beauty, the love of art for art's sake has most; for art comes to you professing frankly to give nothing but the brightest quality to your moments as they pass, and simply for those moments' sake.

Walter Pater (1839-1894).

PART FIVE: EIGHTIES AND NINETIES

One petal of a blood-red tulip pressed
Between the pages of a Baudelaire. . .

Arthur Symons.

Deus est Deus pauperum.

William Morris.

Feed the budding rose of boyhood with the drainage of your sewer.

Alfred, Lord Tennyson.

All can be set right by calomel.

Sir W. S. Gilbert.

220. "FRATER AVE ATQUE VALE"

Row us out from Desenzano, to your Sirmione row!
So they row'd, and there we landed—"O venusta Sirmio!"
There to me thro' all the groves of olive in the summer glow,
There beneath the Roman ruin where the purple flowers grow,
Came that "Ave atque Vale" of the Poet's hopeless woe,
Tenderest of Roman poets nineteen hundred years ago,
"Frater Ave atque Vale"—as we wander'd to and fro
Gazing at the Lydian laughter of the Garda-lake below
Sweet Catullus's all-but-island, olive-silvery Sirmio!

Alfred Tennyson (1809-1892).

221. TO VIRGIL

Written at the request of the Mantuans for the
Nineteenth Centenary of Virgil's Death

I

Roman Virgil, thou that singest
    Ilion's lofty temples robed in fire,
Ilion falling, Rome arising,
    wars, and filial faith and Dido's pyre;

II

Landscape-lover, lord of language
    more than he that sang the Works and Days,
All the chosen coin of fancy
    flashing out from many a golden phrase;

III

Thou that singest wheat and woodland,
    tilth and vineyard, hive and horse and herd;
All the charm of all the Muses
    often flowering in a lonely word;

IV

Poet of the happy Tityrus
    piping underneath his beechen bowers;
Poet of the poet-satyr
    whom the laughing shepherd bound with
        flowers;

V

Chanter of the Pollio, glorying
    in the blissful years again to be,
Summers of the snakeless meadow,
    unlaborious earth and oarless sea;

VI

Thou that seëst Universal
    Nature moved by Universal Mind;
Thou majestic in thy sadness
    at the doubtful doom of human kind;

VII

Light among the vanish'd ages;
    star that gildest yet this phantom shore,
Golden branch amid the shadows,
    kings and realms that pass to rise no more;

VIII

Now thy Forum roars no longer,
    fallen every purple Caesar's dome—
Tho' thine ocean-roll of rhythm
    sound for ever of Imperial Rome—

IX

Now the Rome of slaves hath perish'd,
    and the Rome of freemen holds her place,
I, from out the Northern Island
    sunder'd once from all the human race,

x

I salute thee, Mantovano,
  I that loved thee since my day began,
Wielder of the stateliest measure
  ever moulded by the lips of man.

     Alfred Tennyson (1809-1892).

222. OH, HOLLOW! HOLLOW! HOLLOW!

WHAT time the poet hath hymned
The writhing maid, lithe-limbed,
 Quivering on amaranthine asphodel,
How can he paint her woes,
Knowing, as well he knows,
 That all can be set right with calomel?

When from the poet's plinth
The amorous colocynth
 Yearns for the aloe, faint with rapturous thrills,
How can he hymn their throes,
Knowing, as well he knows,
 That they are only uncompounded pills?

Is it, and can it be,
Nature hath this decree,
 Nothing poetic in the world shall dwell?
Or that in all her works
Something poetic lurks,
 Even in colocynth and calomel?
   I cannot tell.

     Sir W. S. Gilbert (1836-1911).

223. DOUBT

THE beneficent demon, doubt, whose name is Legion and who
dwells amongst the tombs of old faiths, enters into mankind
and thenceforth refuses to be cast out. Sacred customs, vener-

I

able dooms of ancestral wisdom, hallowed by tradition and professing to hold good for all time, are put to the question. Cultured reflection asks for their credentials; judges them by its own standards; finally, gathers those of which it approves into ethical systems, in which the reasoning is rarely more than a decent pretext for the adoption of foregone conclusions.

T. H. Huxley (1825-1895).

224. THE VERY FOOLISH SUNSET

(NATURE NOT ACCORDING TO RUSKIN)

NATURE contains the elements, in colour and form, of all pictures, as the keyboard contains the notes of all music.

But the artist is born to pick, and choose, and group with science, these elements, that the result may be beautiful—as the musician gathers his notes, and forms his chords, until he bring forth from chaos glorious harmony.

To say to the painter, that Nature is to be taken as she is, is to say to the player, that he may sit on the piano.

That Nature is always right, is an assertion, artistically, as untrue, as it is one whose truth is universally taken for granted. Nature is very rarely right, to such an extent even, that it might almost be said that Nature is usually wrong: that is to say, the condition of things that shall bring about the perfection of harmony worthy a picture is rare, and not common at all.

This would seem, to even the most intelligent, a doctrine almost blasphemous. So incorporated with our education has the supposed aphorism become, that its belief is held to be part of our moral being, and the words themselves have, in our ear, the ring of religion. Still, seldom does Nature succeed in producing a picture.

The sun blares, the wind blows from the east, the sky is bereft of cloud, and without, all is of iron. The windows of the Crystal Palace are seen from all points of London. The holiday-maker rejoices in the glorious day, and the painter turns aside to shut his eyes.

How little this is understood, and how dutifully the casual in Nature is accepted as sublime, may be gathered from the unlimited admiration daily produced by a very foolish sunset.

J. M. Whistler (1834-1903).

225. AN AESTHETIC SHAM

Am I alone,
   And unobserved? I am!
Then let me own
   I'm an aesthetic sham!
This air severe
   Is but a mere
     Veneer!
This cynic smile
   Is but a wile
     Of guile!
This costume chaste
   Is but good taste
     Misplaced!

Let me confess!
A languid love for lilies does *not* blight me!
Lank limbs and haggard cheeks do *not* delight me!
   I do *not* care for dirty greens
     By any means.
   I do *not* long for all one sees
     That's Japanese.
   I am *not* fond of uttering platitudes
     In stained-glass attitudes.
In short, my mediaevalism's affectation,
Born of a morbid love of admiration!

Song

If you're anxious for to shine in the high aesthetic line as a
   man of culture rare,
You must get up all the germs of the transcendental terms, and
   plant them everywhere.

You must lie upon the daisies, and discourse in novel phrases
    of your complicated state of mind,
The meaning doesn't matter if it's only idle chatter of a trans-
    cendental kind.
        And every one will say,
        As you walk your mystic way,
"If this young man expresses himself in terms too deep for *me*,
    Why what a very singularly deep young man this deep young
    man must be!"

Be eloquent in praise of the very dull old days which have long
    since passed away,
And convince 'em, if you can, that the reign of good Queen
    Anne was Culture's palmiest day.
Of course you will pooh-pooh whatever's fresh and new, and
    declare it's crude and mean,
For Art stopped short in the cultivated court of the Empress
    Josephine.
        And everyone will say,
        As you walk your mystic way,
"If that's not good enough for him which is good enough for *me*,
    Why what a very cultivated kind of youth this kind of youth
    must be!"

Then a sentimental passion of a vegetable fashion must excite
    your languid spleen,
An attachment *à la* Plato for a bashful young potato, or a not-
    too-French French bean!
Though the Philistines may jostle, you will rank as an apostle
    in the high aesthetic band,
If you walk down Piccadilly with a poppy or a lily in your
    mediaeval hand.
        And everyone will say,
        As you walk your flowery way,
"If he's content with a vegetable love, which would certainly
    not suit *me*,
    Why what a most particularly pure young man this pure
    young man must be!"

                    Sir W. S. Gilbert (1836-1911).

226. THE MERE AND THE LILY

. . My life is as a wood, where owls and jays
 Hoot in the heavy boughs, and magpies rail,
Till I am weary. Then, beyond all praise,
 I hear thy rapture, O my nightingale.

My life is as a lonely woodland mere,
 Whose sullen waters without sun repose:
And thou one ivory lily floating here,
 Marble and white, flushed with a hint of rose. . .
     Lord de Tabley (1835-1895).

227. *From* "DOROTHY: A COUNTRY STORY"

i

DOROTHY goes with her pails to the ancient well in the courtyard
 Daily at grey of morn, daily ere twilight at eve;
Often and often again she winds at the mighty old windlass,
 Still with her strong red arms landing the bucket aright:
Then, her beechen yoke press'd down on her broad square
  shoulders,
 Stately, erect, like a queen, she with her burden returns:
She with her burden returns to the fields that she loves, to the
  cattle
 Lowing beside the troughs, welcoming her and her pails.
Dorothy—who is she? She is only a servant-of-all-work;
 Servant at White Rose Farm, under the cliff in the vale:
Under the sandstone cliff, where martins build in the spring-
  time,
 Hard by the green level meads, hard by the streams of the
  Yore.
Oh, what a notable lass is our Dolly, the pride of the dairy!
 Stalwart and tall as a man, strong as a heifer to work:
Built for beauty, indeed, but certainly built for labour—
 Witness her muscular arm, witness the grip of her hand! . . .

ii

. . *Winter*—she help'd old John, a-laying down straw for the
      cattle;
   Clean'd out the stable and byres, nothing afraid of the
      bull;
   Help'd at the pig-killing too, and clean'd out the pigsty
      after;
   She never thought, not she, *that* was a trouble to do:
Spring—she look'd after the lambs, and the calves that
      wanted suckling;
   Work'd in the fields too, a bit, cleaning the land, or at
      plough.
Well can our Dorothy plough—as a girl, she learnt it and
      loved it;
   Leading the teams, at first, follow'd by Master himself;
Then, when she grew to the height and the strength of a
      muscular woman,
   Grasping the stilts in her pride, driving the mighty
      machine.
Ah, what a joy for her, at early morn, in the springtime,
   Driving from hedge to hedge furrows as straight as a
      line!
Seeing the crisp brown earth, like waves at the bow of a
      vessel,
   Rise, curl over, and fall, under the thrust of the share;
Orderly falling and still, its edges all creamy and crumbling,
   But, on the sloping side, polish'd and purple as steel;
Till all the field, she thought, looked bright as the bars of
      that gridiron
   In the great window at church, over the gentlefolks' pew:
And evermore, as she strode, she had cheerful companions
      behind her;
   Rooks and the smaller birds, following after her plough;
And, ere the ridges were done, there was gossamer woven
      above them,
   Gossamer dewy and white, shining like foam on the
      sea. . .

iii

'Twas but a poor little room; a farm-servant's loft in a garret;
  One small window and door; never a chimney at all:
One little stool by the bed, and a remnant of cast-away
      carpet;
  But on the floor, by the wall, carefully dusted and bright,
Stood the green-painted box, our Dorothy's closet and wardrobe,
      Holding her treasures, her all—all that she own'd in the
      world!
Linen and hosen were there, coarse linen and home-knitted
      hosen;
  Handkerchiefs bought at the fair, aprons and smocks not a
      few;
Kirtles for warmth when afield, and frocks for winter and
      summer;
  Blue-spotted, lilac, grey; cotton and woollen and serge;
All her simple attire, save the clothes she felt most like herself
      in—
  Rough coarse workaday clothes, fit for a labourer's wear.
There was her Sunday array—the boots, and the shawl, and
      the bonnet,
  Solemnly folded apart, not to be lightly assumed:
There was her jewelry too; 'twas a brooch (she had worn it
      this evening)
  Made of a cairngorm stone—really too splendid for her!
Which on a Martlemas Day Mr. Robert had bought for a
      fairing;
  Little she thought, just then, how she would value it now!
As for her sewing gear, her housewife, her big brass thimble,
  Knitting and suchlike work, such as her fingers could do,
That was away downstairs, in a dresser-drawer in the kitchen,
  Ready for use of a night, when she was tidied and clean.
Item, up there in the chest were her books: *The Dairyman's
      Daughter*:
  Ballads: *The Olney Hymns*: Bible and Prayer-book, of
      course:
That was her library; these were the limits of Dorothy's
      reading;

Wholesome, but scanty indeed: was it then all that she
    knew?
Nay, for like other good girls, she had profited much by her
    schooling
    Under the mighty three—Nature, and Labour, and Life:
Mightier they than books; if books could have only come
    after,
    Thoughts of instructed minds filtering down into hers.
That was impossible now; what she had been, she was, and she
    would be;
    Only a farm-serving lass—only a peasant, I fear!

Well—on the green-lidded box, her name was painted in
    yellow;
    Dorothy Crump were the words. Crump? what a horrible
    name!
Yes, but they gave it to her, because (like the box) 'twas her
    mother's;
    Ready to hand—though of course *she* had no joy in the
    name:
She had no kin—and indeed, she never had needed a surname;
    Never had used one at all, never had made one her own:
"Dolly" she was to herself, and to every one else she was
    "Dolly";
    Nothing but "Dolly"; and so, that was enough for a name.
Thus then, her great green box, her one undoubted possession,
    Stood where it was; like her, "never went nowhere" at all;
Waited, perhaps, as of old some beautiful Florentine bride-
    chest,
    Till, in the fulness of time, He, the Beloved, appears. . .

                 A. J. Munby (1828-1910).

228. THE CHURCHYARD ON THE SANDS

My love lies in the gates of foam,
    The last dear wreck of shore;
The naked sea-marsh binds her home,
    The sand her chamber door.

The grey gull flaps the written stones,
   The ox-birds chase the tide;
And near that narrow field of bones
   Great ships at anchor ride.

Black piers with crust of dripping green,
   One foreland, like a hand,
O'er intervals of grass between
   Dim lonely dunes of sand.

A church of silent weathered looks,
   A breezy reddish tower,
A yard whose mounded resting-nooks
   Are tinged with sorrel flower.

In peace the swallow's eggs are laid
   Along the belfry walls;
The tempest does not reach her shade,
   The rain her silent halls.

But sails are sweet in summer sky,
   The lark throws down a lay;
The long salt levels steam and dry,
   The cloud-heart melts away.

But patches of the sea-pink shine,
   The pied crows poise and come;
The mallow hangs, the bindweeds twine,
   Where her sweet lips are dumb.

The passion of the wave is mute;
   No sound or ocean shock;
No music save the trilling flute
   That marks the curlew flock.

But yonder when the wind is keen,
   And rainy air is clear,
The merchant city's spires are seen,
   The toil of men grows near.

Along the coast-way grind the wheels
  Of endless carts of coal;
And on the sides of giant keels
  The shipyard hammers roll.

The world creeps here upon the shout,
  And stirs my heart in pain;
The mist descends and blots it out,
  And I am strong again.

Strong and alone, my dove, with thee;
  And, tho' mine eyes be wet,
There's nothing in the world to me
  So dear as my regret.

I would not change my sorrow, sweet,
  For others' nuptial hours;
I love the daisies at thy feet
  More than their orange flowers.

My hand alone shall tend thy tomb
  From leaf-bud to leaf-fall,
And wreathe around each season's bloom
  Till autumn ruins all.

Let snowdrops, early in the year,
  Droop o'er her silent breast;
And bid the later cowslip rear
  The amber of its crest.

Come hither, linnets tufted-red,
  Drift by, O wailing tern;
Set pure vale lilies at her head,
  At her feet lady-fern.

Grow, samphire, at the tidal brink,
  Wave, pansies of the shore,
To whisper how alone I think
  Of her for evermore.

Bring blue sea-hollies thorny, keen,
    Long lavender in flower;
Grey wormwood like a hoary queen,
    Stanch mullein like a tower.

O sea-wall mounded long and low,
    Let iron bounds be thine;
Nor let the salt wave overflow
    That breast I held divine.

Nor float its sea-weed to her hair,
    Nor dim her eyes with sands:
No fluted cockle burrow where
    Sleep folds her patient hands.

Tho' thy crest feel the wild sea's breath,
    Tho' tide-weight tear thy root,
Oh, guard the treasure house, where Death
    Has bound my darling mute.

Tho' cold her pale lips to reward
    With Love's own mysteries,
Ah, rob no daisy from her sward,
    Rough gale of eastern seas!

Ah, render sere no silken bent,
    That by her head-stone waves;
Let noon and golden summer blent
    Pervade these ocean graves.

And, ah, dear heart, in thy still nest,
    Resign this earth of woes,
Forget the ardours of the west,
    Neglect the morning glows.

Sleep, and forget all things but one,
    Heard in each wave of sea,—
How lonely all the years will run
    Until I rest by thee.
                    Lord de Tabley (1835-1895).

229. THE SNOW AND THE WRECK

THE snow lies sprinkled on the beach,
And whitens all the marshy lea:
The sad gulls wail adown the gale,
The day is dark and black the sea.
   Shorn of their crests the blighted waves
With driven foam the offing fleck:
The ebb is low and barely laves
The red rust of the giant wreck. . .

            Robert Bridges (1844-1930).

230. A PASTORAL

(*Venetian School*)

ARCADIAN spaces of great grass arise;
   Crisp lambs are merry: hoary vales are laid,
Studded with roe-deer and wild strawberries;
   In one a shepherd tabours near a maid;

Who teases at the button of his cloak,
   Where rarely underneath them grows the herb;
A squirrel eyes the lovers from an oak,
   And speckled horses pasture without curb,

In a fair meadow set with tulip-heads,
   A water-mill rolls little crested falls
Of olive torrent, broken in grey threads.
   A grave-yard crowds black crosses in square walls.

And up behind in a still orchard close
   The apples ripen, crushing down the trees,
In millions, russet-green and amber-rose,
   Fit for the gardens of the Hesperides.

Such colour as the morning brings the skies,
  Such mirage as our dreams in childhood gave,
Infinite cadence of ethereal dyes,
  The radiance of a rainbow-burnished wave.

Quaint pastoral Arcadia, where are set
  Thy rainy lands and reddish underwoods?
Earth has not held thy fabled sunsets yet,
  Though lovers build their palace on thy roods.

Lord de Tabley (1835-1895).

231. *From* "THE TEN O'CLOCK LECTURE"

LISTEN! There never was an artistic period.

There never was an Art-loving nation.

In the beginning, man went forth each day—some to do battle, some to the chase; others again to dig and to delve in the field—all that they might gain and live, or lose and die. Until there was found among them one, differing from the rest, whose pursuits attracted him not, and so he stayed by the tents with the women, and traced strange devices with a burnt stick upon a gourd.

This man, who took no joy in the ways of his brethren—who cared not for conquest, and fretted in the field—this designer of quaint patterns—this deviser of the beautiful—who perceived in Nature about him curious curvings, as faces are seen in the fire—this dreamer apart, was the first artist.

And when from the field and from afar, there came back the people, they took the gourd—and drank from it.

And presently there came to this man another—and, in time, others—of like nature, chosen by the Gods—and so they worked together; and soon they fashioned, from the moistened earth, forms resembling the gourd. And with the power of creation, the heirloom of the artist, presently they went beyond the slovenly suggestion of Nature, and the first vase was born, in beautiful proportion.

And the toilers tilled and were athirst; and the heroes returned from fresh victories, to rejoice and to feast; and all drank alike from the artists' goblets, fashioned cunningly, taking no note the while of the craftsman's pride, and understanding not his glory in his work; drinking at the cup, not from choice, not from a consciousness that it was beautiful, but because, forsooth, there was none other!

And time, with more state, brought more capacity for luxury, and it became well that men should dwell in large houses, and rest upon couches, and eat at tables; whereupon the artist, with his artificers, built palaces and filled them with furniture, beautiful in proportion and lovely to look upon.

And the people lived in marvels of art—and ate and drank out of masterpieces—for there was nothing else to eat and drink out of, and no bad building to live in; no article of daily life, of luxury, or of necessity, that had not been handed down from the design of the master, and made by his workmen.

And the people questioned not, *and had nothing to say in the matter.*

So Greece was in its splendour, and Art reigned supreme— by force of fact, not by election—and there was no meddling from the outsider. The mighty warrior would no more have ventured to offer a design for the temple of Pallas Athene than would the sacred poet have proffered a plan for constructing the catapult.

And the Amateur was unknown—and the Dilettante undreamed of!

And history wrote on, and conquest accompanied civilization, and Art spread, or rather its products were carried by the victors among the vanquished from one country to another. And the customs of cultivation covered the face of the earth, so that all peoples continued to use what *the artist alone produced.*

And centuries passed in this using, and the world was flooded with all that was beautiful, until there arose a new class, who discovered the cheap, and foresaw fortune in the facture of the sham.

Then sprang into existence the tawdry, the common, the gewgaw.

The taste of the tradesman supplanted the science of the artist, and what was born of the million went back to them, and charmed them, for it was after their own heart; and the great and the small, the statesman and the slave, took to themselves the abomination that was tendered, and preferred it—and have lived with it ever since!

And the artist's occupation was gone, and the manufacturer and the huckster took his place.

And now the heroes filled from the jugs and drank from the bowls—with understanding—noting the glare of their new bravery, and taking pride in its worth.

And the people—this time—had much to say in the matter —and all were satisfied. And Birmingham and Manchester arose in their might—and Art was relegated to the curiosity shop.

J. M. Whistler (1834-1903).

232. THE UPPER SKIES ARE PALEST BLUE

THE upper skies are palest blue
Mottled with pearl and fretted snow:
With tattered fleece of inky hue
Close overhead the storm-clouds go.

The shadows fly along the hill
And o'er the crest mount one by one:
The whitened planking of the mill
Is now in shade and now in sun.

Robert Bridges (1844-1930).

233. *From* "THE VALES OF MEDWAY"

. . Here on the Medway flood, where a hundred bright little
        islands
    Shine on the broad full tide, stars of its widespreading blue,
    Here are the ships coming in, with sails fullset to the breezes,
    Types of the hope that appears, fraught with adventure,
        to us:
    And on the hundred isles, on the beautiful breast of the
        waters,
    Sunlight gleams and glides, changed with the changeable
        clouds.

Here on the Medway hills, where the land slopes suddenly
   seaward,
Green grows the flush of the corn, moist with the lustre
   of dew.
Yes, and the old brown woods, though they seem still dead
   from a distance,
They too are filling with life, quick with the pulses of
   Spring:
Witness the steel-like sheen that glosses the bark of the
   saplings,
Witness the tassell'd blooms hung from the willows below.
What should I speak of the banks and the wild and wander-
   ing hedgerows,
What of the lanes between, winding from village to farm?
Beautiful they with buds, the red-nippled buds of the
   hawthorn,
Harbouring too in the grass nests of the earliest flowers.
Also by hamlet and fold, by many a trim cottage-dwelling,
Each with its ivied porch, each with its old hooded well,
Daffodils nod at the gate, and wealth is abroad in the
   garden—
Silver of snowdrop tufts, crocuses given for gold.
Now come away to the fields, where the men of the country
   are working;
Men—aye, and women too—working all day with a will:
Here in the vale hard by, stout women are barking the
   hop-poles;
There are the men at plough, cheerily guiding the teams;
Yonder, where lasses and lads in summer time went to the
   milking,
Now they are standing a-row, each with her shovel and sieve,
Opening the straw-cover'd hoard, where fodder is kept
   through the Winter,
Sifting the bad from the good, food for the cattle and swine.
Hark! from yon high grey Downs the tremulous musical
   sheep-bells
Call us to come and behold all that our shepherds can show;
Who with their low-wheel'd huts abide in the field for the
   lambing,

Watching night and day over the weak of the fold.
Ah! from those high grey Downs, what a height, what a
  scope, of enjoyment!
Songs of the mating birds heard in the hollows afar—
Songs of the lark in air, or the clamorous chirp of the
  starlings,
Seated aloft in crowds, talking together at eve.

You who would know what it is to rejoice in the beauty of
  England,
Come to these high grey Downs; come in an evening of
  Spring—
Come in the Autumn noons, or come in a sweet Summer
  morning—
Stand upon Darland Heights, gaze on the glories around!
Look to the east, far down, where the broad white Roman
  highway
Scores the green flank of the hills, stately and sound as of old:
Look to the east, far down, where Medway sweeps to the
  ocean,
Meeting the broader Thames, surging away to the Nore.
There, by the tall sea banks, by the low rich pastures of
  Essex,
There go the ships, far off, bearing the wealth of the world;
Bearing it on the tide, to the port and harbour of London,
Bearing it thence in turn out to the ocean again.
Near, o'er the Medway stream, look down on an humbler
  traffic—
Fishermen's craft alone, barges and boats of the shore:
Yes, and yon giant hulks, where soldiers live as in barracks,
Learning their terrible trade, disciplined daily to war.
Ah, look away from them, look away from the forts in the
  channel
(Needed and wanting once, soon to be needed again),
Look to the smiling shores, to the villages set in the wood-
  land,
Orchards and red-roof'd farms, churches and castles and all.
Then to the west turn round, and see right on to the land-
  ward,

Fold upon fold, the hills rising like waves of the sea:
But at your feet, low down, lies the silent valley of Darland,
Winding in many a curve up to the highlands afar;
Steep are its purple sides, where folded flocks are a-slumber,
And on the further slope, warm in the depth of the vale,
Cluster'd hop-poles stand, like the tents of an army
    encamping,
Soon to be sever'd and ranged, soon to be leafy and green.
Over against us here, on the opposite height, on the summit,
Hempstead stands alone, grey with its gables and barns;
And from Hempstead farm, right on to the western horizon,
Fold upon fold, our hills rise like the waves of the sea;
Crested with high dim lawns, and tufted with copses and
    timber,
Till on the lucid sky loftier ridges appear.
Yes, that is Bluebell Hill, that far in the golden distance
Looks over Maidstone town on to the Garden of Kent;
Looks on those fallen fanes, that wonderful House of the
    Druids,
Oldest of all things old now on the face of the land.

See, into this fair scene, these hills and valleys and waters,
Comes the majestic sun, sobering down to his rest:
He, who was shining above, unapproachable sovereign of
    all things,
Now, at the eventide, friendly, familiar and near,
Glows among purple clouds, his solemn and mournful
    attendants,
Dies as a King should die, gracious and calm to the end.
Then, what a triumph of life, what a gorgeous apotheosis
Mounts from the place of his death up to the zenith on high!
Then, what a blaze of light, of various infinite colour,
Out of his open tomb springs like a fountain of hope!
First, through those purple clouds, and under and in and
    around them,
Bars of ruby red, vivid, intense as a flame;
Paler crimson above, and mellowing softening saffron
Melt through a liquid green into the ultimate blue:
Up to the final blue, where clear cold stars are awaiting,

Till with the luminous dark they shall have leave to appear.
Come, come away—let us go; let us saunter silently
  homeward—
Under these clear cold stars, under this luminous sky;
Thinking, with hearts that are full of enchanting and
  exquisite beauty,
"Ah, what a land is this—ah, what an Eden is here!"

Yes—what an Eden is here, if men were able to know it,
Able to see with their eyes, willing and able to feel!
But they are not: not a man, nor a child, nor even a woman
Cares that the land of their birth still should be pure as
  of old.
What? If they loved greensward, sweet air, and life-giving
  waters,
Would they stand mute, as they do, seeing all these dis-
  appear?
Seeing their mountain lakes fast stolen and spoilt by the
  stranger,
Seeing the streams of the vale blacken'd and poison'd and
  foul;
Seeing the air they breathe, the needful breath of their
  nostrils,
Changed into filthiest gloom, acrid with sulphur and soot;
Seeing their hideous towns, their mean and comfortless
  dwellings,
Sprawl o'er the innocent fields, ugly and aimless and bare:
Yes! for Beauty is dead, and the excellent craft of the
  builder
Fail'd, when the builder himself ceased to be honest and
  true.

What shall be done then for these—for a people besotted as
  this is,
Making such haste to be rich, caring for nothing but greed?
Nay, if they will not turn, and ask their fathers before them
How to discern the Good, whether in Nature or Art;
How to transmit it, increased by the labour of each genera-
  tion,

Weeded of evil, indeed, but with a delicate hand;
Never destroying a good, except for the sake of a better,
Hating the bad alone, keeping their vengeance for that:
Nay, if they will not turn, there is blackness of darkness
    before them;
Lurid with lights that lead only to uttermost hell;
Indolence sapping their wealth, and cowardice offer'd for
    courage;
Knowledge that is but a name—bastard of folly and pride;
Peace trodden down by war; divine Humility dying;
Reverence shamed with scorn; Love going out in despair.

A. J. Munby (1828-1910).

234. SONG

WHY fadest thou in death,
    Oh yellow waning tree?
Gentle is autumn's breath,
    And green the oak by thee.

But with each wind that sighs
    The leaves from thee take wing;
And bare thy branches rise
    Above their drifted ring.

R. W. Dixon (1833-1900).

235. KRAKATOA SUNSETS

i

. . Which said, when he agreed, she spake no more,
    But left him to his task, and took her way
    Beside the ripples of the shell-strewn shore,
    The southward stretching margin of a bay,
    Whose sandy curves she pass'd, and taking stand
    Upon its taper horn of furthest land,
    Lookt left and right to rise and set of day.

Fair was the sight; for now, though full an hour
The sun had sunk, she saw the evening light
In shifting colour to the zenith tower,
And grow more gorgeous ever and more bright.
Bathed in the warm and comfortable glow,
The fair delighted queen forgot her woe,
And watch'd the unwonted pageant of the night.

Broad and low down, where late the sun had been
A wealth of orange-gold was thickly shed,
Fading above into a field of green,
Like apples ere they ripen into red;
Then to the height a variable hue
Of rose and pink and crimson freak'd with blue,
And olive-border'd clouds o'er lilac led.

High in the opposèd west the wondering moon
All silvery green in flying green was fleec't;
And round the blazing South the splendour soon
Caught all the heaven, and ran to North and East;
And Aphrodite knew the thing was wrought
By cunning of Poseidon, and she thought
She would go see with whom he kept his feast. . .

                    Robert Bridges (1844-1930).

                              ii

The glow is intense, this is what strikes everyone; it has
prolonged the daylight, and optically changed the season; it
bathes the whole sky, it is mistaken for the reflection of a
great fire; at the sundown itself and southwards from that on
December 4, I took a note of it as more like inflamed flesh
than the lucid reds of ordinary sunsets. On the same evening
the fields facing west glowed as if overlaid with yellow wax.

But it is also lustreless. A bright sunset lines the clouds so
that their brims look like gold, brass, bronze, or steel. It
fetches out those dazzling flecks or spangles which people call
fish-scales. It gives to a mackerel or dappled cloudrack the

appearance of quilted crimson silk, or a ploughed field glazed
with crimson ice. These effects may have been seen in the late
sunsets, but they are not the specific after-glow; that is without
gloss or lustre.

The two things together, that is intensity of light and want
of lustre, give to objects on the earth the peculiar illumination
which may be seen in studios and other well-like rooms, and
which itself affects the practice of painters and may be seen in
their work, notably Rembrandt's disguising or feebly showing
the outlines and distinctions of things, but fetching out white
surfaces and coloured stuffs with a rich and inward and seemingly self-luminous glow. . . . Four colours in particular have
been noticeable in these after-glows, and in a fixed order of
time and place—orange lowest and nearest the sundown;
above this, and broader, green; above this, broader still, a
variable red, ending in being crimson; above this a faint lilac.
The lilac disappears; the green deepens, spreads and encroaches
on the orange, till at last one red, varying downwards from
crimson to scarlet or orange fills the west and south. . . . Ordinary
sunsets have not this order; this, so to say, fixed and limited
palette. The green in particular is low down when it appears.
There is often a trace of olive between the sundown and the
higher blue sky, but it never develops, that I remember, into
a fresh green.   *Gerard Manley Hopkins* (1844-1889).

236. "WINTER WILL FOLLOW"

THE heaving roses of the hedge are stirred
By the sweet breath of summer, and the bird
Makes from within his jocund voice be heard.

The winds that kiss the roses sweep the sea
Of uncut grass, whose billows rolling free
Half drown the hedges which part lea from lea.

But soon shall look the wondering roses down
Upon an empty field cut close and brown,
That lifts no more its height against their own.

And in a little while those roses bright,
Leaf after leaf, shall flutter from their height,
And on the reaped field lie pink and white.

And yet again the bird that sings so high
Shall ask the snow for alms with piteous cry,
Take fright in his bewildering bower, and die.

                    R. W. Dixon (1833-1900).

237. THE THREE BADGERS

THERE be three Badgers on a mossy stone
   Beside a dark and covered way:
Each dreams himself a monarch on his throne,
     And so they stay and stay—
Though their old Father languishes alone,
     They stay, and stay, and stay.

There be three Herrings loitering around,
   Longing to share that mossy seat:
Each Herring tries to sing what she has found
     That makes Life seem so sweet.
Thus, with a grating and uncertain sound,
     They bleat, and bleat, and bleat.

The Mother-Herring, on the salt sea-wave,
   Sought vainly for her absent ones:
The Father-Badger, writhing in a cave,
     Shrieked out "Return, my sons!
You shall have buns," he shrieked, "if you'll behave!
     Yea, buns, and buns, and buns!"

"I fear," said she, "your sons have gone astray.
   My daughters left me while I slept."
"Yes 'm," the Badger said: "it's as you say.
     They should be better kept."
Thus the poor parents talked the time away,
     And wept, and wept, and wept.

"Oh, dear beyond our dearest dreams,
　　Fairer than all that fairest seems!
　　To feast the rosy hours away,
　　To revel in a roundelay!
　　　　How blest would be
　　　　A life so free—
　　Ipwergis-Pudding to consume,
　　And drink the subtle Azzigoom!

"And if, in other days and hours,
　　Mid other fluffs and other flowers,
　　The choice were given me how to dine—
　　'Name what thou wilt: it shall be thine!'
　　　　Oh, then I see
　　　　The life for me—
　　Ipwergis-Pudding to consume,
　　And drink the subtle Azzigoom!"

The Badgers did not care to talk to Fish:
　　They did not dote on Herrings' songs:
They never had experienced the dish
　　To which that name belongs:
"And oh, to pinch their tails," (this was their wish,)
　　"With tongs, yea, tongs, and tongs!

"And are not these the Fish," the Eldest sighed,
　　"Whose Mother dwells beneath the foam?"
"They *are* the Fish!" the Second one replied,
　　"And they have left their home!"
"Oh, wicked Fish," the Youngest Badger cried,
　　"To roam, yea, roam, and roam!"

Gently the Badgers trotted to the shore—
　　The sandy shore that fringed the bay:
Each in his mouth a living Herring bore—
　　Those aged ones waxed gay:
Clear rang their voices through the ocean roar,
　　"Hooray, hooray, hooray!"

                                   Lewis Carroll (1832-1898).

238. MAD MARGARET'S SONG

CHEERILY carols the lark
    Over the cot.
Merrily whistles the clerk
    Scratching a blot.
      But the lark
      And the clerk,
      I remark,
    Comfort me not!

Over the ripening peach
    Buzzes the bee.
Splash on the billowy beach
    Tumbles the sea.
      But the peach
      And the beach
      They are each
    Nothing to me!

      And why?
      Who am I?
Daft Madge! Crazy Meg!
Mad Margaret! Poor Peg!
    He! he! he! he! he!

Sir W. S. Gilbert (1836-1911).

239. THE MAD GARDENER'S SONG

HE thought he saw an Elephant,
    That practised on a fife:
He looked again, and found it was
    A letter from his wife.
"At length I realise," he said,
    "The bitterness of Life!"

He thought he saw a Buffalo
  Upon the chimney-piece:
He looked again, and found it was
  His Sister's Husband's Niece.
"Unless you leave this house," he said,
  "I'll send for the Police!"

He thought he saw a Rattlesnake
  That questioned him in Greek:
He looked again, and found it was
  The Middle of Next Week.
"The one thing I regret," he said,
  "Is that it cannot speak!"

He thought he saw a Banker's Clerk
  Descending from the bus:
He looked again, and found it was
  A Hippopotamus:
"If this should stay to dine," he said,
  "There won't be much for us!"

He thought he saw a Kangaroo
  That worked a coffee-mill:
He looked again, and found it was
  A Vegetable-Pill.
"Were I to swallow this," he said,
  "I should be very ill!"

He thought he saw a Coach-and-Four
  That stood beside his bed:
He looked again, and found it was
  A Bear without a Head.
"Poor thing," he said, "poor silly thing!
  It's waiting to be fed!"

He thought he saw an Albatross
　　That fluttered round the lamp:
He looked again, and found it was
　　A Penny-Postage-Stamp.
"You'd best be getting home," he said:
　　"The nights are very damp!"

He thought he saw a Garden-Door
　　That opened with a key:
He looked again, and found it was
　　A Double Rule of Three:
"And all its mystery," he said,
　　"Is clear as day to me!"

He thought he saw an Argument
　　That proved he was the Pope:
He looked again, and found it was
　　A Bar of Mottled Soap.
"A fact so dread," he faintly said,
　　"Extinguishes all hope!"

Lewis Carroll (1832-1898).

240. THE LORD CHANCELLOR'S SONG,
from "IOLANTHE"

WHEN you're lying awake with a dismal headache, and repose
　　is taboo'd by anxiety,
I conceive you may use any language you choose to indulge in,
　　without impropriety;
For your brain is on fire—the bedclothes conspire of usual
　　slumber to plunder you:
First your counterpane goes, and uncovers your toes, and your
　　sheet slips demurely from under you;
Then the blanketing tickles—you feel like mixed pickles—
　　so terribly sharp is the pricking,
And you're hot, and you're cross, and you tumble and toss till
　　there's nothing 'twixt you and the ticking.

Then the bedclothes all creep to the ground in a heap, and you
   pick 'em all up in a tangle;

Next your pillow resigns and politely declines to remain at its
   usual angle!

Well, you get some repose in the form of a doze, with hot
   eyeballs and head ever aching,

But your slumbering teems with such horrible dreams that
   you'd very much better be waking;

For you dream you are crossing the Channel, and tossing about
   in a steamer from Harwich—

Which is something between a large bathing-machine and a
   very small second-class carriage—

And you're giving a treat (penny ice and cold meat) to a party
   of friends and relations—

They're a ravenous horde—and they all came on board at Sloane
   Square and South Kensington Stations.

And bound on that journey you find your attorney (who started
   that morning from Devon);

He's a bit undersized, and you don't feel surprised when he
   tells you he's only eleven.

Well, you're driving like mad with this singular lad (by-the-
   bye the ship's now a four-wheeler),

And you're playing round games, and he calls you bad names
   when you tell him that "ties pay the dealer";

But this you can't stand, so you throw up your hand, and you
   find you're as cold as an icicle,

In your shirt and your socks (the black silk with gold clocks),
   crossing Salisbury Plain on a bicycle:

And he and the crew are on bicycles too—which they've
   somehow or other invested in—

And he's telling the tars, all the particu*lars* of a company he's
   interested in—

It's a scheme of devices, to get at low prices, all goods from
   cough mixtures to cables

(Which tickled the sailors) by treating retailers, as though they
   were all ve*ge*tables—

You get a good spadesman to plant a small tradesman (first
   take off his boots with a boot-tree),

And his legs will take root, and his fingers will shoot, and they'll
    blossom and bud like a fruit-tree—
From the greengrocer tree you get grapes and green pea,
    cauliflower, pineapple and cranberries,
While the pastry-cook plant, cherry brandy will grant, apple
    puffs, and three-corners, and Banburys—
The shares are a penny, and ever so many are taken by Roths-
    child and Baring,
And just as a few are allotted to you, you awake with a shudder
    despairing—
You're a regular wreck, with a crick in your neck, and no wonder
    you snore, for your head's on the floor, and you've needles
    and pins from your soles to your shins, and your flesh is
    a-creep, for your left leg's asleep, and you've cramp in
    your toes, and a fly on your nose, and some fluff in your
    lung, and a feverish tongue, and a thirst that's intense,
    and a general sense that you haven't been sleeping in
    clover;
But the darkness has passed, and it's daylight at last, and the
    night has been long—ditto ditto my song—and thank
    goodness they're both of them over!

                                        Sir W. S. Gilbert (1836-1911).

241. THE KING-FISHER SONG

King Fisher courted Lady Bird—
  Sing Beans, sing Bones, sing Butterflies!
  "Find me my match," he said,
  "With such a noble head—
  With such a beard, as white as curd—
    With such expressive eyes!"

  "Yet pins have heads," said Lady Bird—
  Sing Prunes, sing Prawns, sing Primrose-Hill!
  "And, where you stick them in,
    They stay, and thus a pin
  Is very much to be preferred
    To one that's never still!"

"Oysters have beards," said Lady Bird—
Sing Flies, sing Frogs, sing Fiddle-strings!
"I love them, for I know
    They never chatter so:
They would not say one single word—
    Not if you crowned them Kings!"

"Needles have eyes," said Lady Bird—
Sing Cats, sing Corks, sing Cowslip-tea!
"And they are sharp—just what
    Your Majesty is *not*:
So get you gone—'tis too absurd
    To come a-courting *me*!"

                    Lewis Carroll (1832-1898).

242. THE BURGHERS' BATTLE

THICK rise the spear-shafts o'er the land
That erst the harvest bore;
The sword is heavy in the hand,
And we return no more.
The light wind waves the Ruddy Fox,
Our banners of the war,
And ripples in the Running Ox,
And we return no more.
Across our stubble acres now
The teams go four and four;
But out-worn elders guide the plough,
And we return no more.
And now the women heavy-eyed
Turn through the open door
From gazing down the highway wide,
Where we return no more.
The shadows of the fruited close
Dapple the feast-hall floor;

There lie our dogs and dream and doze,
And we return no more.
Down from the minster tower to-day
Fall the soft chimes of yore
Amidst the chattering jackdaws' play:
And we return no more.
But underneath the streets are still;
Noon, and the market's o'er!
Back go the goodwives o'er the hill;
For we return no more.
What merchants to our gates shall come?
What wise man bring us lore?
What abbot ride away to Rome,
Now we return no more?
What mayor shall rule the hall we built?
Whose scarlet sweep the floor?
What judge shall doom the robber's guilt,
Now we return no more?
New houses in the streets shall rise
Where builded we before,
Of other stone wrought otherwise;
For we return no more.
And crops shall cover field and hill
Unlike what once they bore,
And all be done without our will,
Now we return no more.
Look up! the arrows streak the sky,
The horns of battle roar;
The long spears lower and draw nigh,
And we return no more.
Remember how beside the wain,
We spoke the word of war,
And sowed this harvest of the plain,
And we return no more.
Lay spears about the Ruddy Fox!
The days of old are o'er;
Heave sword about the Running Ox!
For we return no more.

                    William Morris (1834-1896).

243. THE DEMOCRATIC KINGS

RISING early in the morning,
  We proceed to light our fire,
Then our Majesty adorning
  In its workaday attire,
    We embark without delay
    On the duties of the day.

First, we polish off some batches
Of political despatches,
    And foreign politicians circumvent;
Then, if business isn't heavy,
We may hold a Royal *levée*,
    Or ratify some acts of parliament.
Then we probably review the household troops—
With the usual "Shalloo humps!" and "Shalloo hoops!"
Or receive with ceremonial and state
An interesting Eastern potentate.
    After that we generally
    Go and dress our private *valet*—
(It's a rather nervous duty—he's a touchy little man)—
    Write some letters literary
    For our private secretary—
He is shaky in his spelling, so we help him if we can.
    Then, in view of cravings inner,
    We go down and order dinner;
Then we polish the Regalia and the Coronation Plate—
    Spend an hour in titivating
    All our Gentlemen-in-Waiting;
Or we run on little errands for the Ministers of State.
    Oh, philosophers may sing
    Of the troubles of a king;
Yet the duties are delightful, and the privileges great;
    But the privilege and pleasure
    That we treasure beyond measure
Is to run on little errands for the Ministers of State.

After luncheon (making merry
On a bun and glass of sherry),
  If we've nothing particular to do,
We may make a Proclamation,
Or receive a Deputation—
  Then we possibly create a Peer or two.
Then we help a fellow-creature on his path
With the Garter or the Thistle or the Bath.
Or we dress and toddle off in semi-State
 Toa festival, a function, or a *fête*.
  Then we go and stand as sentry
  At the Palace (private entry),
Marching hither, marching thither, up and down and
  to and fro,
  While the warrior on duty
  Goes in search of beer and beauty
(And it generally happens that he hasn't far to go).
  He relieves us, if he's able,
  Just in time to lay the table,
Then we dine and serve the coffee, and at half-past twelve
  or one,
  With a pleasure that's emphatic,
  We retire to our attic
With the gratifying feeling that our duty has been done!
  Oh, philosophers may sing
  Of the troubles of a King,
But of pleasures there are many and of troubles there are
  none;
  And the culminating pleasure
  That we treasure beyond measure
Is the gratifying feeling that our duty has been done!

       Sir W. S. Gilbert (1836-1911).

244. DOWN AMONG THE DEAD MEN

Come, comrades, come, your glasses clink;
Up with your hands a health to drink,
The health of all that workers be,
In every land, on every sea.

        K

And he that will this health deny,
Down among the dead men, down among the dead men,
Down, down, down, down,
Down among the dead men let him lie!

Well done! now drink another toast,
And pledge the gath'ring of the host,
The people armed in brain and hand,
To claim their rights in every land.
    And he that will, etc.

There's liquor left; come, let's be kind,
And drink the rich a better mind,
That when we knock upon the door,
They may be off and say no more.
    And he that will, etc.

Now, comrades, let the glass blush red,
Drink we the unforgotten dead
That did their deeds and went away,
Before the bright sun brought the day.
    And he that will, etc.

The Day? Ah, friends, late grows the night;
Drink to the glimmering spark of light,
The herald of the joy to be,
The battle-torch of thee and me!
    And he that will, etc.

Take yet another cup in hand
And drink in hope our little band;
Drink strife in hope while lasteth breath,
And brotherhood in life and death;
    And he that will this health deny,
    Down among the dead men, down among the dead men,
    Down, down, down, down,
    Down among the dead men let him lie!
                    William Morris (1834-1896).

245. THE INDIAN UPON GOD

I PASSED along the water's edge below the humid trees,
My spirit rocked in evening light, the rushes round my knees,
My spirit rocked in sleep and sighs; and saw the moorfowl pace
All dripping on a grassy slope, and saw them cease to chase
Each other round in circles, and heard the eldest speak:
Who holds the world between His bill and made us strong or weak
Is an undying moorfowl, and He lives beyond the sky.
The rains are from His dripping wing, the moonbeams from
    His eye.
I passed a little further on and heard a lotus talk:
Who made the world and ruleth it, He hangeth on a stalk,
For I am in His image made, and all this tinkling tide
Is but a sliding drop of rain between His petals wide.
A little way within the gloom a roebuck raised his eyes
Brimful of starlight, and he said: *The Stamper of the Skies,*
He is a gentle roebuck; for how else, I pray, could He
Conceive a thing so sad and soft, a gentle thing like me?
I passed a little further on and heard a peacock say:
Who made the grass and made the worms and made my feathers
    gay,
He is a monstrous peacock, and He waveth all the night
His languid tail above us, lit with myriad spots of light.

W. B. Yeats (1865-1939).

246. LATE VICTORIAN PAINTING:
FINE ART BIT BY BIT—

As to *form*, we demand that a painter should choose for his
theme beautifully-shaped objects, such as human figures, male
or female, in graceful attitudes, nude and exquisitely formed,
with rounded limbs, or clothed in flowing drapery, Greek or
Roman, Oriental or Florentine; animals like the fawn, the
panther, the Arab charger, the swan, and the butterfly; mountain peaks, bossy hills, winding bays; the cataract leaping in an
arch from the crag; Naples and Vesuvius, Tivoli and Niagara,

the curved horizon of ocean, the thousand inlets of a highland loch; graceful pottery, elegantly-moulded goblets, flagons, and vases, slender beakers and shapely chalices; the domes and minarets of Stamboul, the sweeping arches of Tintern and Poitiers, the columns of Pæstum, the rounded tiers and galleries of the amphitheatre. On the other hand, the painter generally avoids (except for some special effect of colour or contrast) lean, harsh, and angular limbs or features, constrained and graceless clothing, awkward postures and actions; heavy, ungainly, or shapeless animal forms, such as the bear, the cart-horse, the goose, and the slug; flat monotonous plains; the still ocean unbroken by a winding shore or bluff headland, unrelieved by a ship with bellied sails or a tempest curling the breakers on the beach; straight streets, plain rectangular houses, square windows, and flat façades destitute of arch or column, dome or portico.

Grant Allen (1848-1899).

247. —AND IMPRESSIONISM AT LAST

i

PERSONAL preference, artistic impressionability, the counsel of a passing mood, the testimony of a sensitive eye, are not these sufficient reasons for the appearance of some given form in a picture? Moreover, a picture cannot be the efficient, the first cause of a picture; all true art originates in the personal pre-dilections of an individual mind, and in personal sensitiveness to external nature. The rest is disguised copying, artistic or inartistic mannerism.

ii

The largeness, the dignity, the swim of nature seen under a distributed attention is continually contradicted by the appearances which result from separate observations made upon smaller fields of sight. . .

I have often seen men painting sunsets who would shade out the sky with a hat or hand that they might see what they were pleased to call the true colour of the ground. Of course the

grass instantly became of quite another colour to what it had
been when the sky entered the painter's eyes at the same time.
But they seemed unaware that they were painting by this
process two quite different effects in one frame.

                                    R. A. M. Stevenson (1847-1900).

248. JUSTUS QUIDEM TU ES, DOMINE

*Justus quidem tu es, Domine, si disputem tecum :
verumtamen justa loquar ad te : Quare via impiorum
prosperatur ?*

THOU art indeed just, Lord, if I contend
With thee; but, sir, so what I plead is just.
Why do sinners' ways prosper? and why must
Disappointment all I endeavour end?

   Wert thou my enemy, O thou my friend,
How wouldst thou worse, I wonder, than thou dost
Defeat, thwart me? Oh, the sots and thralls of lust
Do in spare hours more thrive than I that spend,
Sir, life upon thy cause. See, banks and brakes
Now, leavèd how thick! lacèd they are again
With fretty chervil, look, and fresh wind shakes
Them; birds build—but not I build; no, but strain,
Time's eunuch, and not breed one work that wakes.
Mine, O thou lord of life, send my roots rain.
                        Gerard Manley Hopkins (1844-1889).

249. THE MEDITATION OF THE OLD FISHERMEN

YOU waves, though you dance by my feet like children at play,
Though you glow and you glance, though you purr and you dart,
In the Junes that were warmer than these are, the waves were
        more gay,
When I was a boy with never a crack in my heart.

The herring are not in the tides as they were of old;
My sorrow! for many a creak gave the creel in the cart
That carried the take to Sligo town to be sold,
When I was a boy with never a crack in my heart.

And ah, you proud maiden, you are not so fair when his oar
Is heard on the water, as they were, the proud and apart,
Who paced in the eve by the nets on the pebbly shore,
When I was a boy with never a crack in my heart.

W. B. Yeats (1865-1939).

250. THE WOODS OF ARCADY ARE DEAD

THE woods of Arcady are dead,
And over is their antique joy;
Of old the world on dreaming fed;
Grey truth is now her painted toy;
Yet still she turns her restless head. . .

W. B. Yeats (1865-1939).

251. EARTH, HESPER, MARS

. . Hesper, whom the poet call'd the Bringer home of all good
    things.
  All good things may move in Hesper, perfect peoples,
    perfect kings.

  Hesper—Venus—were we native to that splendour or in
    Mars,
  We should see the Globe we groan in, fairest of their evening
    stars.

  Could we dream of wars and carnage, craft and madness,
    lust and spite,
  Roaring London, raving Paris, in that point of peaceful light?

Might we not in glancing heavenward on a star so silver-
    fair,
Yearn, and clasp the hands and murmur, "Would to God
    that we were there?" . .

                 Alfred Tennyson (1809-1892).

252. MY EPITAPH

HERE lies a bard, let epitaphs be true,
His vices many, and his virtues few;
Who always left religion in the lurch
But never left a tavern for a church,
Drank more from pewter than Pierian spring
And only in his cups was known to sing;
Laugh'd at the world, however it may blame,
And died regardless of his fate or fame.

               H. J. Daniel (1818-1889).

253. CHAOS, COSMOS! COSMOS, CHAOS!

. . Chaos, Cosmos! Cosmos, Chaos! once again the sickening
    game;
Freedom, free to slay herself, and dying while they shout
    her name.

Step by step we gain'd a freedom known to Europe, known
    to all ;
Step by step we rose to greatness,—thro' the tonguesters we
    may fall.

You that woo the Voices—tell them "old experience is a
    fool,"
Teach your flatter'd kings that only those who cannot read
    can rule.

Pluck the mighty from their seat, but set no meek ones in
    their place;
Pillory Wisdom in your markets, pelt your offal at her face.

Tumble Nature heel o'er head, and, yelling with the yelling
street,
Set the feet above the brain and swear the brain is in the
feet.

Bring the old dark ages back without the faith, without the
hope,
Break the State, the Church, the Throne, and roll their
ruins down the slope.

Authors—atheist, essayist, novelist, realist, rhymester, play
your part,
Paint the mortal shame of nature with the living hues
of Art.

Rip your brothers' vices open, strip your own foul passions
bare;
Down with Reticence, down with Reverence—forward—
naked—let them stare.

Feed the budding rose of boyhood with the drainage of your
sewer;
Send the drain into the fountain, lest the stream should
issue pure.

Set the maiden fancies wallowing in the troughs of Zolaism,—
Forward, forward, ay and backward, downward too into the
abysm.

Do your best to charm the worst, to lower the rising race
of men;
Have we risen from out the beast, then back into the beast
again?

Only "dust to dust" for me that sicken at your lawless din,
Dust in wholesome old-world dust before the newer world
begin. . .

Alfred Tennyson (1809-1892).

254. CALIBAN

THE nineteenth century dislike of Realism is the rage of Caliban seeing his own face in a glass.

The nineteenth century dislike of Romanticism is the rage of Caliban not seeing his own face in a glass. . .

Oscar Wilde (1856-1900).

255. HISTORY

IF the Past has been an obstacle and a burden, knowledge of the Past is the safest and the surest emancipation. And the earnest search for it is one of the signs that distinguish the four centuries of which I speak from those that went before. The Middle Ages, which possessed good writers of contemporary narrative, were careless and impatient of older fact. They became content to be deceived, to live in a twilight of fiction, under clouds of false witness, inventing according to convenience, and glad to welcome the forger and the cheat. As time went on, the atmosphere of accredited mendacity thickened, until, in the Renaissance, the art of exposing falsehood dawned upon keen Italian minds. It was then that History as we understand it began to be understood, and the illustrious dynasty of scholars arose to whom we still look both for method and material. Unlike the dreaming prehistoric world, ours knows the need and the duty to make itself master of the earlier times, and to forfeit nothing of their wisdom or their warnings, and has devoted its best energy and treasure to the sovereign purpose of detecting error and vindicating entrusted truth.

Lord Acton (1834-1902).

256. THE GODS ARE DEAD!

THE gods are dead? Perhaps they are! Who knows?
Living at least in Lemprière undeleted,
The wise, the fair, the awful, the jocose,
Are one and all, I like to think, retreated
In some still land of lilacs and the rose.

K*

Once high they sat, and high o'er earthly shows
With sacrificial dance and song were greeted.
Once . . . long ago. But now, the story goes,
     The gods are dead.

It must be true. The world, a world of prose,
Full-crammed with facts, in science swathed and sheeted,
Nods in a stertorous after-dinner doze!
Plangent and sad, in every wind that blows
Who will may hear the sorry words repeated:—
     "The Gods are Dead!"

      W. E. Henley (1849-1903).

257. A PRAYER

SEARCHER of souls, you who in heaven abide,
To whom the secrets of all hearts are open,
Though I do lie to all the world beside,
From me to thee no falsehood shall be spoken.
Cleanse me not, Lord, I say, from secret sin
But from those faults which he who runs can see.
'Tis these that torture me, O Lord, begin
With these and let the hidden vices be;
If you must cleanse these too, at any rate
Deal with the seen sins first, 'tis only reason,
They being so gross, to let the others wait
The leisure of some more convenient season;
 And cleanse not all even then, leave me a few.
 I would not be—not quite—so pure as you.
     Samuel Butler (1835-1902).

258. A THUNDERSTORM IN TOWN

(A REMINISCENCE: 1893)

SHE wore a new "terra-cotta" dress,
And we stayed, because of the pelting storm,
Within the hansom's dry recess,
Though the horse had stopped; yea, motionles
 We sat on, snug and warm.

Then the downpour ceased, to my sharp, sad pain
And the glass that had screened our forms before
Flew up, and out she sprang to her door:
I should have kissed her if the rain
      Had lasted a minute more.

                              Thomas Hardy (1840-1928).

259. VILLON'S STRAIGHT TIP TO ALL CROSS COVES

" Tout aux tavernes et aux filles"

SUPPOSE you screeve? or go cheap-jack?
      Or fake the broads? or fig a nag?
Or thimble-rig? or knap a yack?
      Or pitch a snide? or smash a rag?
      Suppose you duff? or nose and lag?
Or get the straight, and land your pot?
      How do you melt the multy swag?
Booze and the blowens cop the lot.

Fiddle, or fence, or mace, or mack;
      Or moskeneer, or flash the drag;
Dead-lurk a crib, or do a crack;
      Pad with a slang, or chuck a fag;
      Bonnet, or tout, or mump and gag;
Rattle the tats, or mark the spot;
      You can not bank a single stag;
Booze and the blowens cop the lot.

Suppose you try a different tack,
      And on the square you flash your flag?
At penny-a-lining make your whack,
      Or with the mummers mug and gag?
      For nix, for nix the dibbs you bag!
At any graft, no matter what,
      Your merry goblins soon stravag:
Booze and the blowens cop the lot.

It's up the spout and Charley Wag
With wipes and tickers and what not.
Until the squeezer nips your scrag,
Booze and the blowens cop the lot.

W. E. Henley (1849-1903).

260. THE FALL OF OSCAR WILDE (1895)

i. *Oscar Wilde to Lord Alfred Douglas*

MY OWN BOY,

Your sonnet is quite lovely, and it is a marvel that those
red rose-leaf lips of yours should have been made no less for
music of song than for madness of kisses. Your slim gilt soul
walks between passion and poetry. I know Hyacinthus, whom
Apollo loved so madly, was you in Greek days.

Why are you alone in London, and when do you go to
Salisbury? Do go there to cool your hands in the grey twilight
of Gothic things, and come here whenever you like. It is a
lovely place—it only lacks you; but go to Salisbury first.

Always, with undying love,

Yours,

OSCAR.

ii. *But Mr. Wilde is a poet. . .*

SIR EDWARD CLARKE (for Wilde). The words of that letter,
gentlemen, may appear extravagant to those in the habit
of writing commercial correspondence (Laughter), or those
ordinary letters which the necessities of life force upon one
every day; but Mr. Wilde is a poet, and the letter is considered by him as a prose sonnet, and one of which he is in no
way ashamed and is prepared to produce anywhere as the
expression of true poetic feeling, and with no relation whatever
to the hateful and repulsive suggestions put to it in the plea
in this case.

iii. *Wilde versus Carson*

CARSON.   Where was Lord Alfred Douglas staying when you wrote that letter to him?

WILDE.   At the Savoy; and I was at Babbacombe, near Torquay.

CARSON.   It was a letter in answer to something he had sent you?

WILDE.   Yes, a poem.

CARSON.   Why should a man of your age address a boy nearly twenty years younger as "My own boy"?

WILDE.   I was fond of him. I have always been fond of him.

CARSON.   Do you adore him?

WILDE.   No, but I have always liked him. I think it is a beautiful letter. It is a poem. I was not writing an ordinary letter. You might as well cross-examine me as to whether *King Lear* or a sonnet of Shakespeare was proper.

CARSON.   Apart from art, Mr. Wilde?

WILDE.   I cannot answer apart from art.

CARSON.   Suppose a man who was not an artist had written this letter, would you say it was a proper letter?

WILDE.   A man who was not an artist could not have written that letter.

CARSON.   Why?

WILDE.   Because nobody but an artist could write it. He certainly could not write the language unless he were a man of letters.

CARSON.   I can suggest, for the sake of your reputation, that there is nothing very wonderful in this "red rose-leaf lips of yours"?

WILDE.   A great deal depends on the way it is read.

CARSON.   "Your slim gilt soul walks between passion and poetry." Is that a beautiful phrase?

WILDE.   Not as *you* read it, Mr. Carson. You read it very badly.

CARSON.   I do not profess to be an artist; and when I hear you give evidence, I am glad I am not. . .

261. A PERSIAN STAR-TILE

WHEN regarded in a certain light in which the shine of the glaze is not perceptible the lustre pigment appears of a delicate fawn or raw-siena tint admirably harmonising with the blue and green. Alter the angle of vision ever so slightly, and the lustre flashes forth in amethyst and ruby, sapphire and emerald, so as to appear almost alive. The only substance to which it may be compared is the Labrador felspar familiarly known as Pavement of Paradise, wherein seems to be reflected all the gorgeous effulgence of an oriental sunset. The lustre effect is nothing less than magical, and witnessing this startling transformation one is not surprised at the Persian belief in magic.

Henry Wallis (1830-1916).

262. A PORTRAIT

I AM a kind of farthing dip,
　Unfriendly to the nose and eyes;
A blue-behinded ape, I skip
　Upon the trees of Paradise.

At mankind's feast, I take my place
　In solemn, sanctimonious state,
And have the air of saying grace
　While I defile the dinner plate.

I am "the smiler with the knife,"
　The battener upon garbage, I—
Dear Heaven, with such a rancid life,
　Were it not better far to die?

Yet still, about the human pale,
　I love to scamper, love to race,
To swing by my irreverent tail
　All over the most holy place. . .

R. L. Stevenson (1850-1894).

263. "I SAW THE WOOD FOR WHAT IT WAS"

. . Thick round me in the teeming mud
   Brier and fern strove to the blood:
   The hooked liana in his gin
   Noosed his reluctant neighbours in:
   There the green murderer throve and spread,
   Upon his smothering victims fed,
   And wantoned on his climbing coil.
   Contending roots fought for the soil
   Like frightened demons: with despair
   Competing branches pushed for air.
   Green conquerors from overhead
   Bestrode the bodies of their dead:
   The Caesars of the sylvan field,
   Unused to fail, foredoomed to yield:
   For in the groins of branches, lo!
   The cancers of the orchid grow.
   Silent as in the listed ring
   Two chartered wrestlers strain and cling;
   Dumb as by yellow Hooghly's side
   The suffocating captives died;
   So hushed the woodland warfare goes
   Unceasing; and the silent foes
   Grapple and smother, strain and clasp
   Without a cry, without a gasp.
   Here also sound thy fans, O God,
   Here too thy banners move abroad:
   Forest and city, sea and shore,
   And the whole earth, thy threshing-floor!
   The drums of war, the drums of peace,
   Roll through our cities without cease,
   And all the iron halls of life
   Ring with the unremitting strife. . .

                                        R. L. Stevenson (1850-1894).

264. WE'LL TO THE WOODS

"*Allons au bois le may cueillir.*"—Charles d'Orléans.

WE'LL to the woods and gather may
Fresh from the footprints of the rain.
We'll to the woods, at every vein
To drink the spirit of the day.

The winds of spring are out at play,
The needs of spring in heart and brain.
We'll to the woods and gather may
Fresh from the footprints of the rain.

The world's too near her end, you say?
Hark to the blackbird's mad refrain!
It waits for her, the vast Inane?
Then, girls, to help her on the way
We'll to the woods and gather may.

W. E. Henley (1849-1903).

265. I TALKED ONE MIDNIGHT

I talked one midnight with the jolly ghost
Of a gray ancestor, Tom Heywood hight ;
And, "Here's," says he, his old heart liquor-lifted—
"Here's how we did when Gloriana shone :"

All in a garden green
    Thrushes were singing;
Red rose and white between,
    Lilies were springing;
It was the merry May;
    Yet sang my Lady:—
"Nay, Sweet, now nay, now nay!
    I am not ready."

Then to a pleasant shade
    I did invite her:
All things a concert made,
    For to delight her;
Under, the grass was gay;
    Yet sang my Lady:—
"Nay, Sweet, now nay, now nay!
    I am not ready."

                  W. E. Henley (1849-1903).

266. THE GIFT OF THE SEA

THE dead child lay in the shroud,
    And the widow watched beside;
And her mother slept, and the Channel swept
    The gale in the teeth of the tide.

But the mother laughed at all.
  "I have lost my man in the sea,
And the child is dead. Be still," she said,
  "What more can ye do to me?"

The widow watched the dead,
    And the candle guttered low,
And she tried to sing the Passing Song
    That bids the poor soul go.

And "Mary take you now," she sang,
  "That lay against my heart."
And "Mary smooth your crib to-night,"
  But she could not say "Depart."

Then came a cry from the sea,
  But the sea-rime blinded the glass,
And "Heard ye nothing, mother?" she said,
  "'Tis the child that waits to pass."

And the nodding mother sighed.
"'Tis the lambing ewe in the whin,
For why should the christened soul cry out
    That never knew of sin?"

"O feet I have held in my hand,
    O hands at my heart to catch,
How should they know the road to go,
    And how should they lift the latch?"

They laid a sheet to the door,
    With the little quilt atop,
That it might not hurt from the cold or the dirt,
    But the crying would not stop.

The widow lifted the latch
    And strained her eyes to see,
And opened the door on the bitter shore
    To let the soul go free.

There was neither glimmer nor ghost,
    There was neither spirit nor spark,
And "Heard ye nothing, mother?" she said,
    "'Tis crying for me in the dark."

And the nodding mother sighed:
    "'Tis sorrow makes ye dull;
Have ye yet to learn the cry of the tern,
    Or the wail of the wind-blown gull?"

"The terns are blown inland,
    The grey gull follows the plough.
'Twas never a bird, the voice I heard,
    O mother, I hear it now!"

"Lie still, dear lamb, lie still;
    The child is passed from harm,
'Tis the ache in your breast that broke your rest,
    And the feel of an empty arm."

She put her mother aside,
 "In Mary's name let be!
For the peace of my soul I must go," she said,
   And she went to the calling sea.

In the heel of the wind-bit pier,
   Where the twisted weed was piled,
She came to the life she had missed by an hour,
   For she came to a little child.

She laid it into her breast,
   And back to her mother she came,
But it would not feed and it would not heed,
   Though she gave it her own child's name.

And the dead child dripped on her breast,
   And her own in the shroud lay stark;
And "God forgive us, mother," she said,
 "We let it die in the dark!"

                    Rudyard Kipling (1865-1936).

267. TWILIGHT

THE pale grey sea crawls stealthily
Up the pale lilac of the beach;
A bluer grey, the waters reach
To where the horizon ends the sea.

Flushed with a tinge of dusky rose,
The clouds, a twilit lavender,
Flood the low sky, and duskier
The mist comes flooding in, and flows

Into the twilight of the land,
And darkness, coming softly down,
Rustles across the fading sand
And folds its arms about the town.

                    Arthur Symons (1865-1945).

268. MANDOLINE

(After Paul Verlaine)

THE singers of serenades
Whispers their fated vows
Unto fair listening maids
Under the singing boughs.

Tircis, Aminte, are there,
Clitandre has waited long,
And Damis for many a fair
Tyrant makes many a song.

Their short vests, silken and bright,
Their long pale silken trains,
Their elegance of delight,
Twine soft blue silken chains.

And the mandolines and they,
Faintlier breathing, swoon
Into the rose and grey
Ecstasy of the moon.

Arthur Symons (1865-1945).

269. TO MY WIFE

(A FRAGMENT)

LONG must elapse ere you behold again
Green forest frame the entry of the lane—
The wild lane with the bramble and the briar,
The year-old cart-tracks perfect in the mire,
The wayside smoke, perchance, the dwarfish huts,
And ramblers' donkey drinking from the ruts:—
Long ere you trace how deviously it leads,
Back from man's chimneys and the bleating meads

To the woodland shadow, to the sylvan hush,
When but the brooklet chuckles in the brush—
Back from the sun and bustle of the vale
To where the great voice of the nightingale
Fills all the forest like a single room,
And all the banks smell of the golden broom;
So wander on until the eve descends,
And back returning to your firelit friends,
You see the rosy sun, despoiled of light,
Hung, caught in thickets, like a schoolboy's kite.

Here from the sea the unfruitful sun shall rise,
Bathe the bare deck and blind the unshielded eyes;
The allotted hours aloft shall wheel in vain
And in the unpregnant ocean plunge again.
Assault of squalls that mock the watchful guard,
And pluck the bursting canvas from the yard,
And senseless clamour of the calm, at night
Must mar your slumbers. By the plunging light,
In beetle-haunted, most unwomanly bower
Of the wild-swerving cabin, hour by hour. . .

Schooner "Equator."

                              R. L. Stevenson (1850-1894).

270. HALLUCINATION

ONE petal of a blood-red tulip pressed
Between the pages of a Baudelaire:
No more; and I was suddenly aware
Of the white fragrant apple of a breast
On which my lips were pastured; and I knew
That dreaming I remembered an old dream.
Sweeter than any fruit that fruit did seem,
Which, as my hungry teeth devoured it, grew
Ever again, and tantalised my taste.
So, vainly hungering, I seemed to see
Eve and the serpent and the apple-tree,
And Adam in the garden, and God laying waste

Innocent Eden, because man's desire,
Godlike before, now for a woman's sake
Descended through the woman to the snake.
Then as my mouth grew parched, stung as with fire
By that white fragrant apple, once so fair,
That seemed to shrink and spire into a flame,
I cried, and wakened, crying on your name:
One blood-red petal stained the Baudelaire.

Arthur Symons (1865-1945).

271. DIRGE OF THE MUNSTER FOREST. 1581

[*When the Geraldine rebellion collapsed in* 1581, *and
Munster was desolated after a war, the horrors of
which were extreme, the woods of Munster were to be
destroyed so as to drive the Earl of Desmond and his
starving followers from shelter. Thousands of the
Irish were killed in the fighting or hanged.*]

BRING out the hemlock! bring the funeral yew!
The faithful ivy that doth all enfold;
Heap high the rocks, the patient brown earth strew,
And cover them against the numbing cold.
Marshal my retinue of bird and beast,
Wren, titmouse, robin, birds of every hue;
Let none keep back, no, not the very least,
Nor fox, nor deer, nor tiny nibbling crew,
Only bid one of all my forest clan
Keep far from us on this our funeral day.
On the grey wolf I lay my sovereign ban,
The great grey wolf who scrapes the earth away;
Lest, with hooked claw and furious hunger, he
Lay bare my dead for gloating foes to see—
Lay bare my dead, who died, and died for me.

For I must shortly die as they have died,
And lo! my doom stands yoked and linked with theirs;
The axe is sharpened to cut down my pride:
I pass, I die, and leave no natural heirs.

Soon shall my sylvan coronals be cast;
My hidden sanctuaries, my secret ways,
Naked must stand to the rebellious blast;
No Spring shall quicken what this Autumn slays.
Therefore, while still I keep my russet crown,
I summon all my lieges to the feast.
Hither, ye flutterers! black, or pied, or brown;
Hither, ye furred ones! Hither every beast!
Only to one of all my forest clan
I cry, "Avaunt! Our morning revels flee!"
On the grey wolf I lay my sovereign ban,
The great grey wolf with scraping claws, lest he
Lay bare my dead for gloating foes to see—
Lay bare my dead, who died, and died for me.

Emily Lawless (1845-1913).

272. THE CAP AND BELLS

THE jester walked in the garden:
The garden had fallen still;
He bade his soul rise upward
And stand on her window-sill.

It rose in a straight blue garment,
When owls began to call:
It had grown wise-tongued by thinking
Of a quiet and light footfall;

But the young queen would not listen;
She rose in her pale night-gown;
She drew in the heavy casement
And pushed the latches down.

He bade his heart go to her,
When the owls called out no more;
In a red and quivering garment
It sang to her through the door.

It had grown sweet-tongued by dreaming
Of a flutter of flower-like hair;
But she took up her fan from the table
And waved it off on the air.

"I have cap and bells," he pondered,
"I will send them to her and die";
And when the morning whitened
He left them where she went by.

She laid them upon her bosom,
Under a cloud of her hair,
And her red lips sang them a love-song
Till stars grew out of the air.

She opened her door and her window,
And the heart and the soul came through,
To her right hand came the red one,
To her left hand came the blue.

Thy set up a noise like crickets,
A chattering wise and sweet,
And her hair was a folded flower
And the quiet of love in her feet.

W. B. Yeats (1865-1939).

273. DANNY DEEVER

"What are the bugles blowin' for?" said Files-on-Parade.
"To turn you out, to turn you out," the Colour-Sergeant said.
"What makes you look so white, so white?" said Files-on-Parade.
"I'm dreadin' what I've got to watch," the Colour-Sergeant said.
> For they're hangin' Danny Deever, you can hear the
> Dead March play,
> The regiment's in 'ollow square—they're hangin'
> him to-day;
> They've taken of his buttons off an' cut his stripes
> away,
> An' they're hangin' Danny Deever in the mornin'.

"What makes the rear-rank breathe so 'ard?" said Files-on-
Parade.
"It's bitter cold, it's bitter cold," the Colour-Sergeant said.
"What makes that front-rank man fall down?" says Files-on-
Parade.
"A touch o' sun, a touch o' sun," the Colour-Sergeant said.
>They are hangin' Danny Deever, they are marchin'
>   of 'im round,
>They 'ave 'alted Danny Deever by 'is coffin on the
>   ground;
>An' 'e'll swing in 'arf a minute for a sneakin' shootin'
>   hound—
>O they're hangin' Danny Deever in the mornin'!

"'Is cot was right-'and cot to mine," said Files-on-Parade.
"'E's sleepin' out an' far to-night," the Colour-Sergeant said.
"I've drunk 'is beer a score o' times," said Files-on-Parade.
"'E's drinkin' bitter beer alone," the Colour-Sergeant said.
>They are hangin' Danny Deever, you must mark 'im
>   to 'is place,
>For 'e shot a comrade sleepin'—you must look 'im
>   in the face;
>Nine 'undred of 'is county an' the regiment's disgrace,
>While they're hangin' Danny Deever in the mornin'.

"What's that so black agin the sun?" said Files-on-Parade.
"It's Danny fightin' 'ard for life," the Colour-Sergeant said.
"What's that that whimpers over'ead?" said Files-on-Parade.
"It's Danny's soul that's passin' now," the Colour-Sergeant
said.
>For they're done with Danny Deever, you can 'ear
>   the quickstep play,
>The regiment's in column, an' they're marchin' us
>   away;
>Ho! the young recruits are shakin', an' they'll
>   want their beer to-day,
>After hangin' Danny Deever in the mornin'.
>   *Rudyard Kipling* (1865-1936).

274. MR. KIPLING

HE who would stir us now by fiction must either give us an entirely new background, or reveal to us the soul of man in its innermost workings. The first is for the moment being done for us by Mr. Rudyard Kipling. As one turns over the pages of his *Plain Tales from the Hills*, one feels as if one were seated under a palm-tree reading life by superb flashes of vulgarity. The bright colours of the bazaar dazzle one's eyes. The jaded, second-rate Anglo-Indians are in exquisite incongruity with their surroundings. The mere lack of style in the story-teller gives an odd journalistic realism to what he tells us. From the point of view of literature Mr. Kipling is a genius who drops his aspirates. From the point of view of life he is a reporter who knows vulgarity better than anyone has known it. Dickens knew its clothes and its comedy. Mr. Kipling knows its essence and its seriousness. He is our first authority on the second-rate, and has seen marvellous things through keyholes, and his backgrounds are real works of art.

Oscar Wilde (1856-1900).

275. IN VALLEYS GREEN AND STILL

IN valleys green and still
  Where lovers wander maying
They hear from over hill
  A music playing.

Behind the drum and fife,
  Past hawthornwood and hollow,
Through earth and out of life
  The soldiers follow.

The soldier's is the trade:
  In any wind or weather
He steals the heart of maid
  And man together.

The lover and his lass
   Beneath the hawthorn lying
Have heard the soldiers pass,
   And both are sighing.

And down the distance they
   With dying note and swelling
Walk the resounding way
   To the still dwelling.

              A. E. Housman (1859-1936).

276. IN TENEBRIS

"*Heu mihi, quia incolatus meus prolongatus est!
Habitavi cum habitantibus Cedar; multum incola
fuit anima mea.*"—Ps. cxix.

THERE have been times when I well might have passed and the
    ending have come—
Points in my path when the dark might have stolen on me,
    artless, unrueing—
Ere I had learnt that the world was a welter of futile doing:
Such had been times when I well might have passed, and the
    ending have come!

Say, on the noon when the half-sunny hours told that April
    was nigh,
And I upgathered and cast forth the snow from the crocus-
    border,
Fashioned and furbished the soil into a summer-seeming order,
Glowing in gladsome faith that I quickened the year thereby.

Or on that loneliest of eves when afar and benighted we stood,
She who upheld me and I, in the midmost of Egdon together,
Confident I in her watching and ward through the blackening
    heather,
Deeming her matchless in might and with measureless scope
    endued.

Or on that winter-wild night when, reclined by the chimney-
　　nook quoin,
Slowly a drowse overgat me, the smallest and feeblest of folk
　　there,
Weak from my baptism of pain; when at times and anon I
　　awoke there—
Heard of a world wheeling on, with no listing or longing to join.

Even then! while unweeting that vision could vex or that
　　knowledge could numb,
That sweets to the mouth in the belly are bitter, and tart, and
　　untoward,
Then, on some dim-coloured scene should my briefly raised
　　curtain have lowered,
Then might the Voice that is law have said "Cease!" and the
　　ending have come.

　1896.　　　　　　　　　　　　*Thomas Hardy* (1840-1928).

277. LAUSANNE,

IN GIBBON'S OLD GARDEN: 11-12 P.M.

June 27, 1897

[The 110th anniversary of the completion of the
Decline and Fall at the same hour and place.]

　　A SPIRIT seems to pass,
　Formal in pose, but grave withal and grand
　He contemplates a volume in his hand,
And far lamps fleck him through the thin acacias.

　Anon the book is closed,
　With "It is finished!"　And at the alley's end
　He turns, and when on me his glances bend
As from the Past comes speech—small, muted, yet composed

"How fares the Truth?—Ill?
—Do pens but slily further her advance?
May one not speed her but in phrase askance?
Do scribes aver the Comic to be Reverend still?

"Still rule those minds on earth
At whom sage Milton's wormwood words were hurled:
' *Truth like a bastard comes into the world*
Never without ill-fame to him who gives her birth'?"

Thomas Hardy (1840-1928).

278. INTO MY HEART AN AIR THAT KILLS

INTO my heart an air that kills
    From yon far country blows:
What are those blue remembered hills,
    What spires, what farms are those?

That is the land of lost content,
    I see it shining plain,
The happy highways where I went
    And cannot come again.

A. E. Housman (1859-1936).

NOTES AND SOURCES

The numbers are of items, not pages. Poems given in full are taken from the standard editions and, generally, their sources are not indicated.

1. *The Gardener's Daughter.* Tennyson thought " The mellow ouzel fluted in the elm " one of his best lines.
2. *Past and Present*, 1843.
3. *Charles Kingsley: His Letters and Memories of his Life*, 1877.
4. *Ibid.*
5. The picture was " Returning from the Ball," exhibited in the Academy in 1845, and now in the Tate.
7. *The Gardener's Daughter.*
9. *Past and Present*, 1843.
10. *Victorian Street Ballads*, edited by W. Henderson, 1937.

How curious it is to compare the honest language of the street ballads with the Latinate, silver dishonesty of the language of so many Victorian poets, Tennyson included ! The illiterate and the psychopathic writers of delightful nonsense (Lear and Carroll) escape a legitimate condemnation ; though once the sentence is delivered one may enjoy, falsity or no, the melody and the skill, the wonderful embroidery with *ersatz* silks. By the Sixties (see Mayhew's *London Labour and London Poor*) the street poets were dying out. Mayhew cross-examined one of them who made four shillings a week in the best weeks by putting new bottoms in old tin teapots, and three shillings in a good week or a shilling in a poor week by writing poems for the printers. He was very fond of Goldsmith, and complained : " The printers like hanging subjects best and I don't." This man had been brought up to hawking wire-work all over England and Wales. " We lost count of the days sometimes in wild parts ; but if we did lose count, or thought we had, I could always tell when it was Sunday morning by the look of nature ; there was a mystery and beauty about it as told me."

It is high time the whole mass of the street ballads was sifted and anthologized ; and not only the ballads, but the popular songs from Victorian days to our own. More poetry is hidden away in the ballads and the songs than we realize ; or perhaps will realize for another fifty years.

11. *Modern Street Ballads*, edited by John Ashton, 1888.
16. *Literary Works of James Smetham*, edited by William Davies, 1893.

He was an artist of distinction, a wordpainter, and a critic (in his separately published *Letters*) of sane and warm perception. Smetham's friends were Rossetti, Ruskin, and Frederic Shields,

and Ford Madox Brown—all admirers of his painting. He died
of religious melancholy, overloaded with the sense of his un-
worthiness and his sins. Most of his pictures are privately
owned or lost ; though a few may be seen in Oxford at the
Ashmolean Museum.

18. *In Memoriam.* Verlaine to Yeats : he had once tried to translate
In Memoriam, but could not because Tennyson was " too noble,
too Anglais, and, when he should have been broken-hearted,
had many reminiscences " (*The Cutting of an Agate*).

19. See No. 16.

24. From Millais' Diary, quoted in *Life and Letters of Sir John Millais*,
1899.

25. *Modern Painters.*

26. In the " Historical Sketch of the Progress of Opinion on the
Origin of Species " which Darwin prefixed to his own great
book, he wrote of the *Vestiges of Creation* that " from its powerful
and brilliant style, though displaying in the earlier editions little
accurate knowledge and a great want of scientific caution,"
it had at once a wide circulation. " In my opinion it has done
excellent service in this country in calling attention to the
subject, in removing prejudice, and in thus preparing the ground
for the reception of analogous views."

    Tennyson was quick to read the *Vestiges*. How disconcerting
it must have been for pious amateur geologists (see note on
No. 77) that their delightful science should now be betraying
them ! That the solid rocks should be preserving all the
insolidities of doubt ! An Early Victorian nightmare for bishop
or vicar : lying sleepless on a pillow and a feather-bed lumpy
with fossils. Bishop's, or vicar's, head changes into a huge
stony sea-urchin, geologically hammered at by Chambers or
Lyell ! It breaks. Hundreds of hungry Chartists think the
pieces are bread, and try to eat them.

29. See No. 11.

30. *Ibid.*

31. " A Walk in the Workhouse," in *Reprinted Pieces*.

32. See too what Newman had to say about the exclusive possession of
enjoyments (No. 75). Peacock's poem is taken from *Fifty
Years of Public Work*, 1884, by his friend Sir Henry Cole.

35. " North Devon," in *Prose Idylls*, 1873.

36. See No. 10.

37. *Modern Painters.*

38. " The Woodman's Daughter," in *Poems*, 1844.

39. *Modern Painters* : preface to the second edition, 1857.

41. *Sonnets from the Portuguese.*

42. Lear's *Book of Nonsense* came out in 1846. Lewis Carroll wrote
these limericks in 1845 when he was thirteen years old. I have
heard it remarked that perhaps in nonsense alone did the

Victorians express themselves in honest language. Perhaps, until Hopkins. But Hopkins is, after all, the Victorian word-painter who paints both clearest *and deepest* of all. Limericks were current at least a quarter of a century before the *Book of Nonsense*.

43. One hears people complaining that Lear left his limericks so to say *open*, by not finding a third rhyming word. But of course. It was this that made the nonsense complete nonsense.

44. *The Princess*, 1848.

45. " Sir Hubert," in *Poems*, 1844.

46. See No. 44.

47. *Modern Painters*.

48. See No. 44.

49. " The Religion of the Day," in *Parochial and Plain Sermons*.

50. *Life of Frederick Denison Maurice*, 1884.

51. *Ibid.* For Maurice looking rather the agonized man than the saint, see the portrait of him as one of the two brain-workers in Ford Madox Brown's " Work."

52. This was in the first number of *The Germ* (January 1850), the Pre-Raphaelite magazine.

54. From *The Germ*, No. 4, May 1850—or rather *Art and Poetry* as they rechristened it. Deverell died young ; but might obviously have been poet as well as painter. He was unlucky after death, since several of his few pictures have been burnt. The best that survives must, I conclude, be " The Irish Vagrants " in Johannesburg Art Gallery.

55. *Household Words*, June 15, 1850. Dickens had had plenty of time since the opening of the Academy exhibition to judge that the article was just what his middle-class public required. *Household Words* was young, and Dickens was building it up, and assuring its popularity.

56. *The Germ* (*Art and Poetry*), March 1850. Rossetti spoilt this poem later by enlarging it and weakening its Pre-Raphaelite clarity. It is in the collected editions as " The Sea-Limits."

57. See No. 52.

58. " Dipsychus."

59. The opening of *Bleak House*, 1852.

60. See No. 16.

61. " A Walk to Amington," in *A Rhyming Chronicle of Incidents and Feelings*, 1850. Jean Ingelow was an unsophisticated amateur ; a poet of one poem and several bits.

64. See No. 11.

66. *Notes sur l'Angleterre*, 1872, which was translated and, as it deserved to be, often reprinted. Indeed, this brilliant examination of ourselves, or our grandfathers, ought to be kept in print as a classic of observation. Taine was here, with his sharp eyes and unsentimental intelligence, in 1858.

67. See No. 11.
68. *The Stones of Venice.*
71. " A Boy's Poem."
72. *Thomas Woolner, R.A.*, by Amy Woolner, 1917. Woolner, sculptor and Pre-Raphaelite Brother, was on his way back from Australia, to which he had emigrated in search of better fortune. He became a rather trying and self-important figure ; and as a sculptor he gets left out whenever the P.R.B. is discussed. I could not say whether his statuary or drawing ever equalled his writing—at least his writing in prose, since his verse is feeble. He was very friendly with the Tennysons. It was Woolner who suggested the subject of *Enoch Arden* ; and his journal, at sea and in Australia, shows he could well have suggested some of the colour.
74. *Angel in the House*, Canto XI.
75. *Lectures on Certain Difficulties felt by Anglicans in submitting to the Catholic Church*, No. VIII, 1850.
76. " Song of Myself." Victorian reaction to Whitman was a curious blend of sympathetic attraction and moral repulsion.
77. *Aurora Leigh*, 1857, Fifth Book. One of the most movingly alive of Victorian narrative poems. And a long gallery of word-paintings.

Had Mr. John Betjeman been alive in 1857, unconverted or converted by Father Newman, man of letters or incumbent, he would have been also a geologist. Geology was the cultural hobby then, as architecture (especially the neo-Gothic) is now. Thus an advertisement in Murray's *Handbook Advertiser* for 1856 (at the end of all the Murrays):

GEOLOGY AND MINERALOGY

A knowledge of these interesting branches of science adds greatly to the pleasure of the traveller in all parts of the world, and may lead to important discoveries. Mr. TENNANT, Mineralogist to her Majesty, 149, STRAND, gives *Practical Instruction* in MINERALOGY and GEOLOGY. He can supply Geological Maps, Hammers, and Bottles, Blow-pipes, and all the recent Works on Mineralogy, Conchology, Chemistry, and Geology.

Elementary Collections of Minerals, Rocks, and Fossils, at Two, Five, Ten, Twenty, Fifty, and One Hundred Guineas each, etc.

78. *Angel in the House*, Canto VIII.
79. *Letters of James Smetham*, 1891. See No. 16.
80. *Aurora Leigh*, 1857, Seventh Book.
81. *Balder*, 1854. Cf. D. H. Lawrence's " Ballad of Another Ophelia."
82. See No. 79.

83. *Brick and Marble in the Middle Ages : Notes of a Tour in the North of Italy*, 1855.   Street designed the Law Courts (see No. 172) ; and many country churches.   He is more or less the Pre-Raphaelite architect, mediaevalizing in a " modern " way.

If there is one thing which seems wrong about so much architecture of Street's time, before you look more into detail and form, it is the colour of the bricks.   How ironical that it was so meant to give us delight!   "Our buildings are, in nine cases out of ten, cold, colourless, insipid, academical studies, and our people have no conception of obtaining rich colour, and no sufficient love for it when successfuly obtained.   The task, therefore, and duty of architects at the present day is mainly that of awakening and then satisfying this feeling ; and one of the best and most ready vehicles for doing this exists, no doubt, in the rich-coloured brick so easily manufactured in this country, which, if properly used, may become so effective and admirable a material."—Street once more, in his last chapter.

84. *Aurora Leigh*, 1857, First Book.

85. *As We Were*, 1930.

86. See No. 84.

87. *Angel in the House*, Canto X.

88. *Ibid.*, Canto XI.

89. See No. 84.

90. See No. 79.

91. *The Brook.*

92. *Aurora Leigh*, 1857, Second Book.

93. "Thoughts on Beauty and Art," *Macmillan's Magazine*, May-Oct. 1861.

94. *Aylmer's Field.*

95. *Praeterita.*

96. *Glaucus*, 1855.

97. See No. 93.

98. i. "The Marriage of Geraint," *Idylls of the King.*   ii. P. H. Gosse's *A Naturalist's Rambles on the Devonshire Coast*, 1853.

99. See No. 83.

100. *Aurora Leigh*, 1857, Fifth Book.

101. " De Gustibus— ", 1855.

102. As Thomas Maitland, Buchanan attacked Rossetti in " The Contemporary Review," October 1871, in the famous and scurrilous article *The Fleshly School of Poetry—D. G. Rossetti.*

105. See No. 66.

108. " A Lover's Quarrel," 1855.

109. *Origin of Species*, 1859.

110. *The Idea of a University.*

112. See No. 109.

114. *Apologia pro Vita Sua*, 1864.

115. Charles Tennyson Turner : Tennyson's elder brother. He changed his name as a young man, on succeeding to an estate.
116. Dixon was an undergraduate friend of Burne-Jones, a North-country cleric, and a correspondent upon poetry with Hopkins. His own poetry must have been damaged by isolation.
117. *The Naturalist on the River Amazons*, 1863. A book of fact, and colour, which fitted into the moment and established itself quickly. It was ripe for such *virile* exoticism.—cf. Ballantyne's *Martin Rattler, or a Boy's Adventures in the Forests of Brazil*, 1858, and his *Coral Island*, 1858. Then Tennyson's *Enoch Arden* in 1864.
   Hooker the botanist told Tennyson his island vegetation, his tropical vegetation, " was all right."
118. " Victories of Love."
119. See No. 116.
120. See No. 35.
121. " The Four Bridges."
122. *Ibid.*
124. See No. 118.
125. See No. 115.
127. " Not sing at Night."
128. See No. 117.
129. *Laurence Bloomfield in Ireland*, 1864. Allingham wrote three remarkable things—" Up the Airy Mountain," his diary, and this long poem, straightforward, simple, and exciting ; and seldom read.
132. See No. 116.
133. See No. 117.
134. " George Eliot," in *Essays, Classical and Modern.*
135. " James Lee's Wife," 1864.
136. See No. 115.
138. " Hill or Dell." Coventry Patmore, who admired Barnes's poetry, believed that only he and Barnes in their day had kept a literary conscience ; also that Barnes did a small thing well, while the other poets did a big thing ill. He hardly belongs to an age. Some of his cleanest-cut poems I put into *The Romantics* (perhaps wrongly) and do not like now to repeat them. I believe Patmore was right about his " classic " quality. The major Victorians have no such quality—save for Hopkins now and then, and Thomas Hardy in a few poems. But, diversely, Barnes is the pure classic, and classic still more purely are Lewis Carroll and Edward Lear.
139. See No. 115.
140. See No. 66.
141. From " Bacchanalia ; or the New Age."
145. See No. 117.
147. *Note-Books.*

148. *William Allingham. A Diary*, 1907.

150. See No. 148.

151. *Enoch Arden*, 1864.

152. Review of *Enoch Arden* and Browning's *Dramatis Personae*, in the *National Review*, November 1864.

153. *Enoch Arden.*

156. Hardy near to Swinburne—time's freakish behaviour makes us forget that these two were separated in birth only by three years. Hardy admired him (even to imitation—see Hardy's " Friends Beyond ")—and kept in his head such lines as the one on Man,—that " Save his own soul he hath no star." He wrote bitterly, when Swinburne died : " Was there ever such a country—looking back at the life, work, and death of Swinburne—is there any other country in Europe whose attitude towards a deceased poet of his rank would have been so ignoring and almost contemptuous ? . . . A few months ago, when old and enfeebled, he was honoured by a rumour that he had been offered a complimentary degree at Oxford."
    Hardy on the *Poems and Ballads* of 1866 :

> " It was as though a garland of red roses
> Had fallen about the hood of some smug nun
> When irresponsibly dropped as from the sun,
> In fullth of numbers freaked with musical closes,
> Upon Victoria's formal middle time
>   His leaves of rhythm and rhyme. . ."

158. See No. 16. The image of the quivering lip whitening round the world should be enough to make this a famous poem. Essentially it is one of Victorian turbulence and dismay. Europe felt the sea in the nineteenth century. English poets swung between its waves ; but did they fight ? Did they fight as man fights with the sea and yet loves it in Baudelaire's *L'Homme et la Mer* ?—

> " Homme libre, toujours tu chériras la mer !
> La mer est ton miroir ; tu contemples ton âme
> Dans le deroulement infin de sa lame,
> Et ton esprit n'est pas un gouffre moins amer. . .

> " Et cependant voilà des siècles innombrables
> Que vous vous combattez sans pitié ni remord,
> Tellement vous aimez le carnage et la mort,
> O lutteurs éternels, ô frères implacables ! "

159. See No. 117.

161. *The Ring and the Book*, in the " Conclusion."

162. *Ibid.*, Book I. Hopkins on *The Ring and the Book*, to R. W. Dixon : " I remember a good case of ' the impotent collection of

particulars' of which you speak in the description of the market place at Florence where he found the book of the trial : it is a pointless photograph of still life, such as I remember in Balzac, minute upholstery description ; only that in Balzac, who besides is writing prose, all tells and is given with a reserve and simplicity of style which Browning has not got. Indeed I hold with the old-fashioned criticism that Browning is not really a poet, that he has all the gifts but the one needful and the pearls without the string; rather one should say nuggets and rough diamonds. I suppose him to resemble Ben Jonson, only that Ben Jonson has more real poetry."

164. Tennyson, Morris, Swinburne—here they all are :

> " And folks did ask her in the street
> ' How fared it with her long pale feet ? ' "

Du Maurier published this parody in *Punch* in 1866—the year in which Swinburne's *Poems and Ballads* exploded upon the world ; and with each part went a strongly outlined Pre-Raphaelite drawing, in middle Pre-Raphaelitism between Hunt and Burne-Jones. Hopkins had no great care for the Victorian mediaevalists or for archaism. He wrote of Swinburne : " His poetry seems a powerful effort at establishing a new standard of poetic diction, of the rhetoric of poetry ; but to waive every objection it is essentially archaic, biblical a good deal, and so on : now that is a thing that can never last ; a perfect style must be of its age." Another time he mentions Swinburne's " delirium-tremendous imagination." About Morris, Hopkins was less severe. He felt Morris's want of style, but knew his charm and unspeculative clarity.

165. *The Earthly Paradise.* Morris's poetry is somewhat rolled out, and rolled thin. But his Arthurian Age and Middle Ages are just around the corner : walk out of Red Lion Square and you are in a straightforward forest, or under the walls of a straightforward castle. Or you stand in front of a church (as in *The Dream of John Ball*) newly built, with the white chips of stone on the ground ; and *not* designed by G. E. Street. The language is not " magic," or strong. Like the upper Thames, it is a little watery; but clear. And the loosestrife is a little refreshing after the coloured art-silks of Tennyson. His knights rode among flowers or under the thin hornbeams of Epping Forest. The worst of Morris comes in his translations of Icelandic prose. He poeticizes the laconic simplicity and naturalism of the sagas. Basically, the water meadows are more for him than the volcanic triangles and gauntnesses of Iceland. But it is not always stuffy on the upper Thames. Duller than Farringford, but, *happier*, for a change.

167. *Kilvert's Diary*, vol. 1, 1938. This Wiltshire clergyman, who died young a few weeks after his marriage, was a prose writer of tenderness, strength, and distinction. A Victorian " wordpainter "—yes, but there were diamonds mixed in toughly with his easier sentiment. His curiosity was strangely unimpeded. A corpse, a mental defective, a suicide, roses and mountains, young girls—never as he collects and describes such a miscellany could one think of using Dixon's phrase— " the impotent collection of particulars."

168. " Gareth and Lynette," in the *Idylls of the King*.

170. *The Earthly Paradise*.

171. See No. 167. Kilvert, in the Radnorshire parish where he was curate, finishes this Easter Eve by watching how the people dress the graves for the resurrection morning. Before they finish, the moon has risen again ; and Kilvert walks down through the churchyard noting how the flowery graves looked " as if the people had laid down to sleep for the night out of doors, ready dressed to rise early on Easter morning." Kilvert felt the curves, the warmth, the colours, and the bones of life.

172. " Religion as a Fine Art," in *Essays on Freethinking and Plain-speaking*, 1873.

173. " Gray and his School," in *Hours in a Library*, vol. iv, 1907.

Hardy quotes this remark with approval, in 1879. Stephen (whose daughter, ironically as one may think, was the late Virginia Woolf) begins a realistic and welcome scouring of his century and its Alexandrine shams and evasions. Hardy admired him, as he admired Carlyle, and Mill ; noting " Leslie Stephen as a critic. His approval is disapproval minimized." But there was much to disapprove of. Ten years later Hardy was telling himself how modern literature was beset with insincerity : " Half its utterances are qualified, even contradicted, by an aside, and this particularly in morals and religion. When dogma has to be balanced on its feet by such hair-splitting as the late Mr. M. Arnold's it must be in a very bad way."

174. *The Lower Slopes*, 1894.

175. *Note-Books*, 1912. As Coleridge wrote of Crabbe, but with more justice, one could say that Butler was absolutely deficient in the higher imagination. His use was to be a solvent to the overlayers of Victorian varnish. But, for example, what a cheapness reveals itself in so many of his notes, so much of his writing—and especially in his celebrated piece about Montreal, the stuffed owl, and the Discobolus !

177. " The Regrets of a Mountaineer," in *The Playground of Europe*, 1871. There is just a touch of priggishness about the Victorian agnostic on the high Alpine eyries, among the pure snow, and where the mere you and I will never climb. The common

element in mountaineers—the rebellious Byron setting Manfred on the Jungfrau, the radical John Martin painting Manfred among the peaks ; then the Victorian freethinkers up, where the Byrons, the Martins, the Turners had only fancied themselves up. Tyndall making the first ascent of the Weisshorn, Stephen the first ascents of the Schreckhorn and Rothhorn, Whymper (brilliantly able to draw and engrave his high mountain scenery) conquering the Matterhorn, Chimborazo and Cotapaxi : Englishmen, from the Fifties, scurrying and scrambling round to all the mountains of the world. Mountaineers from the ironic Stephen down (in letters) to Dr. I. A. Richards, in his scepticism. How many *critics* (Stephen, Sir Martin Conway, Dr. Richards, Michael Roberts . . .) are mountaineers ? How much are the high Alps a substitute for high climbs in the imagination, and also (as Stephen suggested) a concomitant of social nonconformity of one kind or another ? How is it that this Alpinism breaks out in the Fifties ? And among the English ? And gathers and increases through the century ? A pathography of Victorianism would have to answer that question.

179. *Physiological Aesthetics*, 1877.
181. (i) " The Mission of St. Bernard," in *Historical Sketches*, vol. ii, 1872-73.
182. " Autobiography," in *Collected Essays*, vol. i, 1893.
183. *The City of Dreadful Night*, first printed in 1874.

I find Thomson's poems, the murky ones, all too like big, blotched funguses growing out of his misery. The misery, though nothing else about him, was profound, and the mushrooms are coarse eating. Thomson's friend Bradlaugh was not one of the Muses or an under-clerk of Apollo : and it does not do to take misery mixed with overripe romanticism as even one of the lesser eminences of Victorian verse. Fungus or bog, or the two together.

Yet . . . How can it be explained ? If you know Bristol, you must know that the mock Gothic tower of the University at the head of Park Street is fake architecture, but that the fake does rear itself high, does acquire, or appear to, some grandeur in the right light, or when you are looking not too clearly.

There is a terrible description of events on the day before Thomson's death (after which he was buried in unconsecrated ground). William Sharp was called and went into the bedroom in the dark : " Stooping, I caught his whispered words to the effect that he was dying ; upon which I lit a match, and in the sudden glare beheld his white face on the blood-stained pillow. He had burst one or more blood-vessels, and the haemorrhage was dreadful." Thomson exists somewhere in between De Quincey and the sordid verbatim of an inquest.

Amblongus pie : serve up in a clean dish and throw the whole out of a window as fast as possible ?

184. *Nonsense Songs, Stories, Botany and Alphabets*, 1871.

185. See No. 183.

186. See No. 172.

187. *The Rod, The Root, The Flower*, 1895.

188. *The Light of Asia*, 1879.

189. See No. 177.

190. " Cowper and Rousseau," *Hours in a Library*, vol. iii, 1879.

194. An Amblongus pie made up of Poe mixed with Tennyson.

195. *Poems*, 1891. Seven stanzas left out. O'Donnell was a busy journalist in Ireland and London, who contributed verse to *The Nation* and later to *All the Year Round*. He is buried at Kensal Green. He may have written as good or better things hidden away in periodicals.

196. See No. 195. Four lines from " A July Dawn."

197. Enter from Brasenose the cultured devil with languors and impressionism. This (see also No. 219) comes from the celebrated, and then omitted, and then modified and restored " Conclusion " in *Studies in the History of the Renaissance*, 1873. Thomas Hardy, when he first met Pater in the Eighties, recorded how his manner was " that of one carrying weighty ideas about without spilling them."

Brasenose has been a very different college in our day. No wonder.

199. See No. 195. From " Happy Christmasses."

200. *Congal*, 1872. From the conclusion to his long epic. Ferguson's delightful lyrics belong to his early life and are romantic rather than Victorian.

201. See No. 115.

202. See No. 172.

203. From the fragmentary " Woodlark," written in 1876. Hopkins is the extraordinary heir to Pre-Raphaelitism in painting and poetry. He peers into detail, he likes fact, but does not feebly embroider fact and detail into a moral sampler, or enjoy them like a jackdaw, or rely on them. He begins, that is much of the point, by being in love with words, and is always in love with them.

206. A climacteric, this libel case in 1878, more profoundly so than the trial of Oscar Wilde seventeen years later. Despite butter-flies, Japanese prints and nocturnes, art over here goes this way : Whistler–Sickert–Wyndham Lewis–Moore. The other way was Burne-Jones (detail, composition, finish)–Beardsley–Ricketts–Extinction. Too crude a schematization, of course. Fine Art ends, and art, naked without that indecent adjective, at any rate begins over again.

207. *Songs and Romances*, Dublin, 1878.

208. " Winckelmann," in *Studies in the History of the Renaissance*, 1873.
209. *The Rod, The Root, The Flower*.
210. From *The Unknown Eros*.
211. See No. 209.
212. *Life of Thomas Hardy*, by Florence Hardy, vol. i, 1933.
214. *Pictures and Songs*, Dublin, 1880.
215. Another of the Pre-Raphaelities, more or less. The poem is from *Annus Amoris*, 1876. Admired by Ruskin, and a friend of Patmore and Swinburne. So much have his pictures gone from sight that not one of them was exhibited in any of the 1948 exhibitions celebrating the centenary of Pre-Raphaelitism. Yet " The Moorland " is in the Tate. " More exquisite in its finish of lichenous rock painting than any work I have ever seen "—Ruskin, on its exhibition in the Academy, 1855.
219. See No. 197.
220. Written in 1880.
223. " Evolution and Ethics," the Romanes Lecture of 1893, in *Collected Essays*, vol. ix.
224. " Ten O'Clock Lecture " (1885), in *The Gentle Art of Making Enemies*.
225. *Patience*, 1881. Pater by origin, Wilde, conveniently, by transference.
226. From " An Invocation."
227. A. J. Munby is one of the smaller poets, following after Browning, who ought not to be forgotten altogether ; though most of his writing is tame. A barrister, he was touched, it seems, by the morality of Pre-Raphaelitism ; and from 1860 to 1870 he taught Latin at the Working Men's College. Several Pre-Raphaelites, affected by the Christian Socialism of Kingsley and Maurice, married " beneath them,"—just as the rich Christian Socialist meant to do in *Aurora Leigh*. True, the wives were not infrequently beautiful, and before or after marriage their husbands set about having them educated. Rossetti had his " Guggum," Morris the daughter of an Oxford groom. Frederic Stephens, P.R.B., married a girl whom he had to reprove for her aitches and mispronunciations. Frederic Shields sent his wife off to school. The daughter of one poet is said to have married a working man, whom she left quick enough. Munby in 1873 married his servant; and it was kept a secret : " Owing to the refusal of his wife to quit her station, the marriage . . ., though known to her relations and to three of her husband's friends, had never been made known to his own family " (*D.N.B.*).

A queer situation, the wife working on, it seems, faithfully and sensibly in the kitchen ; and the husband turning the business over and over in his mind and being impelled by it to write many of his poems. In *Dorothy* (1880) and elsewhere he recurs again and again to one mark displayed by the virtuous servant—her *red arms*. He seems arguing or refusing to argue with his conviction that the marriage was right. And to his poems he added an anthology he named *Faithful Servant : Epitaphs and Obituaries*.

It is revealing that the virtue and beauty of the illegitimate Dorothy, " Built for beauty, indeed, but certainly built for labour," are ascribed partly to the fact that, though her mother was a country girl, her father was a gentleman. In Charles Reade's Pre-Raphaelite novel, *Christie Johnstone* (1853), this balm is applied in reverse. Charles Gatty, the gentleman and the artist, does marry Christie the Scottish fishgirl. But Christie is not, so to say, ennobled by a genetic fifty per cent. Instead, old Mrs. Gatty is discovered to have been a cook, who had married a greengrocer.

228. Lord de Tabley's plants in this poem—the loveliest and most moving he wrote—are botanists' plants. De Tabley, Crabbe, Cowley, and Jacobsen (De Tabley's contemporary, who translated *The Origin of Species* into Danish) are the only poets I can recall who had more than an amateur knowledge of botany. De Tabley compiled a valuable *Flora of Cheshire*.

229. *Shorter Poems* : first stanza of No. 27 in Book iv. It suggests a Thames bank painting by Greaves or Cecil Lawson. Detail is thinning out to a tactile colour or two.

231. See No. 224.

233. *Vestigia Retrorsum*, 1891. See No. 227.

235. (i) Four stanzas out of *Eros and Psyche* (March), which was first printed in 1885. Two years before, in the Sunda Strait between Java and Sumatra, Krakatoa had stupendously erupted. Dust broke into the upper atmosphere and spread and was carried over most of the world, fantastically altering the sunsets. In England these evening pageants were seen late in the year. They gave Bridges these lines ; or rather Bridges saw them and also read the brilliant analysis of the colours which Hopkins sent from Stonyhurst to *Nature*.

(ii) Part of this letter by Hopkins, which is reprinted in *The Correspondence of Gerard Manley Hopkins and Richard Watson Dixon*, edited by C. C. Abbott, 1935.

Hopkins, with his skill of sensuous observation, had absorbed and was familiar with all the normal qualities of light and colour in sunset. He explains easily enough the differences— as no scientist could have done, and perhaps few artists except a Turner or a Danby.

242. Here in this poem (as in " The God of the Poor ") mediaevalism goes left; as it does also in the prose of *The Dream of John Ball*.

243. *The Gondoliers*, 1889.

245. Yeats walks in, with the *Wanderings of Oisin and Other Poems* (1889), out of Pre-Raphaelitism, Pater, Morris, Ireland, Ferguson, magic, Mme Blavatsky—and Balzac. . . .

Balzac : Hopkins respected Balzac, Yeats admired Balzac. George Eliot and Lewes, as she recorded in her journal,—to the delighted instruction of Henry James—finished reading *Père Goriot* together and found it a *hateful* book.

Another moral story. The man who bought Holman Hunt's "Awakened Conscience" found the face of the kept girl too agonizing to live with. Hunt changed the face : Hunt, the moral realist, diluted his own morality.

246. *Physiological Aesthetics*, 1877—a book, and a fascinatingly silly one, derived out of Herbert Spencer, and so out of Darwin misunderstood. One may think of this passage in terms of Alma Tadema and Leighton, the plays of Stephen Phillips, and perhaps a little of Bridges, and much of Sturge Moore.

247. *Velasquez*, 1899. Stevenson, painter and critic, cousin of R. L. Stevenson. He wrote with great understanding ; and his book —a notable piece of writing anyway—is one of the stones which squash the precious afterlife of the Pre-Raphaelites in England.

250. "The Song of the Happy Shepherd."

251. "Locksley Hall Sixty Years After" (1886).

252. Daniel came of shopkeepers in Lostwithiel in Cornwall. He wrote much verse—most of it dead and flat. A Victorian Byronist, a careless liver and a wild drinker.

253. In taking leave of Tennyson, being skilfully querulous in "Locksley Hall Sixty Years After" (1886), I am tempted to insert a piece out of *The Foresters*, just to show for once in this anthology how the great wordpainter could slip out of his painted music and crash into bathos. He wrote it in his old age. But at all ages he could whistle and sing, and then slip on his own orange peel :

> *Titania on a hill, Fairies on either side of her,*
> *the moon above the hill.*

1ST FAIRY.	Evil fairy ! do you hear ?
	So said he who lieth here.
2ND FAIRY.	We be fairies of the wood.
	We be neither bad nor good.
1ST FAIRY.	Back and side and hip and rib,
	Nip him, nip him, for his fib.
TITANIA.	Nip him not, but let him snore.
	We must flit for evermore.
1ST FAIRY.	Tit, my queen, must it be so ?
	Wherefore, wherefore should we go ?
TITANIA.	I, Titania, bid you flit,
	And you dare to call me Tit!

1ST FAIRY.	Tit, for love and brevity, Not for love of levity.
TITANIA.	Pertest of our flickering mob, Wouldst thou call my Oberon Ob ?
1ST FAIRY.	Nay, an please your Elfin Grace, Never OB before his face.
TITANIA.	Fairy realm is breaking down When the fairy slights the Crown.

If this was a picture, long lost, which reappeared in the sale-room, art experts would not be wanting to deny it to the master upon stylistic grounds.

254. Preface to *The Picture of Dorian Gray*, 1891.

255. " Inaugural Lecture on the Study of History " (1895), in *Lectures on Modern History*, 1921.

257. *Note-Books*, 1912.

261. Henry Wallis painted the " Death of Chatterton " in the Tate. I suspect that the scandal of his life has to do with the little we know either of him or his pictures. He was not altogether a Pre-Raphaelite moralist. He did not marry a working-class girl. Instead, he eloped—to Capri—with the wife of George Meredith. Meredith had sat, or reclined, to him for the green, handsome face of the dead poet in the sapphire breeches.

Wallis became an expert in ceramics, Egyptian, Persian, Italian. This piece of verbal lustre, indeed, comes from one of his privately printed books—*Persian Lustre Vases. With Illustrations by the Author*, 1899 ; in which he also remarks of the Persians of the Middle Ages that " dauntless in arms, splendid in arts, ' free, learn'd, and valiant,' they embody our conception of mediaeval chivalry in its most brilliant aspect."

Nothing, I think, has been written on Wallis except a disappointing pamphlet—*Henry Wallis*, 1830-1916, by A. van de Put (Bollettino del Museo Internazionale delle Ceramiche in Faenza, 1917). There is no life of him in the *D.N.B.*

263. From " The Woodman."

271. *With the Wild Geese*, 1902.

272. This early poem came to Yeats in a dream.

274. " The Critic As Artist," Part ii, first published in the *Nineteenth Century* in 1890.

INDEX OF AUTHORS

(Item numbers, not page numbers, are given)